THE EQUILIBRIUM ECONOMICS
OF LÉON WALRAS

THE EQUILIBRIUM ECONOMICS OF LÉON WALRAS

Jan van Daal and Albert Jolink

London and New York

First published 1993
by Routledge
11 New Fetter Lane, London EC4P 4EE

Simultaneously published in the USA and Canada
by Routledge
29 West 35th Street, New York, NY 10001

Typeset in Scantext 10 on 12 point Times
by Leaper and Gard Ltd, Bristol
Printed and bound in Great Britain by
Mackays of Chatham PLC, Chatham, Kent

British Library Cataloguing in Publication Data
A catalogue record for this book is available from the British Library

Library of Congress Cataloging in Publication Data
Daal, J. van.
The equilibrium economics of Léon Walras/Jan van Daal and Albert Jolink.
p.   cm.
Includes bibliographical references and index.
ISBN 0-415-00157-9
1. Equilibrium (Economics)—Mathematical models.   2. Walras, Léon,
1834–1910.   I. Jolink, Albert, 1962-   II. Title.
HB145.D23   1993
330.15′7—dc20
93–16567
CIP

ISBN 0-415-00157-9

CONTENTS

CONTENTS

CONTENTS

viii

PREFACE

From his own days until now, most of the attention to the works of Léon Walras (1834–1910) has been restricted to his work on general economic equilibrium as exposed in his *Eléments d'économie politique pure ou théorie de la richesse sociale* (first edition 1874/1877). Two main reasons may be put forward for this nearly exclusive attention to the *Eléments*. First, Walras himself attached much value to his work on economic equilibrium, as appears from the fact that during his lifetime he published four editions of the *Eléments*. The way in which he altered, rearranged and supplemented the contents of this book several times provides clear evidence that the issue of general economic equilibrium was never out of his mind.

Second, notwithstanding the fact that his work was aimed at contributing to policy matters, he felt (and indeed was) obliged, as so many of the first-generation academic economists, to provide an overall picture of the whole field. Starting with pure theory, however, he ran out of time and did not succeed in writing the two other treatises he had planned, namely, *Eléments d'économie politique appliquée* and *Eléments d'économie sociale*. These two volumes were to deal with their subjects in the same fundamental and systematic way as the *Eléments d'économie politique pure* did with respect to pure economic theory. Feeling his strength wavering, however, Walras published instead the *Etudes d'économie sociale* (1896) and the *Etudes d'économie politique appliquée* (1898). Both *Etudes* consist of a collection of already existing papers. In this form they could not compete with the *Eléments d'économie politique pure* and therefore the latter book received most of the attention.

The *Eléments* and the two *Etudes* contain the essence of Walras's economic work. There are two main conclusions that can be drawn from these books.

1   In his analytical economics of free competition Walras was thinking in terms of what we now call temporary equilibrium, i.e. he stylized economic life into consecutive periods during which trade and production

ix

take place in a situation of equilibrium. Capital, including money, was to carry over value from period to period, and economic growth was to be brought about by net saving.

2 In his normative economics Walras extended the working of equilibrium beyond the strict boundaries imposed by free competition and by the traditional social institutions. He did so because his models of equilibrium were primarily meant as instruments within the framework of a broader design, namely to unfold an optimal economic order, from which prescriptions for reaching this ideal could be derived.

The first point is even now not fully recognized and about the second point much ignorance exists. Without the work of the two most outstanding modern Walras scholars, William Jaffé and Donald A. Walker, this situation would undoubtedly have been even worse. Jaffé's translation and careful annotation of the *Eléments*, the publication of Walras's *Correspondence* by Jaffé, and the three dozen papers by Jaffé and by Walker on Walras have made Walras's person and his work known to a wider audience.

But, however important, these papers mainly deal with separate aspects of Walras's work. Moreover, we have the impression that one of the implicit premises of most of them is that Walras's work is already known to the readers of those papers. Walras's *Eléments*, even in its English translation, is too complicated a book for such an optimistic premise. The two *Etudes*, poorly composed as they are, are even less known.[1] A comprehensive review and analysis of his whole work does not yet exist.

In this book we have tried to present such an exposé with respect to Walras's equilibrium models. In Part I and Part II we elaborate the first of the two points mentioned above; the second point will be dealt with briefly in Part III.

In Part I we deal with Walras's method and with some fundamental notions he developed. For a correct understanding of his use of mathematics and of the development of his thinking on utility we had to rely upon unpublished manuscripts in the Walras Archives in the Universities of Lausanne and Lyon.

In Part II we elaborate upon Walras's models of general economic equilibrium. We not only represent his chain of equilibrium models, from the one of exchange of two goods only to that with fixed capital, circulating capital and money, but we also sketch the development of these models through the respective editions of the *Eléments*. Moreover, we present interpretations that may differ from those known from the literature; this is in particular the case for the issues of flexible coefficients of production, of the optimality of capital formation, and of money. We thus hope to contribute to clearing up obscurities in the interpretations of the work of Léon Walras.

In Part III we shall speculate on how Walras, had he had more time to work, would possibly have extended his models of general economic equilibrium with elements of monopoly, public goods and state ownership of the land. These elements have been extensively dealt with by Walras in his two *Etudes* and it was always his intention to insert them in what he called his 'complete mathematical theory of economic equilibrium'. Regrettably, he did not come to such a synthesis. We subject our ideas on how this task could be performed to the judgement of the competent reader.

The three parts of the book have been written in such a way that they are independently readable. This necessarily entailed a certain degree of repetition.

The book ends with five appendices. The first two, dealing with Walras's life and works, have been included in order to give an impression of the personality of Léon Walras. Appendices III and IV are of a more technical character. In Appendix V we deal with the existence of solutions of Walras's equilibrium models and with *tâtonnement*. The relegation of the latter issue to an appendix expresses our view that *tâtonnement* has been overrated in comparison with other issues in Walras's models of general economic equilibrium; in particular its presumed implications for dynamics in Walras's theory have been overestimated.

We wish to stress here that our main source of inspiration is the work of Léon Walras himself. This book is in the first place an exposition of how we understand Walras, in particular his static equilibrium models. References to secondary literature are only included to illustrate or to complement the exposition; we did not aim at completeness in this respect.

Although the book may serve as an introduction to Walras's general equilibrium economics, it should not be considered as a surrogate for reading Walras's books and articles, but rather as a stimulus for studying the works themselves; Appendix II may be helpful in this respect.

We hope that readers who have already acquired opinions on Walras will find much in the book that will bring them to (re-)read his works and that this will stimulate a discussion that will further improve our understanding of modern general economic equilibrium theory through a better understanding of Walras.

Jan van Daal
Albert Jolink

ACKNOWLEDGEMENTS

The present book has benefited greatly from remarks, suggestions and corrections made by many people. The support ranged from simple but helpful remarks made in passing, to extensive answers to our questions. We wish to thank all these colleagues and friends. Our special thanks go to Roger Backhouse, Harm Booy, Hans Brems, Pascal Bridel, Neil de Marchi, Pierre Dockès, Rien Dullaart, Bruna Ingrao, Philip Mirowski, Claude Mouchot, Fred Muller, Jean-Pierre Potier, Cor van Eijk and Donald Walker.

We acknowledge with pleasure the hospitality and helpfulness we met with during our numerous trips to the Walras archives in the Universities of Lausanne and Lyon; further, we shall not forget the endless conversations we had in Lyon on all aspects of the life and works of the two Walrases, father and son.

Mr Edward Elgar of Edward Elgar Publishing Limited, Aldershot, kindly granted us permission to use the material from our article 'On Walras's "general general equilibrium model"', published originally as Chapter 9 of Volume IX of *Perspectives on the History of Economic Thought*, Edward Elgar Publishing Limited, 1993.

We are likewise indebted to the History of Economics Society for permission to include material from our article 'Léon Walras's mathematical economics and the mechanical analogies', published in the *History of Economics Society Bulletin*, 11 (1) (Spring 1989): 25–32.

Furthermore, we thank Donald Walker, in his position as literary executor of William Jaffé's estate, for permission to quote extensively from the English translation by Jaffé of Walras's *Eléments d'économie politique pure*.

We are grateful to Erasmus University Rotterdam, in particular the Faculty of Economics, for the generous way they provided research facilities for us.

Finally, we thank our publisher for his kind patience and for the beautiful appearance of the book.

CONVENTIONS

The mathematical notation in this book is that used by Walras. The formulae have been numbered by chapter by the authors.

All French citations in the text have been translated into English. Those from the fourth and the definitive edition of Walras's *Eléments d'économie politique pure* are taken from the English translation *Elements of Pure Economics* by William Jaffé. All other translations have been provided by the authors. We only present the original French texts of citations when their source was an unpublished or very recently published manuscript.

The following abbreviations are used.

Eléments is used for *Eléments d'économie politique pure ou théorie de la richesse sociale*. If no edition is mentioned, the citation refers to the fifth, definitive one; it can then also be found in all former editions.

EES stands for *Etudes d'économie sociale*; the citation in general refers to the first edition (1896).

EPA stands for *Etudes d'économie politique appliquée*; the citation refers to the first edition (1898).

Mélanges denotes *Mélanges d'économie politique et sociale* (1987).

Part I

PROLOGUE

Evidemment! Il faudrait prouver que
la libre concurrence procure le maximum
d'utilité.

Léon Walras
(*EPA*, p. 466)

1

ON THE USE OF MATHEMATICS IN ECONOMIC *ANALYSIS*[1]

Léon Walras may rightfully be considered as one of the founding fathers of mathematical economics. Much of mathematical economics developed since Walras's time has gradually become common knowledge in economics. This means that Walras directly and indirectly has had a marked influence upon our science as it stands now. It is therefore important to know how Walras came to his results, what these results are, and to what end the results were used or were intended to be used.

As far as pure mathematical economics is concerned, Walras's aim was to provide, by means of a mathematical solution of the problem of the determination of current prices, a proof of optimality of free competition in terms of utility (see *Eléments*, preface to the first edition, and *EPA*, p. 466). In this part of the present book we shall deal with mathematics in economics, free competition, and price determination under a regime of free competition and utility, elements which are basic in Walras's theory of pure economics. The synthesis of these elements is dealt with in Part II.

MATHEMATICS AND ECONOMIC THEORY

In Walras's day the use of mathematical theorems and techniques in the treatment of problems of economic theory was not at all obvious. And indeed, Walras had great difficulty in convincing his contemporaries of the necessity for the application of mathematics to economics. One of the reasons, Walras claimed, for the opposition to his mathematical approach lies in the misunderstanding of the nature of mathematics. In the first place we should distinguish between mathematics as such and the *application* of mathematics. Further, in discussing the application of mathematics we should, according to Walras, distinguish between application to economic theory and application to economic practice.[2]

Walras's mathematics in economic theory has a strongly Cartesian flavour. It can be asserted that it is similar to Descartes's 'Mathesis Universalis' (universal mathematics). The Mathesis provides a process of discovery. Descartes stated that his order of study was to start with the

3

simplest and easiest of disciplines and to master them before moving on. In this sense Mathesis Universalis is a general introduction to 'higher disciplines':

> There must be some general science to explain everything which can be asked concerning measure and order not predicated of any special subject matter. This, I perceived, was called Mathesis Universalis.[3]

In its application universal mathematics is restricted to those matters

> in which order or measure are investigated, and in that it makes no difference whether it be numbers, figures, stars, sounds, or any other object that the question of measure arises.[4]

It is in this light that Walras's introduction of mathematics can be seen. His purpose, therefore, was not that of 'mathematicizing' economics (whatever that means), at least not at this stage. With the introduction of mathematics Walras intended to present a method to discover 'universal truths'. Although Walras does not seem to be very explicit about it, his manner of proceeding runs parallel with Descartes's: all the objects of rational knowledge somehow subsist in deductive chains and are ordered from the simple to the complex, or from the 'absolute' to the 'relative'. This is prior to any application.

With the *application*, then, of mathematics to economic theory there is more to it. In the case of application, Walras would have to show that economic matters can be posed mathematically. As Walras wrote:

> All these operations: choice of variables and of functions; adoption of notation that is both simple and expressive; use of geometry, as Descartes says, to 'consider particular relationships better' and 'to represent them more distinctly to the imagination and to the intellect'; adoption of the algebraic mode to 'retain them or to understand several of them together'; use of the method of reduction or of analysis, and use of the method of deduction or of synthesis; all these are delicate operations. For them to be successful it is less essential to possess some rather elementary mathematical knowledge than to have economic data drawn always carefully from experience. Be that as it may, what I have just said truly indicates wherein consists the problem of the application of mathematics to economic theory and to applied economics.

> (*Mélanges*, p. 314)[5]

At this stage one would expect Walras to find an identification between the objects of mathematics and those of economics, as Descartes does for the case of mathematical physics. Indeed, Walras described this identification in the *Eléments* (Section 30) as follows:

4

The pure theory of economics ought to take over from experience certain type concepts, like those of exchange, supply, demand, market, capital, income, productive services and products. From these real-type concepts the pure science of economics should then abstract and define ideal-type concepts in terms of which it carries on its reasoning.[6]

In this sense we could speak of Walras's mathematical economics, as contained in his *Eléments d'économie politique pure*. In the case of pure economic theory, according to Walras, we study and explain facts, and the use of mathematics, then, is motivated by the need for a *method of analysis*. The mathematical expressions are, and should be, general, undetermined, non-numerical. Though Walras was dealing with magnitudes, problems of measurement are beside the point. Or, as he wrote (*Mélanges*, pp.,311–12):

There are [certain elements], such as utility, for example, which, though being magnitudes, are not appreciable magnitudes. But what does this imply for the analysis?

MATHEMATICS AND ECONOMIC PRACTICE

Quite distinct is the application of mathematics to practical problems. In economic practice, according to Walras, mathematics is used to evaluate certain consequences of an economic measure. The application of mathematics, in this case, is motivated by the necessity of calculation. In the case of economic practice, therefore, the magnitudes have to be measured and the relations between them have to be given concrete form, with parameters numerically determined. The expressions are specific for given circumstances. This, indeed, poses some restrictions on the possibilities of applying mathematics.

It is this distinction, theoretical application versus practical application, which is of importance for the understanding, and in a sense the justification, of the use of mathematics in Walras's theory. Since Walras spent most of his time on theory, it can be argued that in most cases Walras's mathematics should be regarded as a method of analysis in abstract terms, rather than as a method of calculation. It is this distinction that many of his opponents failed to see. As he stated in his article 'Une branche nouvelle de la mathématique' (*Mélanges*, pp. 306–7):

Of these two modes, the theoretical, abstract, and analytical application, and the practical, concrete, and numerical application, the people to whom one speaks of applying mathematics to economics can conceive of only the second .... Our adversaries absolutely neglect the first mode of application of mathematics to economics, that which consists in speaking and reasoning about value in exchange, about demand and supply, about utility and quantity, which are magnitudes, in the language of magnitudes, and which consists in following the method of the science of magnitudes. They neglect the first mode, that consists in doing those things and in treating the magnitudes as functions of others, thus making the knowledge of the properties of functions contribute to the study of economic phenomena.

WALRAS AND THE OBJECTIONS AGAINST THE USE OF MATHEMATICS

The objections of Walras's contemporaries to the use of mathematics in economics can be summarized in four points.[7]

1 Mathematics has no heuristic role to play in economics.
2 The complexities and subtleties of economic reality cannot be reduced to mathematical formulae of any practical significance.
3 Mathematics is too difficult to understand for economists who are not mathematicians.
4 Mathematical economics does not provide unambiguous results.

Persisting in the use of mathematics as a method of analysis in economic theory, Walras spent quite some time in answering the objections. To the objection on the minor heuristic role of mathematics Walras replied that his own work proved the contrary. It was only through the mathematical method that Walras had been able to obtain the results in the *Eléments*. The inability to reduce the complexities and subtleties of economic reality to mathematical formulae of any practical significance was, according to Walras, an objection valid for any generalization; mathematics as such has nothing to do with it. Mathematics could, however, be of practical relevance by formulating *general* rules. The third objection, mathematics being too difficult for economists, is overcome by formal education and therefore hardly an argument against the use of mathematics. Walras did admit the objection that mathematical economics does not provide unambiguous results. In reply he stated that it was never a question of finding the absolute truth, but rather of whether mathematics could be of any help in clearing up matters.

WALRAS AND THE MECHANICAL ANALOGIES

It would have been quite legitimate if Walras had restricted himself to arguments for the defence of his approach that lie entirely within the field of economics. However, an alternative line of defence, and, as it turned out, his last, culminated in 1909 in the article 'Economique et mécanique'. The object of the article, which, according to Walras, would provide additional justification for the use of mathematics in economic analysis, is explained in a letter to George Renard (Jaffé 1965: Letter 1722, 21 January 1909, emphasis added):

> But it is not enough to popularize the mathematical method in political economy by elementary education; it also has to be *justified* in the eyes of competent men. This is what I have tried to do in a memoir: 'Economique et Mécanique'.

The central theme in this article was to show the analogy between mathematical *formulations* in economics and those in mechanics. As Descartes asserted, any science dealing with magnitudes can be subjected to the analytical, mathematical method, thus being a mathematical science. These sciences all have one thing in common: the mathematical method.

'Economique et mécanique' stressed that both economics and mechanics deal with magnitudes, though very distinct ones. In the case of economics, according to Walras, we are dealing with '*intime*' phenomena, which happen within ourselves and are therefore individual and subjectively observable. On the other hand, mechanics deals with 'exterior' phenomena, which happen outside ourselves and can be observed by everyone. The fact, then, that both sciences deal with observable phenomena which may be expressed in numerical magnitudes makes a mathematical method applicable in both cases. In this situation, some analogies in mathematical expressions could appear between economics and mechanics because of their common method of analysis. Walras showed in the article that for some particular cases this analogy, indeed, can be found.

By illustrating his ideas with mechanical analogies, however, Walras ran the risk of being misunderstood. Contemporaries as well as present-day authors[8] tended to see the physical idea as the original, after which the economic analogy is found, instead of the other way around. In our opinion, copying physics was never Walras's intention, because of the unbridgeable difference between observed magnitudes originating from *intime* versus exterior phenomena. Therefore Walras's conception does not allow for an analogy between economics and physics as such. A correct understanding of the presence of mechanical analogies needs a correct understanding of Walras's mathematical economics.

2

FREE COMPETITION AND GENERAL EQUILIBRIUM

In a world in which the doctrine of *laissez-faire* is the rule rather than the exception, one may expect a science supporting this doctrine to supply the proofs of the arguments. The doctrine of *laissez-faire*, in terms of economic organization, was stumbled upon by Walras as an accepted view from earlier 'économistes', i.e. the Physiocrats. Walras viewed *laissez-faire* as a stage in a long historical process of organizational progress in society. The optimality of *laissez-faire*, however, was not at all obvious in the second half of the nineteenth century, as was persistently stressed by Saint-Simonists and socially oriented economists. The *laissez-faire* doctrine was therefore rejected on grounds that it propagated absolute freedom on ill-founded arguments.

FREE COMPETITION

Walras's investigation of the mechanism of free competition, as an economic consequence of *laissez-faire*, was motivated by his dissatisfaction with the state of orthodox economic science. This investigation, as it seemed, would supply the knowledge on the limitations of orthodox economic doctrine. The limits would follow from the restrictions set by the assumptions of free competition. Hence, rather than simply refuting *laissez-faire*, Walras's very intention was to demonstrate the limitations of free competition.

Free competition was considered to represent the process of exchange in a setting of competition unhampered by institutional obstructions. In this setting, the offer and demand of goods and services would unconditionally give rise to exchange values for each and every product. This unconditional process, however, presumed that buyers and sellers not only have full information about the prices in the market but can also participate in market transactions in an unrestricted manner. Hence, the assumptions more or less limit the applicability of free competition to an ideal type of market, or to a very specific type of market, to which these assumptions apply.

Markets which according to Walras resembled the free competition ideal were characterized by a high degree of organization: in particular they were those markets in which the transactions are centralized, such as auctions, and the terms of trade are made known openly to all market participants who, in turn, are given the opportunity to react to the prevailing prices. In Walras's representation of centralized transactions, the (Paris) Stock Exchange seems to have been at the back of his mind. This gave rise to all sorts of abstractions inspired by the pricing mechanism of the Stock Exchange itself. Although Walras did not claim any similarity of his theoretical price-adjustment scheme to the actual pricing mechanism, the outcome of both the theoretical scheme and the practical process were bound to coincide in his opinion. This circumstance, as it seems, was considered by Walras as a clear-cut demonstration of the validity of his theoretical solutions:

> What must we do in order to prove that the theoretical solution is identically the solution worked out by the market? Our task is very simple: we need only show that the upward and downward movements of prices solve the system of equations of offer and demand by a process of groping [par *tâtonnement*].
>
> (*Eléments*, Section 125)

The question remains, of course, whether this was actually proved by Walras.

Apart from being a typical representation of free competition, the Stock Exchange seemed to have another characteristic which would be advantageous in the investigation of the exchange process: the transactions take place between a limited number of stockbrokers, acting on behalf of a multiplicity of buyers and sellers. As such, the Stock Exchange aggregates the individual supplies and demands into 'macro' supply and demand. The 'macro' perspective is typically present in all of Walras's models. This approach is advantageous when general laws are sought for, although at the same time it blurs observations of individual behaviour.

The exchange operations in the theoretical market of free competition were represented by bidding procedures similar to the procedure at the Stock Exchange. Hence, the market participants would try to buy or sell their goods and services according to their preferences. When supply did not match demand, sellers would underbid their competitors or buyers would outbid other potential buyers.

The matching system of supply and demand was at one time imagined by Walras by means of a 'calculateur'.[1] This calculateur would receive all potential orders and accordingly determine the equilibrium price. At another instance, Walras investigated the process of bidding itself. In the case of excess demand, buyers would raise their bids, whereas in the case of excess supply the sellers would lower their price. This will bring demand

and supply closer to each other. In the final situation supply equals demand and the equilibrium price is determined.[2]

This (theoretical) price-adjustment mechanism in Walras's theory, known as the *tâtonnement* process, has been the subject of numerous discussions and ample confusion. One of the problems associated with the *tâtonnement* process is the question to what extent it represents reality, in other words, whether it is a dynamic process or an imaginary procedure in a static framework. This problem also gives rise to a second problem: does the *tâtonnement* process actually converge to a situation of equilibrium? In our view, both problems are only partially relevant for a description of Walras's equilibrium economics. If one is interested in the investigation of equilibrium situations, the problem of the nature of *tâtonnement*, as well as its possible effects, falls outside the scope of interest. For better or worse, Walras cannot be credited for having described situations of disequilibrium since his free competition models are simply static equilibrium models. In this light, the *tâtonnement* process is no more than a hypothetical scheme of what might have happened when the general bidding rules are applied to a pre-equilibrium situation. The *tâtonnement* process may therefore be seen as no more than a possible price-adjustment mechanism which leads to the same theoretical solution as is empirically achieved in practice.

By relating this theoretical result to the practical result, Walras believed his theory to be in conformity with the actual situation in the real world. As such, his theoretical results could be applied to actual policy matters. This application of theoretical results, as we shall see below, did not imply an implementation of policy rules but rather a comparison between an ideal, although theoretical, situation and a practical, although not very ideal, situation. Taking free competition as a theoretically optimal situation, an application of the results of the analysis of free competition gave way to normative rules to approach these results in practice. Hence, free competition implied the introduction of at least some regulation as opposed to a *laissez-faire* policy.

GENERAL EQUILIBRIUM

A dominant concept in Walras's description of a market organization with free competition is the concept of equilibrium. It seems that the concept was quite natural at the time[3] and needed no introduction by Walras. Equilibrium, as such, was considered to represent a state of market transactions in which supply of a product would match the demand for it. The ideas of Jean-Baptiste Say, but also those of Auguste Walras, were clearly the general views on economic transactions inherited by Léon Walras. The early writings by Walras on market processes, such as the 'tentatives',[4] clearly exhibit these received views of a simple idea of equilibrium. However, with the introduction of several commodities and several markets, the concept of equilibrium also became more complex.

As was rightfully acknowledged by Walras in the early 1870s, the exchange of several commodities created an opportunity for arbitrage. This opportunity resulted from the fact that when commodities, taken two at a time, were in a state of equilibrium with respect to each other, this would not necessarily imply that these same two commodities were automatically in equilibrium with a third commodity. Hence, arbitrageurs would be offered an opportunity to gain a profit by exchanging the two commodities at a more advantageous rate through the intermediation of such a third commodity. Although one could speak in terms of equilibrium as far as the commodities were taken in pairs, the possibility of arbitrage would make it an imperfect equilibrium. With the publication of the *Eléments* an idea of general market equilibrium was introduced:

> *We do not have* perfect *or general market equilibrium unless the price of one of any two commodities in terms of the other is equal to the ratio of the prices of these two commodities in terms of any third commodity.*

(*Eléments*, Section 111; emphasis in original)

The origin of Walras's general market equilibrium has often been attributed to Louis Poinsot's *Eléments de statiques*.[5] In particular William Jaffé[6] has described this book as the *fons et origo* of the conception of general equilibrium, based on similarities of the mathematical representation of equilibrium. In addition, Jaffé has tried to support his thesis by claiming that Poinsot's book was Walras's life-time companion-book.

To some extent, however, Jaffé's thesis is not very convincing. First, one may point to the fact that Walras did not develop the concept of general market equilibrium until 1874, whereas the multi-equational systems were elaborated by him at a much earlier date, without this specific conception of equilibrium, as follows from the 'tentatives'. If Poinsot had served as the prime inspiration for the general market equilibrium conception Walras could have developed it much earlier than 1874. Second, Walras acknowledged that he read Poinsot's work in 1853, but only reported this fact as late as 1901. In addition, Walras acknowledged having read several mathematical textbooks which he consulted during his career, such as Haton de la Goupillière's *Eléments de calcul infinitésimal* (1860).[7] In our opinion, none of these books, however, can be singled out as the *fons et origo* of the general market equilibrium concept. We therefore consider this matter as unsettled.

As will be set out in the following chapters, the concept of general equilibrium is applied by Walras throughout the different versions of the models. Hence in the model of exchange, equilibrium is a state in which effective demand and supply of commodities are equal and a stationary equilibrium price can be established. Similarly, in the production model,

11

equilibrium is the state in which also effective demand and supply of services are equal and a stationary equilibrium price can be observed in the services market. In addition, equilibrium in Walras's production models implies that the selling prices of the commodities equal the costs of the productive services entering into these commodities. The latter condition of equilibrium assumes that the selling price of commodities in equilibrium leaves no profits, or losses, for the entrepreneurs. In this situation no entrepreneurs will tend to flow into or out of the production sector in which equilibrium has been established nor will any entrepreneur tend to expand or decrease production. A situation of general equilibrium, therefore, represents a situation of rest.

It is generally acknowledged by Walras that equilibrium is not a real state but rather an ideal. In this respect, a setting of free competition is of crucial importance. Only in a situation of free competition, in which entrepreneurs are free to flow in and out of production sectors, will the market transactions tend to a state of equilibrium, which as such is denominated by Walras 'the normal state'. Nevertheless, in an attempt to approximate reality as closely as possible, Walras was aware that in a 'continuous market' general equilibrium is never attained:

> Such is the continuous market, which is perpetually tending towards equilibrium without ever attaining it, because the market has no other way of approaching equilibrium except by groping, and, before the goal is reached, it has to renew its efforts and start over again....
>
> (*Eléments*, Section 322)

The mathematical models presented by Walras and described in the subsequent chapters, however, only deal with situations of equilibrium. As such they represent neither the continuous market nor a real process of market transactions. This does not make the study of theoretical matters irrelevant for practical situations. It may be argued, as Walras in fact argued, that the better we know the ideal situation the better we shall know how to deal with actual practice.

3

ON THE NOTION OF UTILITY AS DEVELOPED BY WALRAS

SOCIAL WEALTH

The concept of social wealth is the central theme of Walras's work, as was underlined by the subtitle of the *Eléments*: 'The theory of social wealth'. As an element of the theory, social wealth was to relate to 'all things, material or immaterial (it does not matter which in this context), that are *scarce*, that is to say, on the one hand useful to us and, on the other hand, only available to us *in limited quantity*' (*Eléments*, Section 21; emphasis by Walras). This definition of social wealth clearly belonged to the 'Walrasian tradition', since it already formed the anchor in the writings of Auguste Walras, such as *De la nature de la richesse et de l'origine de la valeur* (1831) and *Théorie de la richesse sociale* (1849). Whereas the point of departure for Auguste Walras was above all the nature and origin of property, Léon Walras started his investigations in economic theory by choosing the exchange of social wealth as the subject to be studied in the first instance.

In the 1830s Auguste Walras had concluded that property only relates to those things that are both useful and valuable. Other things, not at the same time useful and valuable, would not be appropriated. Hence, a study of the nature and origin of property would need to go into matters of utility and value. Looking for an appropriate definition of value in the works of the contemporary economists of his day, he was dissatisfied with the accepted labour-commanded or labour-embodied approach. Primarily preoccupied with considerations of natural law and the appropriation of things by man, Auguste Walras found that some 'appropriated' wealth could not be covered with this approach:

> There are values prior to production. And here the facts are in favour of me; .... Spontaneous fruits of the earth, such as trees, wild animals, arable land as a factor of agricultural production, labour itself, or the entirety of man's industrial factors with respect to their primitive and natural characteristics, are things which certainly have value and are not the products of labour.[1]

These same arguments may be found in the works of Léon Walras. The definition of social wealth gave rise to matters of value in exchange, appropriation of scarce goods and the production of scarce goods. The concept of value in exchange was put on a par with the concepts of appropriation and production of scarce goods. All three concepts could then be derived from a more general idea of scarcity:

> *Value in exchange, industry and property* are ... the three generic phenomena of the three orders or groups of specific facts which result from the limitation in quantity of utilities or the scarcity of things. All three are bound up with the whole of social wealth and nothing else.
>
> (*Eléments*, Section 26)

Hence, this definition of social wealth was both an extension to Auguste Walras's work and a schedule to direct Léon Walras's theoretical work.

'VALORIES' AND VALUE IN EXCHANGE

The earliest traces of Walras's pure economics can be found in two manuscripts entitled 'Application des mathématiques à l'économie politique', the first designated as '(1ère tentative, 1860)' and the second as '(2e tentative, 1869–1870)'. In his first attempt to apply mathematics to economics around 1860, Walras looked for a mathematical representation of value in absolute terms. He called the unit of absolute value 'valorie', which was denoted as[2]

$$v = \frac{\text{demand}}{\text{supply}} = \frac{q_d}{q_0} \tag{1}$$

or, in general,

$$v = F(q_0, q_d). \tag{2}$$

Because different goods have their own absolute values, the relative value, or the price, of a good may also be expressed as a relation between absolute values. Confronted with an indeterminacy, Walras already considered at this stage the value of one of the goods to be invariable, say $v_a = 1$, so he could express the absolute values of the other goods in terms of the invariable good A:

> The ratio v_b/v_a is that between the absolute value of good B and the absolute value of good A, or the relative value of good B with respect to good A, or the *price* of one unit of B in units of A.[3]

In other terms:

$$p = \frac{v_b}{v_a} = \frac{v_b}{1}. \tag{3}$$

The price itself, then, may also be considered as a function of demand and supply for these goods:

$$p = F(q_0, q_d).$$ (4)

In part, this functional relation was based on an embryonic idea of exchange of equivalent quantities:

Theorem: Nobody is a demander of a certain quantity of social wealth unless he is supplying a certain other quantity of social wealth.[4]

Supply at this stage was simply considered as the aggregate of the individual amounts *possessed,* rather than offered, of goods A, B, C, ... Demand at this stage was triggered by desires and made manifest by the revealed absolute value of the quantity demanded. Following the above theorem, Walras concluded that the desire α of an individual for good A must equal the value of good A (denoted by v_a) multiplied by its quantity demanded (denoted by a_d):

$$\alpha = v_a a_d.$$ (5)

The aggregate over all the individuals would then be ('Applications', 1ère tentative)

$$\alpha + \alpha' + \alpha'' + \ldots = v_a(a_d + a_d' + a_d'' + \ldots),$$ (6)

$$\beta + \beta' + \beta'' + \ldots = v_a(b_d + b_d' + b_d'' + \ldots),$$ (7)

$$\gamma + \gamma' + \gamma'' + \ldots = v_a(c_d + c_d' + c_d'' + \ldots).$$ (8)

Following the above theorem, in which demand of an individual would necessarily imply a supply by this same individual, Walras concluded that in the market each supply of a good would meet its demand. Hence, taking $S_\alpha, S_\beta, S_\gamma, \ldots$ as the respective sums of desires A, B, C, ..., $A_d, B_d, C_d, \ldots$ as the respective sums of individual demands and $A_0, B_0, C_0, \ldots$ as the respective sums of individual supplies of A, B, C, ..., Walras concluded that total desires must equal the total value of the goods offered:

$$S_\alpha = v_a A_0,$$ (9)

$$S_\beta = v_b B_0,$$ (10)

$$S_\gamma = v_c C_0,$$ (11)

or

$$v_a = \frac{S_\alpha}{A_0},$$ (12)

$$v_b = \frac{S_\beta}{B_0},$$ (13)

15

$$v_c = \frac{S_y}{C_0}. \tag{14}$$

The absolute value is then proportional to the sum of desires and inversely proportional to the sum of provisions.[5]

Although it seemed that Walras had been able to find a practicable expression for the absolute value, in fact he had simply transferred the problem. Whereas the supply, as a sum of provisions, could in principle be measured, the sum of desires would cause more difficulties. Hence Walras concluded:

> There is no unit of demand or of want. From this it follows that one cannot speak in an absolute sense of a piece of social wealth as having a value resulting from confronting some specific demand with some specific offer. In other words, there is no absolute value, there are only relative values.[6]

The interesting point at this stage was the embryonic relation between value and desire which, once elaborated, would later become one of the anchors of Walras's marginal utility theory: the desires could, indeed, influence the value of a good. The main feature of the first tentative, compared with his later work, however, consisted of the fact that the absolute value of a good was considered to be the same for everyone and, as such, was attached to the good itself.

In his second attempt to apply mathematics to economics, around 1870,[7] Walras introduced a concept of utility to express those qualities of a good that are able to satisfy the desires of man:

> Utility of a commodity is supposed to be in proportion to the sum of the wants it satisfies – or the sum of the wants are in proportion to utility.[8]

To relate demand to supply, Walras introduced a concept which he called 'rareté', and which differed in content from the marginal utility meaning he would attach to it some years later. At this stage rareté was defined as the ratio of the utility of a good to the available quantity, or the ratio of demand and supply of a good.[9] By defining rareté as the ratio of demand and supply Walras, in fact, tried to capture the same absolute value he had tried to pursue ten years earlier. To some extent, this may be due to the fact that he had slavishly taken over the term from his father, who had labelled rareté as the limited quantity of useful things. It was clear at this point, however, that value was thus becoming quite a volatile concept. Since rareté was the ratio of demand and supply, and since demand and supply were continually changing, rareté could hardly be considered as an invariable concept. This implied that value in exchange, defined as the relative raretés, was also a continually changing term, as observed by Walras:

16

Value in exchange is measured by a meter of which the magnitude is changing in our hands.[10]

The problems Walras already had encountered in the first tentative thus re-emerged in the second. The problem, in fact, consisted of the impossibility of finding an absolute measure, whether it be 'value' or *rareté*:

The real difficulty in appreciating *rareté* is the absence of a unit of utility. Utility is not susceptible of weighing. Wants are not susceptible of measuring. Utility and wants belong to the things that are within us. This is why *rareté* cannot be measured directly either .... One only measures relative *rareté*.[11]

Although the second tentative did not conclude with an absolute measure, this second step was an important one: this tentative married the concept of utility to the concept of scarcity, as we have seen.

UTILITY AND DEMAND

The conclusions of the two 'tentatives' turned out to be the starting point for Walras from which to develop a theory of exchange on a mathematical basis. The theory, however, only fully matured after his arrival at Lausanne. There he continued the research of values in exchange, but now as ratios of quantities exchanged, i.e. in relative terms, rather than in such esoteric notions as *rareté*. In particular he studied exchange ratios in their causal relationship with utility and scarcity.[12]

During the period 1870–1, Walras elaborated the concept of utility by making a distinction between *virtual* utility and *effective* utility, thereby distinguishing, on the one hand, the total virtual human wants and, on the other, the effective manifestation of utility in terms of wants satisfied.

Virtual utility, then, coincided to some extent with the definition of utility Walras had introduced in the second 'tentative'. Around 1870 it was extended by imposing a double dimension on the virtual wants: the magnitude of the virtual wants in their totality and the urgency of the virtual wants. Hence Walras distinguished *extensive* (virtual) utility, relating to the magnitude of wants, and *intensive* (virtual) utility, relating to the urgency. Extensive utility could be expressed as the amount of goods that would be desired if their prices were not an obstacle, i.e. if prices were equal to zero. Intensive utility expressed the relation between the urgency of the successive wants and the capacity of the commodity to diminish this urgency. At this stage, Walras postulated that the intensive utilities diminished with each consecutive unit of consumption:

I postulate that intensive utilities always diminish from that from the first unit or fraction of a unit consumed to that of the last unit or fraction of a unit consumed.

(*Eléments*, Section 74)

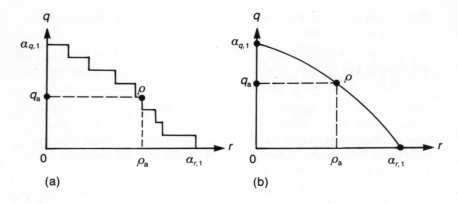

Figure 3.1

This relationship is often called by Walras the good's 'utility equation (function)', whereas nowadays we would refer to it as the good's 'marginal utility function'. In geometrical terms it can be depicted by a graph of one of the two forms of Figure 3.1.

Figure 3.1(a) applies to a commodity that is not perfectly divisible; Figure 3.1(b) applies to a perfectly divisible good. The utility depicted in the figure is the intensive (virtual) utility for good (A) of individual (1).[13] When consumption actually takes place and wants are indeed satisfied, virtual utility becomes realized utility, i.e. the intensive utility *ex ante* is translated into the intensity of the wants satisfied *ex post*. The intensity of wants satisfied can be depicted by the same figure. The intensity of the last wants satisfied by consuming a quantity of good (A) is measured horizontally. If individual (1) consumes in total a quantity q_a of good (A) then Walras calls $0\rho_a = \phi_{a,1}(q_a)$ the rareté of good (A). In other terms, $\phi_{a,1}(q_a)$ is the intensity of the last want satisfied when a quantity q_a of good (A) is consumed, i.e. the marginal utility of (A).

The innovative element in this analysis is that the previously expected utility of a commodity is now translated into the revealed utility in the form of satisfied wants. These wants are now the explanatory factors lying behind the phenomenon of exchange.

In geometrical terms the area $0\alpha_{r,1}\alpha_{q,1}$ in Figure 3.1 represents both virtual utility and the maximum attainable effective utility. Effective utility of the consumption of a quantity q_a of (A) is depicted as the area $0\alpha_{r,1}\rho q_a$. The fact that the curves display both *ex ante* and *ex post* utilities gives the analysis a rather confusing 'double character'. The introduction of virtual utility, in either of its dimensions, seemed in the end to serve no purpose other than to provide an explanation for the 'cause' of the exchange: virtual wants can be satisfied through exchange.

By creating the concept of effective utility Walras, in fact, introduced a clearly defined motivation for exchange. The trading of objects could now be evaluated by the degree of satisfaction of wants. Total effective utility was defined by Walras as the sum of the effective utilities corresponding to the quantities of the various commodities consumed by the individual. By assuming 'that his [the trader's] object in trading is to gratify the greatest possible sum total of wants' (*Eléments*, Section 76) he could now describe an optimal situation as one in which a maximum satisfaction of wants is attained, after the exchange. Exchange of goods, then, partakes of the form of exchange of lower utilities for higher utilities. Following Walras, the exchange will take place when each trader has ensured for himself that a maximum of utility subject to the constraint of the total virtual utility is attainable. This implies that, given the initial quantities possessed and given the prices of the commodities, the *raretés* of each commodity are evaluated. This was later, at the end of his career, explained by Walras in a note intended for Charles Gide (never mailed), which deserves full quotation:

Observation to Mr Gide (June 98)

1^0 Distinction between *final utility* (increment of effective utility) and the *final degree of utility* (rareté).

Final utility is the product of the increment [dq] in quantity, supposed to be infinitesimally small (positive or negative, demand or supply), and the *final degree* [r] *of utility* (rareté):

$$\text{final utility} = dq \times r. \tag{15}$$

2^0 Maximum effective utility of (A) and (B) for a trader at *prices cried* comes about when final utilities are equal:

$$dq_a \times r_a = dq_b \times r_b, \tag{16}$$

$$\frac{r_a}{r_b} = \frac{dq_b}{dq_a} = p_{a,b}. \tag{17}$$

This condition does not determine exchange, but only *demand* and *supply*.[14]

Hence, supply and demand are determined by the principle of utility maximization as we shall elaborate in the next part of this book.

4

WALRAS'S GRAPHIC ANALYSIS OF THE EXCHANGE OF TWO GOODS

Having read Cournot's *Recherches sur les principes mathématiques de la théorie de la richesse social* (1838) Walras was acquainted with the notion of market demand and the corresponding notion of the demand curve. Inspired by these ideas, Walras elaborated market demand in several ways.

1 He considered the market demand curve as an aggregate of individual demand curves.
2 He developed a graphical apparatus for the two-goods case, in which market demand as well as market supply are considered, together determining the equilibrium prices.
3 He underpinned these individual demand curves theoretically as stemming from maximization of utility while taking into account a budget restriction.
4 He generalized Cournot's demand function such that other prices can also influence the demand for a certain good.

In this chapter we shall deal with the first two of these issues.

DEMAND AS AN AGGREGATE

Let the individuals be indicated by (1), (2), (3), ... Individual (1) will consume $a_{d,1}$ units of good (A) if this good is a free good, i.e. when its price is zero. The quantity $a_{d,1}$ is assumed to be finite and not necessarily the same as the quantities $a_{d,2}$, $a_{d,3}$, ... for the other individuals. When the price of (A) increases from 0 to, say, p'_a individual (1) will demand for consumption a quantity of good (A) that is less than $a_{d,1}$. The quantity demanded decreases further when the price increases from p'_a to p''_a. This is depicted in Figure 4.1.

For the case of only two goods the demand schedule can be denoted by the following demand function:

$$d_{a,1} = f_{a,1}(p_a); \tag{1}$$

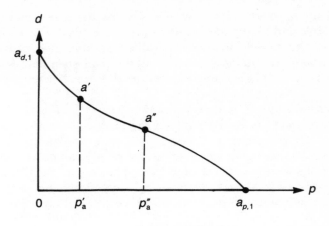

Figure 4.1

its graph is supposed to intersect both co-ordinate axes, but the function $f_{a,1}$ need not be continuous, according to Walras. For the other individuals there are similar demand functions for good (A): $d_{a,2} = f_{a,2}(p_a)$, $d_{a,3} = f_{a,3}(p_a)$, ...

By 'joining to one another all the ordinates corresponding to each abscissa, we obtain a total [or aggregate] demand curve $A_d A_p$' (*Eléments*, Section 52). This is depicted in Figure 4.2(a). In formulae:

$$D_a = f_{a,1}(p_a) + f_{a,2}(p_a) + f_{a,3}(p_a) + \ldots = F_a(p_a). \tag{2}$$

Here we have in Walras's own symbols the very first aggregation procedure ever presented formally in economic theory.[1] Walras was the first economist who built models in which individual demand and supply are explicitly

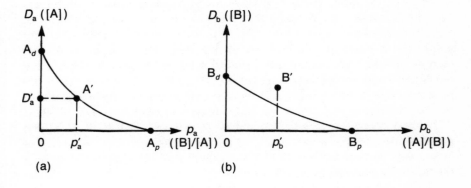

Figure 4.2

21

aggregated at the market level. In this way he developed models that are manageable and surveyable because of their (relatively) small numbers of variables. The models are also determined microeconomically, as we shall see, because the equilibrium values of the total quantities demanded and supplied can be split into micro quantities that are all determinate, and optimal.

The macro function F_a is always considered to be continuous, irrespective of the continuity or discontinuity of the individual demand functions $f_{a,1}$, $f_{a,2}$, $f_{a,3}$, ... comprising it. Following Cournot, Walras tried to justify this continuity by making an appeal to the law of large numbers.[2] Although Cournot was apparently rather doubtful about this argument, Walras made no further point of it. Market demand (and supply) functions are considered to be continuous throughout the *Eléments* without any further comment.

Below we shall investigate how the individual demand functions can be derived from utility maximization by the individuals.

MARKET EQUILIBRIUM

Most modern textbooks of (micro)economics start with the case of the demand for and supply of one good, in one market. There must also be a second good, however, for the simple reason that otherwise there can be no question of exchange. In the above mentioned textbooks, this problem has been solved by assuming that the market parties exchange the good against money or the other way around, where money represents all other goods. The question then arises: why should one not first consider the case of exchanging *directly* two goods against each other? Therefore, Walras started by considering a simple world in which only two goods exist and where there is a group of people possessing a certain quantity of the first good which they wish to exchange, wholly or in part, against some of the other good; the other group of people in this economy consists of holders of only the second good which they wish to exchange for the first good. The underlying assumption that there should be *groups* of holders of (A) and of (B) is essential here. Because Walras desired to analyse the phenomenon of free competition there should be a multiplicity of competing demanders and competing suppliers. For Walras there was therefore no reason to start with analysing a Robinson Crusoe type of economy, nor to start with the case where only two individuals try to exchange two goods.

Let two decreasing demand functions $D_a = F_a(p_a)$ and $D_b = F_b(p_b)$ be given. D_a denotes the *total* quantity of good (A) demanded by the group of individuals that are holders of (B), the other good. D_a is assumed to be a continuously decreasing function of the price p_a, the quantity of (B) that has to be given in exchange for one unit of (A). Likewise one can define D_b, F_b and p_b; hence p_b is the reciprocal of p_a, or $p_a p_b = 1$. The demand

22

functions are considered to be given and to have graphs that intersect both axes; this is depicted in Figure 4.2.

It should be noted that $F_a(p_a)$ is the amount of good (A) that the demanders are willing to buy when the prevailing price is equal to p_a. When the available quantity of (A) is less than $F_a(p_a)$, the demanders try to outbid each other; this is reflected in the negativity of the slope of the demand curve. On the other hand, the available amount of (A), i.e. the quantity offered by the demanders for commodity (B), may be larger than $F_a(p_a)$. In that case the suppliers are considered to underbid each other.

The dimensions of the four magnitudes D_a, p_a, D_b and p_b are indicated in square brackets in Figure 4.2: D_a is measured in quantities of good (A), denoted by [A] in Figure 4.2(a); p_a is measured in quantities of good (B) divided by quantities of good (A), which is indicated by [B]/[A]; the same applies to Figure 4.2(b). Let p'_a be an arbitrary value of the price p_a. Then $0D'_a$ is the total quantity of good (A) that the demanders are willing to buy at that specific price. The area of the rectangle $0D'_aA'p'_a$ is the value in good (B) of the amount $0D'_a$ and therefore has the dimension $[A]([B]/[A]) = [B]$. Let p'_b be such that $p'_ap'_b = 1$ and erect at the point of the horizontal axis with abscissa p'_b in Figure 4.2(b) the vertical line segment p'_bB' with length equal to the area of the rectangle $0D'_aA'p'_a$. Because of what we said above about the dimensions in the figure, no anomalies will arise.

In most cases the point B' at the top of the line segment will not lie on the demand curve B_dB_p. If, however, a value p'_a had been chosen such that its corresponding point B' does lie on the demand curve, we would have found a special price, which we shall call $\tilde{p}_a$. This price will be called the *equilibrium price*. The following relations hold for the equilibrium price:

$$F_a(\tilde{p}_a)\tilde{p}_a = F_b(\tilde{p}_b), \tag{3a}$$

$$\tilde{p}_a\tilde{p}_b = 1. \tag{3b}$$

The left-hand side of (3a) is the amount of (B) that demanders of (A), who are at the same time suppliers of (B), are willing to pay for the quantity $F_a(\tilde{p}_a)$ of (A) if the price is $\tilde{p}_a$. Since this amount is equal to $F_b(\tilde{p}_b)$ with $\tilde{p}_a\tilde{p}_b = 1$, exchange can take place because then the demanders of (A) offer just as much of (B) as the demanders of (B) are willing to buy at the prevailing price $\tilde{p}_b = 1/\tilde{p}_a$.

From the above considerations it follows that an equilibrium price can be found as a point of intersection of the demand curve B_dB_p and the 'offer curve' that can be constructed from the demand curve A_dA_p by plotting in Figure 4.2(b) all points B' that can be constructed for different points p'_a on the segment $0A_p$ of the horizontal axis of Figure 4.2(a). The offer curve is the broken line KLM in Figure 4.3(b). Point K results from a price p_a equal to the length $0A_p$; in this case the inscribed rectangle has become the line segment $0A_p$ which has an area equal to zero. Point L corresponds to the

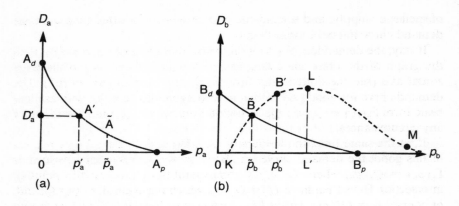

Figure 4.3

largest rectangle of the type $0D'_a A'p'_a$ and M reflects a rectangle with its p'_a very close to 0 on the horizontal axis of Figure 4.3(a). It can easily be seen that the offer curve always has a form like KLM if the demand curve for (A) is continuously decreasing in p_a and intersects both axes. Further, it is clear that there is also an offer curve for good (A) that can be drawn in Figure 4.3(a); this offer curve and the demand curve for (A) intersect each other at a point Ã with abscissa $\tilde{p}_a = 1/\tilde{p}_b$.

That these points of intersection correspond to a stable equilibrium follows from the assumption of free competition, which, among other things, means that the demanders outbid each other in the case of excess demand and that the suppliers underbid each other in the case of excess supply. This may be explained as follows. If, say, p_b is less than $\tilde{p}_b$ (see Figure 4.3(b)) then demanders of good (B) will outbid each other, which results in a higher demand price; suppliers will then offer more and a movement in the direction of $\tilde{p}_b$ sets in. If the price is in the first instance higher than $\tilde{p}_b$, the suppliers will underbid each other; demand will increase and, again, a movement in the direction of $\tilde{p}_b$ will set in. The criterion for stability, as Walras already observed in the first edition of the *Eléments*, is that the offer curve cuts the demand curve such that in a neighbourhood of the point of intersection the demand curve lies above the offer curve for prices lower than the abscissa of the point of intersection and lies under the offer curve for prices above that abscissa. Or, saying it more loosely, the criterion for stability is that the supply curve cuts the demand curve from below.

SOME SPECIAL CASES

Two interesting topics complete Walras's graphical analysis: first the case of inelastic[3] supply, and second the case in which the offer curve and the demand curve intersect more than once.

If, say, the demanders of (A) wish to sell all they have of good (B), then the graph of the offer curve becomes a straight line parallel to the horizontal axis (see the dotted line through Q_b and B in Figure 4.4(b)). The demand curve for good (A) is then an orthogonal hyperbola[4] with as algebraic form $F_a(p_a) = Q_b/p_a$; Q_b is the total quantity of (B) to be sold under any circumstances.

If, at the same time, the holders of (A) also wish to sell all they possess of this good, the demand curve for (B) is likewise a hyperbola; its form is $F_b(p_b) = Q_a/p_b$, where Q_a is the total quantity of (A). At the point of intersection B we then have $Q_b = Q_a/p_b$, which results in $\tilde{p}_b = Q_b/Q_a$ and, of course, $\tilde{p}_a = Q_a/Q_b$. This is in accordance with what could be expected, because the prices are again ratios of quantities exchanged.

In the situations depicted thus far there is always a stable equilibrium price. There may be situations, however, in which the criterion for stability is not met, as Walras already pointed out as early as 1874 (*Eléments*, first edition, Section 60 and Figure 2). The quantity of (B) offered increases if p_b rises from 0K to 0L' (see Figure 4.3(b)). If p_b increases further then that quantity decreases. This is because goods (A) and (B) are the only goods in the economy in question and because of the form of Walras's demand functions: if p_b is low, holders of (B) will ask less (A) against a high price (of (A)); and if p_b is high these holders ask more (A) against a low price. In both cases the quantities of (B) offered are small and they will tend to zero if p_b decreases or increases further, respectively. Consequently, we have 'eventually forward-falling' offer curves, i.e. offer curves that eventually will decrease for increasing prices. This means that the offer curve may

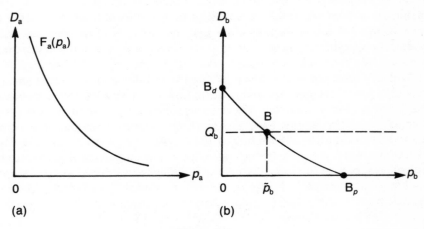

Figure 4.4

25

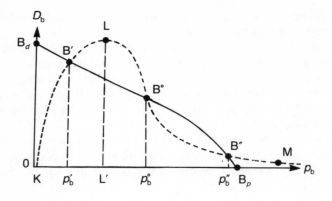

Figure 4.5

have more than one point in common with the demand curve. Such a case is depicted in Figure 4.5, where the two curves have three points in common (see also Walras 1874: Figure 2).

In Figure 4.5 the offer curve and the demand curve intersect at B′, B° and B″. Point B° does not meet Walras's stability criterion mentioned above. If p_b lies between p'_b and $p°_b$ supply exceeds demand and suppliers will underbid each other, which will decrease p_b further, however, until B′ is reached. If p_b lies between $p°_b$ and p''_b then the outbidding will force the price to rise further until B″ is reached. Hence B° is an unstable point of equilibrium. Two other situations (not considered by Walras) would arise if B′ and B° or B″ and B° coincided. In these cases the offer curve touches the demand curve at B° and intersects it at B″ or B′, respectively. It can easily be shown that the point of intersection is a stable equilibrium point. The point of tangency, on the other hand, could be called 'semi-stable': a disturbance from the point of tangency in the direction of the point of intersection leads to a further movement in the same direction until the intersection point is reached; after a disturbance in the other direction, however, the price will eventually come back to the point of tangency.

Walras's geometrical treatment of supply and demand described above provides a clear insight into his ideas on how markets work. Nevertheless, it did not get much following. The reasons for this might be the undeniable complexity of the figures and, above all, the circumstance that it is only applicable in the case of bartering of two goods. We inserted this typically Walrasian piece of theory for its own sake, but also because it provides us in a plain way with the case of a forward-falling supply curve and therefore with 'natural' examples of cases of stability and instability of market prices. Walras unmistakably had a good claim on priority with respect to this matter (see further Walras 1954: Lesson 7, note 5).

26

Part II

WALRAS'S EQUILIBRIUM MODELS

Quant à [ma théorie], j'en réponds: c'est celle du *Grenznutzen* poursuivie dans les derniers détails de l'équilibre économique.

Léon Walras
(Letter 1465 in Jaffé 1965)

5

WALRAS'S EXCHANGE MODEL

Walras's analytical derivation of demand curves is an important element of the *Eléments*. For a long time he considered it as his main achievement and for good reason.

THE THEOREM OF MAXIMUM UTILITY OF COMMODITIES

In Chapter 3 we observed that the individual demand functions are determined by utility maximization. Walras considered the individuals as being able to appreciate in some 'internal, subjective way' the 'value in utility' for them of a certain quantity of each good. Furthermore, he postulated that the effective utility that an individual attaches to a whole basket of goods and services is the sum of the effective utilities yielded by each good and service separately in the basket.

The notion that was instrumental in this analysis is what Walras called the '*rareté*' of a good. A good's *rareté* is defined, in Walras's own words, as 'the intensity of the last want satisfied [l'intensité du dernier besoin satisfait] by any quantity *consumed*' (*Eléments*, Section 75; Walras's italics). Crucial for Walras's theory is now that, for every individual consumer and each good, he assumed a relationship to exist between the quantity consumed of a good on the one hand and the intensity of the last want satisfied by that consumption on the other. Walras called this relationship the good's 'utility function', which has to be considered as 'subjective' because its parameters depend on the individuals' characteristics, but nevertheless, he argued, we may consider it as a normal mathematical function that can be manipulated just as other mathematical functions.[1]

It must be stressed that Walras introduced his intensive utility as the more *fundamental concept* of his system. It is therefore inappropriate to consider intensive utility as the derivative of effective utility. Rather we have to consider effective utility as an integral of intensive utility. For instance, for an individual whose *rareté* function for good (A) is $\phi_{a,1}$ and

29

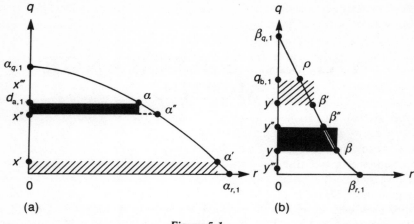

Figure 5.1

who consumes a quantity $q_{a,1}$ of (A), the effective utility u of that consumption is

$$u = \int\limits_0^{q_{a,1}} \phi_{a,1}(q)\mathrm{d}q = \Phi(q_{a,1}). \tag{1}$$

We are now in a position to derive an individual's demand functions from his *rareté* functions. We shall start by considering the process of utility maximization in the simple case in which there are only two goods (A) and (B).

Consider an individual (1), holding only a quantity of good (B), who wishes to exchange (part of) his belongings for a quantity of good (A). It will turn out that the demand for (A) can only be determined on the basis of the individual's *rareté* curve for (A) together with that for (B), which are both supposed to be decreasing continuous functions of the respective quantities. Here we have the first glimpse of the interdependence of all economic variables of a system.

In Figure 5.1 we have depicted the two *rareté* functions $\phi_{a,1}$ and $\phi_{b,1}$ for individual (1). With Walras we measure quantities along the vertical axis and intensive utility along the horizontal axis. The individual's initial holdings of (B) are denoted by $q_{b,1}$ and his initial holdings of (A) are zero. We suppose that the price of (A) in (B) is given as p_a. Further, we suppose that the length $0\alpha_{r,1}$ in Figure 5.1(a) is greater than $q_{b,1}\rho$ in Figure 5.1(b) multiplied by p_a, or

$$\phi_{a,1}(0) > p_a\phi_{b,1}(q_{b,1}). \tag{2}$$

Under Walras's assumption that the individuals strive at maximum total effective utility (2) implies that giving up some (B) for some (A) is profitable. This can be explained as follows. Let x' be a small quantity of good (A) which will be purchased by individual (1) in exchange for $q_{b,1} - y' = p_a x'$ units of (B). Because of (2) we can choose x' such that $\phi_{a,1}(x') > p_a \phi_{b,1}(y')$. Multiplying the two sides of this inequality by $p_a x'$ and $q_{b,1} - y'$ respectively and dividing both sides of the resulting inequality by p_a yields $x'\phi_{a,1}(x') > (q_{b,1} - y')\phi_{b,1}(y')$. This means that the hatched rectangle of Figure 5.1(a) has a greater area than the hatched rectangle of Figure 5.1(b). But then we certainly have that the area of the 'trapezium' $0\alpha_{r,1}\alpha'x'$ of (a) is larger than the area of the 'trapezium' $q_{b,1}\rho\beta'y'$ of (b). This means that the individual's total effective utility has increased as a consequence of this transaction. It is obvious that further exchange of (B) for (A) against the price p_a will likewise be profitable as long as the same inequalities as above hold. Let x'' in Figure 5.1(a) be the result of a chain of utility-increasing transactions with corresponding y'' in Figure 5.1(b) and with $\phi_{a,1}(x'') > p_a \phi_{b,1}(y'')$. However, there must be a situation with a total quantity $d_{a,1}$ of (A) exchanged for a quantity y of (B), and hence with $p_a d_{a,1} = q_{b,1} - y$, such that

$$\phi_{a,1}(d_{a,1}) = p_a \phi_{b,1}(y). \tag{3}$$

The transaction in which $d_{a,1} - x''$ units of (A) are exchanged against $y'' - y$ units of (B) turns out to be still profitable. To show this we note that, because of (3) and because of the fact that the price p_a is always equal to the ratio of two quantities exchanged, or $p_a = (y'' - y)/(d_{a,1} - x'')$, we have $(d_{a,1} - x'')\phi_{a,1}(d_{a,1}) = (y'' - y)\phi_{b,1}(y)$. This means that the two dark rectangles in Figure 5.1 have the same area. But then the area of $d_{a,1}\alpha\alpha''x''$ is larger than that of $y''\beta''\beta y$. Hence this transaction is likewise profitable. A further transaction, indicated by, say, x''' and y''', where $x''' - d_{a,1}$ units of (A) are exchanged against $y - y'''$ of (B), will diminish total effective utility with regard to the total effective utility entailed by a consumption of $d_{a,1}$ units of (A) and y units of (B). This can be argued in the same way as above: additional effective utility of (A) is less than that of (B) given up. This means that consuming $d_{a,1}$ units of (A) and y units of (B) yields maximal effective utility for the individual, given the prices of (A) and (B) (see *Eléments*, Sections 76–9). Walras gives the following verbal conclusion:

> *Given two commodities in a market, each holder attains maximum satisfaction of wants, or maximum effective utility, when the ratio of the intensities of the last wants satisfied* [by each of these goods], *or the ratio of their* raretés, *is equal to the price. Until this equality has been reached, a party to the exchange will find it to his advantage to sell the commodity the* rareté *of which is smaller than its price multiplied by the* rareté *of the other commodity and to buy the other commodity the* rareté *of which is greater than its price multiplied by the* rareté *of the first commodity.*

> (*Eléments*, Section 80; Walras's italics)

THE INDIVIDUAL DEMAND FUNCTIONS

The individual demand functions can now be derived as follows.

Writing $o_{b,1}$ for $q_{b,1} - y$ (the quantity offered of (B)), condition (3) of utility maximization can be written as

$$\phi_{a,1}(d_{a,1}) = p_a \phi_{b,1}(q_{b,1} - o_{b,1}). \tag{4}$$

Since $o_{b,1} = d_{a,1} p_a$, this can be rewritten as

$$\phi_{a,1}(d_{a,1}) - p_a \phi_{b,1}(q_{a,1} - d_{a,1} p_a) = 0. \tag{5}$$

From this $d_{a,1}$ can be found as a function of p_a:

$$d_{a,1} = f_{a,1}(p_a), \tag{6}$$

which is individual (1)'s demand equation (*Eléments*, Section 81).

For the case in which one or both *rareté* functions are step functions, or display other discontinuities, relation (5) cannot in general be fulfilled exactly. Walras discussed this problem neatly in showing how optimal consumption then takes place if (5) is fulfilled 'approximately' and how the ensuing demand equation (6) can be derived (Sections 84–5). Likewise he treated other special cases of the above exchange situation systematically (Sections 85–91) before discussing the more general case in which an individual may initially hold quantities of both goods.

A highly interesting aspect of the above exposition is that Walras succeeded in restricting himself completely to elementary mathematics, with the notion of continuity of functions the most advanced.

For the case of differentiable *rareté* functions Walras provided the following alternative proof. Total effective utility can be written as a function of $d_{a,1}$:

$$u_1(d_{a,1}) = \Phi_{a,1}(d_{a,1}) + \Phi_{b,1}(q_{b,1} - d_{a,1} p_a)$$

$$= \int_0^{d_{a,1}} \phi_{a,1}(q)\mathrm{d}q + \int_0^{q_{b,1} - p_a d_{a,1}} \phi_{b,1}(q)\mathrm{d}q. \tag{7}$$

Differentiating u_1 with respect to $d_{a,1}$ and equating the result to zero yields

$$u_1'(d_a) = \phi_{a,1}(d_{a,1}) - p_a \phi_{b,1}(q_{a,1} - d_{a,1} p_a) = 0. \tag{8}$$

Equation (5) follows from this (*Eléments*, Section 82).

Differentiating once more gives

$$u_1''(d_{a,1}) = \phi_{a,1}'(d_{a,1}) + p_a^2 \phi_{b,1}'(q_{a,1} - d_{a,1} p_a) < 0. \tag{9}$$

The second derivative is negative because the *rareté* functions are declining differentiable functions of quantity and therefore have negative derivatives. This means that (5) is, indeed, the condition for utility maximization.

32

The second-order condition $u_1''(d_{a,1}) < 0$ for maximization of utility appeared for the first time in print in the fourth edition (1900) of the *Eléments*, though it appears from his correspondence that already in 1888 he was aware of it.[2] This throws a clear light on the extent of Walras's technical abilities with respect to mathematics when starting his *Eléments*; one could say he learned it 'on the spot'.

Incidentally, the assumption of differentiability of the *rareté* functions is superfluous because $u'(x)$ is decreasing in x, which means that the solution $d_{a,1}$ of (6) is such that $u'(x) > 0$ for $x < d_{a,1}$ and $u'(x) < 0$ for $x > d_{a,1}$; hence $u(x)$ is increasing for $x < d_{a,1}$ and decreasing for $x > d_{a,1}$. Consequently $u(x)$ attains a maximum for $x = d_{a,1}$. The maximum is global because $u'(x)$ is decreasing throughout its whole range, which means that its sign changes only once.

EXCHANGING TWO GOODS

In the more general case in which an individual initially holds non-zero quantities of both (A) and (B), it depends on these quantities, together with his *rareté* curves and the prices of (A) and (B), whether he will exchange some (A) for (B) or the other way round. Therefore let x_1 and y_1 be the quantities of (A) and (B), respectively, that are traded by individual (1). A negative value of x_1 implies that individual (1) gives up some of his holdings of (A) in exchange for a positive quantity y_1 of (B); in the reverse case he buys x_1 units of (A) and sells some (B). We always have

$$x_1 = -p_a y_1, \tag{10a}$$

$$y_1 = -p_b x_1. \tag{10b}$$

Note that $p_a = 1/p_b$. Using the same reasoning as in the preceding section, it can be proved that for utility maximization the quantities x_1 and y_1 have to fulfil

$$\phi_{a,1}(q_{a,1} + x_1) = p_a \phi_{b,1}(q_{b,1} - p_a x_1), \tag{11a}$$

$$\phi_{b,1}(q_{b,1} + y_1) = p_b \phi_{a,1}(q_{a,1} - p_b y_1). \tag{11b}$$

These equations can be solved for x_1 or y_1, yielding

$$x_1 = f_{a,1}(p_a), \tag{12a}$$

$$y_1 = f_{b,1}(p_b). \tag{12b}$$

Note that x_1 and y_1 are related to each other because $p_a = 1/p_b$.

Likewise there are demand functions for individuals (2), (3), ...:

$$
\begin{aligned}
x_2 &= f_{a,2}(p_a) & y_2 &= f_{b,2}(p_b), \\
x_3 &= f_{a,3}(p_a) & y_3 &= f_{b,3}(p_b), \\
&\vdots
\end{aligned}
\tag{13}
$$

Here, again, x_i is demand in the usual sense of the word when it is positive and it is supply (negative demand) when it is negative.

Now we come to Walras's analytical treatment of the determination of the market price. Total excess demand is defined as

$$X = x_1 + x_2 + x_3 + \ldots$$
$$= f_{a,1}(p_a) + f_{a,2}(p_a) + f_{a,3}(p_a) + \ldots$$
$$= G_a(p_a). \tag{14}$$

Equilibrium, i.e. demand equals supply in both markets and individuals maximize utility, prevails if all market parties' decisions are based on a price $\tilde{p}_a$ which is a solution of

$$G_a(p_a) = 0. \tag{15}$$

Note that, because $y_i = -p_b x_i$, we then also have

$$Y = y_1 + y_2 + y_3 + \ldots$$
$$= f_{b,1}(p_b) + f_{b,2}(p_b) + f_{b,3}(p_b) + \ldots$$
$$= G_b(p_b) = 0 \tag{16}$$

if $p_b = \tilde{p}_b = 1/\tilde{p}_a$.

That the prices $\tilde{p}_a$ and $\tilde{p}_b = 1/\tilde{p}_a$ are indeed equilibrium prices follows from the twofold circumstance that, first, total demand for (A) equals total supply of (A) and the same holds for (B) and, second, all individual quantities demanded and supplied are such that individual effective utility is maximal. The first assertion follows from $X = Y = 0$ if $p_a = \tilde{p}_a$, whereas the second follows from the fact that

$$G_a(\tilde{p}_a) = f_{a,1}(\tilde{p}_a) + f_{a,2}(\tilde{p}_a) + f_{a,3}(\tilde{p}_a) + \ldots = 0, \tag{17}$$

implying that for each individual i the values $\tilde{x}_i = f_{a,i}(\tilde{p}_a)$ and $\tilde{y}_i = -p_a \tilde{x}_i$ are such that

$$\phi_{a,i}(q_{a,i} + \tilde{x}_i) = \tilde{p}_a \phi_{b,i}(q_{b,i} - \tilde{y}_i). \tag{18}$$

Hence, upon completion of the exchange all individuals consume optimal quantities of (A) and (B).

The positive values of $f_{a,1}(p_a)$, $f_{a,2}(p_a)$, $f_{a,3}(p_a)$, $\ldots$ as well as those of $f_{b,1}(p_b)$, $f_{b,2}(p_b)$, $f_{b,3}(p_b)$, $\ldots$ add, respectively, up to the values $F_a(p_a)$ and $F_b(p_b)$ of the preceding chapter. The negative values of the above sequences, when taken in absolute value, add up to the respective offer curves for (A) and (B).

BARTERING AN ARBITRARY NUMBER OF GOODS

The simple case of the foregoing section is necessarily one of so-called barter exchange: the two goods are exchanged directly against each other. The most straightforward generalization to the case of the exchange of m commodities (A), (B), (C), (D), ... for one another is where we suppose that there exist $\frac{1}{2}m(m-1)$ 'trading posts', one for each pair of goods, where two goods can be exchanged directly. Walras was the first to study such a barter economy more or less in detail using mathematical symbols (see Lesson 11 of the *Eléments*).

In this barter model there are m groups of agents: holders of (A) demanding (B), (C), ..., holders of (B) demanding (A), (C), ..., and so on. There are $m(m-1)$ prices: p_{ab} (i.e. the price of (A) measured in (B)), $p_{ac}, \ldots, p_{ba}, p_{bc}, \ldots, p_{ca}, p_{cb}, \ldots$. Likewise there are $m(m-1)$ quantities: D_{ab} (i.e. the quantity of (A) demanded in exchange for (B)), $D_{ac}, \ldots, D_{ba}, D_{bc}, \ldots, D_{ca}, D_{cb}, \ldots$. The holders of (A) are assumed to express their total demands $D_{ba}, D_{ca}, \ldots$ as functions of the $m-1$ prices that are relevant to them: $D_{ba} = F_{ba}(p_{ba}, p_{ca}, \ldots)$ and so on. Similar assumptions are made for the holders of other goods. These demand equations are given, i.e. posited somehow, as aggregates of corresponding individual equations. This results in $m(m-1)$ equations.

There are $\frac{1}{2}m(m-1)$ separate markets: that for (A) and (B), that for (B) and (C) and so on. In the separate market for (A) and (B), for instance, the following two equilibrium conditions prevail:

$$D_{ba} = p_{ab}D_{ab} \qquad D_{ab} = p_{ba}D_{ba}. \tag{19}$$

Likewise there are similar equations for the other separate markets. Hence another $m(m-1)$ equations have to hold good.

All in all this results in $2m(m-1)$ equations with $2m(m-1)$ unknown variables; the latter, according to Walras, can now be determined, where the prices are pairwise each other's inverses.

It should be observed that the above model describes the most strict form of bartering. The $m(m-1)$ equations of type (19) express that eventually the quantity of any good (X) demanded in exchange for any good (Y) equals the quantity of (X) offered in exchange for (Y). Only in this pure barter model can transactions be performed without an intermediary means of exchange.

It seems that Walras did not have such an unrealistic pure barter model in mind, because he replaced the equilibrium equations (19) by the m equilibrium conditions expressing that the total demand for each good has to be equal to its total supply. For good (A), for instance, this would mean

$$D_{ab} + D_{ac} + \ldots = p_{ba}D_{ba} + p_{ca}D_{ca} + \ldots \tag{20}$$

This would allow for indirect barter, but now there are fewer equations than variables.

Walras solved this problem by removing another objection against the pure barter model. In the purest barter model it is by no means certain, as he observed, that the resulting prices are the real unambiguous ratios of exchange because p_{ab}, p_{bc}, ... may be such that traders may benefit from arbitrage, i.e. from the existence of different prices in different situations for the same pair of goods. If, for instance,

$$p_{bc} > \frac{p_{ba}}{p_{ca}} \tag{21}$$

then it is not good business to buy (B) in direct exchange for (C); instead it will be more profitable to sell (C) for (A) first, and then to sell the acquired quantity of (A) in exchange for (B).

It is obvious that in a situation of general economic equilibrium gains by arbitrage are not feasible. This means a reduction in the number of prices in the above system in the sense that, in fact, there are only $m - 1$ independent prices. In addition to $p_{ab} = 1/p_{ba}$, $p_{bc} = 1/p_{cb}$ and so forth (see (19) above), we then also have, as Walras stated,

$$p_{bc} = \frac{p_{ba}}{p_{ca}}, \ldots \tag{22}$$

If we choose good (A) as the so-called *numéraire*, i.e. as a 'standard commodity' in which the prices of the other commodities are measured, and if we replace the symbols p_{ba}, p_{ca}, ... by p_b, p_c, ... (the price of (A) being equal to 1) then we still have $m(m - 1)$ demand equations for the separate markets: $D_{ba} = F_{ba}(p_b, p_c, \ldots)$, $D_{ca} = F_{ca}(p_b, p_c, \ldots)$, ... The m equilibrium equations (20) now become

$$D_{ab} + D_{ac} + \ldots = p_b D_{ba} + p_c D_{ca} + \ldots,$$

$$D_{ba} + D_{bc} + \ldots = \frac{1}{p_b} D_{ab} + \frac{p_c}{p_b} D_{cb} + \ldots,$$

$$D_{ca} + D_{cb} + \ldots = \frac{1}{p_c} D_{ac} + \frac{p_b}{p_c} D_{bc} + \ldots, \tag{23}$$

$$\vdots$$

Multiplying the second of equations (23) on both sides by p_b, multiplying the third by p_c, and so on, and adding the results, we obtain the first of equations (23). Hence, one of the m equations of (23) is redundant, and consequently we end up with $m(m - 1) + m - 1 = (m + 1)(m - 1)$ equations in $(m + 1)(m - 1)$ variables.

EXCHANGING AN ARBITRARY NUMBER OF GOODS

Just as in the case of the exchange of two goods, one would expect that Walras would have continued his exposé with a microeconomic under-pinning of the magnitudes D_{ab}, D_{ac}, D_{ad}, ... In the opening sentence of

Lesson 12 of the *Eléments*[3] he seems to announce this. But further on it turns out that he abstracted from the $\frac{1}{2}m(m-1)$ trading posts and restricted himself to the microeconomic explanation of the m totals $D_{ab} + D_{ac} + D_{ad} + \ldots, D_{ba} + D_{bc} + D_{bd} + \ldots$ etc.

Hence, instead of considering the micro quantities of the type $d_{ab}, d_{ac}, d_{ad}, \ldots, d_{ba}, d_{bc}, d_{bd}, \ldots$ etc., he turned his attention to the explanation of less specific micro quantities, not distinguished by trading posts:

Let $x_1, y_1, z_1, w_1, \ldots$ be the quantities of (A), (B), (C), (D), $\ldots$ respectively which our individual will add to the original quantities held $q_{a,1}, q_{b,1}, q_{c,1}, q_{d,1}, \ldots$ at prices $p_b, p_c, p_d, \ldots$[4] These additions may be positive and consequently represent quantities demanded; or they may be negative so as to represent quantities offered. Inasmuch as the individual trader cannot possibly demand any of these commodities without offering in return a quantity of other commodities having the same value, we can be sure that if some of the quantities $x_1, y_1, z_1, w_1, \ldots$ are positive, others are bound to be negative, and that the following relationship between these quantities will always hold:

$$x_1 + y_1 p_b + z_1 p_c + w_1 p_d + \ldots = 0. \tag{24}$$

(Eléments, Section 118, our numbering)

Using the same arguments as on pages 30–1, it can be argued that maximum satisfaction is achieved for individual (1), in other words, the sum of the effective utilities of (A), (B), (C), (D), $\ldots$ is maximal for him, if

$$\phi_{b,1}(q_{b,1} + y_1) = p_b \phi_{a,1}(q_{a,1} + x_1),$$

$$\phi_{c,1}(q_{c,1} + z_1) = p_c \phi_{a,1}(q_{a,1} + x_1),$$

$$\phi_{d,1}(q_{d,1} + w_1) = p_d \phi_{a,1}(q_{a,1} + x_1), \tag{25}$$

$$\vdots$$

This can also be seen by writing total effective utility u as a function of $y_1, z_1, w_1, \ldots$, making use of relation (24) and assuming the *rareté* functions to be differentiable and decreasing:

$$u = \int_0^{q_{a,1} - p_b y_1 - p_c z_1 - p_d w_1 - \cdots} \phi_{a,1}(q)\mathrm{d}q + \int_0^{q_{b,1} + y_1} \phi_{b,1}(q)\mathrm{d}q$$

$$+ \int_0^{q_{c,1} + z_1} \phi_{c,1}(q)\mathrm{d}q + \int_0^{q_{d,1} + w_1} \phi_{d,1}(q)\mathrm{d}q + \cdots. \tag{26}$$

Differentiating u subsequently with respect to $y_1, z_1, w_1, \ldots$ results in the relations (25). That a solution of (25) indeed yields a maximum of u may be inferred from the fact that the matrix of second derivatives of u is diagonal with negative elements on its main diagonal. These elements are

$$p_b^2 \phi'_{a,1}(q_{a,1} + x_1) + \phi'_{b,1}(q_{b,1} + y_1),$$
$$p_c^2 \phi'_{a,1}(q_{a,1} + x_1) + \phi'_{c,1}(q_{c,1} + z_1),$$
$$p_d^2 \phi'_{a,1}(q_{a,1} + x_1) + \phi'_{d,1}(q_{d,1} + w_1), \tag{27}$$
$$\vdots$$

They are negative because the *rareté* functions are decreasing for increasing quantities.[5]

The equilibrium prices, or the '*current prices*' as they were baptized by Walras, in an exchange economy under free competition can subsequently be determined from equations (25) together with (24). From these first-order conditions for maximum utility one can derive the following demand or supply equations for individual (1):

$$y_1 = f_{b,1}(p_b, p_c, p_d, \ldots),$$
$$z_1 = f_{c,1}(p_b, p_c, p_d, \ldots),$$
$$w_1 = f_{d,1}(p_b, p_c, p_d, \ldots), \tag{28}$$
$$\vdots$$

For individual (2), of course, similar equations exist:

$$y_2 = f_{b,2}(p_b, p_c, p_d, \ldots),$$
$$z_2 = f_{c,2}(p_b, p_c, p_d, \ldots),$$
$$w_2 = f_{d,2}(p_b, p_c, p_d, \ldots), \tag{29}$$
$$\vdots$$

and so forth for (3), (4), ...

Defining total excess demands as

$$X = x_1 + x_2 + x_3 + x_4 + \ldots,$$
$$Y = y_1 + y_2 + y_3 + y_4 + \ldots,$$
$$Z = z_1 + z_2 + z_3 + z_4 + \ldots,$$
$$W = w_1 + w_2 + w_3 + w_4 + \ldots, \tag{30}$$
$$\vdots$$

we can write, as a result of simple addition of the corresponding equations for individuals (1), (2), (3), (4), ..., the aggregate excess demand functions as

$$Y = F_b(p_b, p_c, p_d, \ldots),$$
$$Z = F_c(p_b, p_c, p_d, \ldots),$$

$$W = F_d(p_b, p_c, p_d, \dots), \tag{31}$$
$$\vdots$$

In equilibrium we have

$$Y = 0, \ Z = 0, \ W = 0, \dots. \tag{32}$$

Consequently, we have the following $m - 1$ equations of which the $m - 1$ equilibrium prices are the solutions:

$$F_b(p_b, p_c, p_d, \dots) = 0,$$
$$F_c(p_b, p_c, p_d, \dots) = 0,$$
$$F_d(p_b, p_c, p_d, \dots) = 0, \tag{33}$$
$$\vdots$$

System (33) is a system in which the prices, expressed in *numéraire*, are the endogenous variables that are determined eventually by the system. It is completely in accordance with Walras's starting point: the phenomenon that in markets goods are exchanged against each other in certain quantities and that therefore these exchange ratios are the principal features that have to be described and explained in pure economics. The solution of system (33) is a vector of prices p_b, p_c, p_d, ... of the goods (B), (C), (D), ... in terms of (A) as *numéraire*. If these prices prevail for everybody there is no gain in arbitrage; each individual will achieve maximum satisfaction of his desires by equating the ratios of the *raretés* of each pair of goods to the ratio of the prices of those goods, while markets clear.

Note that, if (33) is satisfied, X will automatically become zero because $p_b Y + p_c Z + p_d W + \dots$ always denotes the total net quantity of (A) exchanged, which is zero if $Y = Z = W = \dots = 0$. Here we recognize what we now call Walras's law.

DISCUSSION

Walras expressed the above result as follows:

> *The exchange of several commodities for one another in a market ruled by free competition is an operation by which all holders of one, several, or all of the commodities exchanged can obtain the greatest possible satisfaction of their wants consistent with the twofold condition: (1) that any two commodities be exchanged for each other in one and the same ratio for all parties and (2) that the two ratios in which these commodities are exchanged against any third commodity be proportional to the ratio in which they are exchanged for each other.*

(Section 131; Walras's italics)

His contemporaries had great difficulties in interpreting this. In particular the question whether or not the sum of all individual utilities, i.e. the total utility for the whole community, is maximized when equilibrium is reached has led to much misunderstanding. In our view, there is no justification for an interpretation of Walras's results in terms of maximal social utility.[6] It would be equally dubious to see in the above quotation a 'premonition' of the Cournot–Nash equilibrium. In our interpretation Walras was simply the first who gave a correct definition (or, rather, a description) of the notion of general economic equilibrium. What Walras tried to achieve by means of his equations (with (14) above as the simplest example) was to demonstrate the plausibility of a 'normal state': a solution of his systems of equations, yielding prices that give rise to a situation of equilibrium in the above sense. It is at these prices that exchange can take place.

From the viewpoint of modern general equilibrium analysis, a reasonable interpretation is that Walras came to the conclusion that there are uniform current prices such that at these prices market clearance may coincide with the greatest possible effective utility for each individual under the further condition that each individual may freely use his initial endowments for own consumption or for exchange.[7]

6

THE NOTION OF CAPITAL

When studying exchange only, one need not bother about the fact that the commodities exchanged are products originating from the combination of production factors. These factors are supplied by the capital owners for use in the production processes. If one wishes to proceed further in the direction of more realism, the exchange of these factors of production should also be taken into consideration. This has been done by Walras in his so-called *production model.* Therefore, as we shall see, he had to distinguish capital goods from consumption goods and had to provide clear practicable definitions of these concepts. Fortunately, he had not to look very far, because his father had already written at length upon the subject.[1]

THE THREE CATEGORIES OF CAPITAL

Following his father, Walras defined the notion of capital goods as all forms of social wealth that are not used up after their first use; in other words, a capital good's duration of life consists of a number of subsequent periods. Apparently he had in mind durable goods in the literal sense of the term. Later, however, from the fourth edition of the *Eléments* onwards, he also introduced what he called 'circulating capital', a notion already touched upon by his father, too.[2] Where his father did not do much more than provide a (useful) taxonomy, Léon Walras took a step further in bringing the above concepts into his analytical framework, thereby maintaining his father's terminology as much as possible.

A capital good is capable of giving rise to a sequence of services during the periods of its existence and therefore the Walrases made a clear distinction between the capital goods themselves and the *services* provided by these capital goods as factors of production. We shall exemplify this crucial distinction in the discussion of the three categories of fixed capital goods that are distinguished:

1   land,
2   human capital,
3   capital proper.

Within each category of capital several subcategories can be distinguished. Corresponding to these categories, individuals can function, alternatively or simultaneously, as

1   land-owners,
2   labourers,
3   capitalists.[3]

Walras's open-mindedness with respect to the economic reality of his time made him adopt wholeheartedly his father's classification. The three categories each have their own specificity that cannot escape the attentive observer. Land is characterized by its availability in fixed quantities and its indestructibility. Human capital is evidently a separate category of production factors. Land and human capital remain exogenous in Walras's models.

Industrialization, i.e. the increasing use of machines, is the evident cause of the spectacular economic progress of the nineteenth century. Machinery or, more generally, capital proper has therefore been given its own place in Walras's analytical framework. In contradistinction to land, capital proper is subject to wear and tear, which decreases its stock; this stock may be increased, however, by the production of new capital.

It will appear that this classification suited Walras very well to underpin his analysis of the notion of property and to ventilate his judgements on that subject. See for this Chapter 19, the finale of this book.

Walras meticulously made a distinction for each capital good between (i) the good itself, (ii) its service in kind and (iii) the money value of the latter. Consequently, he distinguished the following three triples:

1   (i) land(ed capital)   (ii) land services   (iii) rent
2   (i) personal capital   (ii) labour   (iii) wage
3   (i) capital goods proper (ii) capital services (iii) interest[4]

With the word 'income' Walras denoted in the first instance all revenues *in kind* of some capital. Different pieces of land can yield quite different kinds of income. Examples are the pleasure of walking in a public garden, the fertility of a piece of land and a plot's suitability for construction. Because this income is in kind we can speak of the price of a certain type of land service. Similarly, there are many types of human capital, giving rise to many types of labour. Into the third category we place all remaining capital assets, which are neither land nor personal capital: houses, machines, trees, cattle etc. They are all productive of income: shelter, products, fruit, milk and so on.

It should be noted that many of the services, i.e. many types of land services, labour or capital services, may be used in two different ways. First, they can be utilized as consumers' services; for instance, one can live in one's own house, or one can 'consume' one's own labour in the form of leisure. Second, in agriculture, industry or commerce, they can be transformed into products, thus rendering productive services.

CAPITAL IN THE PRODUCTION PROCESS

Throughout the *Eléments* capital goods are invariably considered as being owned by individual capital-owners. They supply capital services for productive purposes. In the production model products are consumption goods only. In this model Walras assumed the capital goods to be given: for the period under consideration, each owner of a certain type of capital is assumed to have at his disposal certain given quantities of capital goods, from which services originate. The owners are supposed to use some of these services for their own consumption and to sell the rest as productive services or for consumption by other individuals. Investment in new capital goods is not considered at this stage, and exchange of capital goods themselves will not take place; this is elaborated in the model of capital formation, in which the phenomenon of wear and tear of capital goods is allowed for and where production of new capital goods takes place in order to replace or to augment the capital stock.

7

THE ENTREPRENEUR

Among Walras's major innovations in economic theory, such as the concepts of *rareté* (marginal utility) and general economic equilibrium, the concept of the entrepreneur is a relatively minor one. Nevertheless, Walras claimed at length that his concept of the entrepreneur differed quite distinctly from both the English and French traditions and as such may be considered as an innovation. To some degree this claim seems to be justified, not because of the relative importance of the entrepreneur in Walras's theory but because of the volatile nature of the theoretical role of the entrepreneur in his models.

THE ENTREPRENEUR

The emphasis placed by Walras on the role of the entrepreneur follows quite naturally from the emergence of an industrializing society and its conceptualization. In an industrializing society, production would be withdrawn from a system of guilds and a new class of 'entrepreneurs' would be given the opportunity to unfold their activities. As a consequence, Walras observed, a division of labour would take place; at the same time the activity of entrepreneurs would induce competition.

This new class of 'entrepreneurs' revealed certain characteristics which would make it quite distinct from the classes of land-owners, labourers and capitalists. The latter classes, as we have seen in Chapter 6, were clearly associated with the categories of capital, i.e. land, human capital and capital proper. The entrepreneur, on the other hand, does not hold any capital. Apart from the land-owner, the labourer and the capitalist, the entrepreneur was one of the theoretical economic agents without predefined 'endowments':

A certain number of economic actors are entrepreneur and need, in that quality, a fund of working-capital comprising stocks of raw materials, products in their shops, and money for paying productive

44

services as well as to replenish the stocks of raw materials anticipating payments of products sold.

(*EPA*, p. 378)

The theoretical distinction between the classes, however, is primarily a functional one; the entrepreneur can only be differentiated from the land-owner, labourer and capitalist through the function he exercises in theory. From this it follows that the owners of the factors of production are the suppliers of these factors and the demanders of the (final) commodities. The demand for the factors of production and, subsequently, the supply of the (final) commodities is attributed to the entrepreneur.

Once translated to the various markets, i.e. the market for factors of production and the market for commodities, the functional distinction between the classes becomes clear. The role of the entrepreneur, then, is to buy productive services from the owners of the factors of production, thus providing rents, salaries and interests. Provided with these productive services the entrepreneurs see to it that production of commodities takes place and offer them at the product market. With this specific role of the entrepreneur Walras believed himself to be at variance with both French and English economists. The French economists, Walras claimed, consid-ered the entrepreneur as a specific type of manager in charge of produc-tion; hence, the entrepreneur was simply one of the labourers. Others, such as Jean-Baptiste Say, failed according to Walras to take account of any entrepreneur. The English economists, on the other hand, were accused by Walras of conflating the capitalist with the entrepreneur.

Walras's quarrel with French and English economists partly follows from the terminology adopted by Walras and not from the conceptualiz-ation of exchange and production. His claims are not substantiated because the models seem to exhibit little of the actual production process. In fact, the entrepreneur in Walras's model is only 'viewed' at the marketplace and is therefore, as we shall see in the next section, simply an intermediate person between providers of production factors on the one hand and consumers on the other. The entrepreneur in Walras's model may very well be the same person as the one who actually produces the commodities, though this is not accounted for in the model. Hence, whether Walras's definition of the entrepreneur excludes the function of a manager in charge of production does not follow from his model at this stage.

Simultaneously, the distinction between entrepreneur and capitalist is only an analytical distinction. In fact, an individual may perform several roles in reality and, as such, combine the various functions in one person. According to Walras, however, this theoretical distinction makes it possible to develop a theory of exchange based on univocal functional relations:

The definition of entrepreneur is, in my opinion, the kernel of the whole economic science. I, for me, consider him exclusively as the person who buys the productive services at the market for services and sells the products at the market for products, thus making a benefit or a loss. If he possesses part of the land or of the capital goods productive in his firm, or if he takes part, in the quality of manager or otherwise, in the activities relating to the transformation of the services into products, he is, for that reason, landowner, capitalist or labourer, and cumulates his own function [i.e. that of entrepreneur] with other, different functions. In practice such a cumulation occurs frequently and may, in general, even be necessary; but I believe that theoretically it [i.e. that cumulation] should be discarded from the analysis.

(Walras to F. A. Walker, 12 June 1887; Jaffé 1965: Letter 800)

In this light Walras's critique laid at the door of the French and English economists seems to serve no other purpose than to distinguish himself from the economists of his day. Nevertheless, since Walras's concept of the entrepreneur mainly served as a basis for his models of exchange, it may be considered as a minor innovation.

PROFITS AND LOSSES

One of the essential elements associated with the role of the entrepreneur in Walras's theory is the element of risk. The entrepreneur sees to it that production takes place but runs the risk that he might sell the produce at a loss or not be able to sell it at all. Hence, the function of the entrepreneur is not only one of intermediating between the services market and the product market but also of being responsible for a proper allocation of factors of production and final commodities. As explained by Walras, this risk extends to anyone involved in the production of commodities and, as such, the 'function' of the entrepreneur may be performed by either individuals, companies or the state:

In order to acquire some product in a society with division of labour one needs a market of services, a market of products and an entrepreneur who buys services at the first market at predetermined prices, has the product produced, and sells it at his risk at the second market. This entrepreneur may be an individual or an association of individuals; it may be a community or the State.

(*EPA*, p. 267)

The element of risk is translated in Walras's exchange models by 'profits' or 'losses' for the entrepreneur. Hence, profits are an expression of, and reward for, running the risk involved in the activities of the entrepreneur. These profits, or losses, are simply calculated by subtracting the costs of inputs from the sales revenues. Since these sales revenues are determined on one market, i.e. the products market, and the costs of inputs are determined on another, i.e. the services market, the entrepreneur is by necessity active on both markets and is thus the link between them.

Since profits and losses are an expression of the risk involved in his activities, the entrepreneur will be able to influence his profit position by increasing or decreasing the (degree of) risk, in other words, by increasing or decreasing production. In this particular circumstance, one can also think of entrepreneurs entering, or retreating from, a certain branch of production. The only motivation of the entrepreneur to influence production, then, is to obtain profits or to avoid losses.

> In fact, under free competition, if the selling price of a product exceeds the cost of the productive services for certain firms and a *profit* results, entrepreneurs will flow towards this branch of production or expand their output, so that the quantity of the product [on the market] will increase, its price will fall, and the difference between price and cost will be reduced; and if [on the contrary] the cost of the productive services exceeds the selling price for certain firms, so that a *loss* results, entrepreneurs will leave this branch of production or curtail their output, so that the quantity of the product [on the market] will decrease, its price will rise and the difference between price and cost will again be reduced. It is to be observed, however, that although the multiplicity of firms conduces to equilibrium in production, such multiplicity is not absolutely necessary in order to bring about this equilibrium, for, theoretically, one entrepreneur alone might do so if he bought his services and sold his products by auction, and if, in addition, he always decreased his output in case of loss and always increased it in case of a profit. That is not all, for now we see that the desire to avoid losses and to make profits is the mainspring of the entrepreneurs' actions in demanding productive services and offering products for sale.
>
> (*Eléments*, Section 188; Walras's italics)

In Walras's production model,[1] the functioning of the entrepreneur can be recognized in the relations expressing the equality of quantities of productive services *used* by the entrepreneur and the quantities of productive services *offered* by the land-owners, labourers and capitalists. Simultaneously, the selling prices of the products become equal to the costs of inputs. Since Walras's models only describe a situation of equilibrium, profits and losses are by necessity equal to zero. Hence, in Walras's production model entrepreneurs make neither profits nor losses.

The fact that Walras's entrepreneurs 'make neither profits nor losses' in a situation of equilibrium has led to much confusion and disagreement. Most of the confusion was based on the observation that in reality entrepreneurs do make profits or losses. Walras's model was therefore denounced as utterly unrealistic or simply false. The critique, however, did not take account of the fact that the profit position of the entrepreneur in equilibrium was simply a matter of definition. Walras's entrepreneur was not designed to represent a person or an institution but rather a function. Hence, as a function the entrepreneur ceased to exist in equilibrium:[2]

> Assuming equilibrium, we may even go so far as to abstract from entrepreneurs and simply consider the productive services as being, in a certain sense, exchanged directly for one another, instead of being exchanged first against products, and then against productive services. It was Bastiat's idea that, in final analysis, services are exchanged against services, but he meant only personal services, while we have in mind the services of land, persons and capital goods.
>
> (*Eléments*, Section 188)

By abstracting from the entrepreneur in equilibrium, Walras's production model also abstracts from the production process and thus only takes account of quantities exchanged. This interpretation of the producer and the entrepreneur only adds to the conviction expressed above that the entrepreneur is not necessarily linked to the production process itself even though he 'commands' the production process. As such, the entrepreneurial activity not only differs substantially from the French and English real-type definition of the entrepreneur but is also, in the Walrasian version, a highly volatile concept.

8

PRODUCTION

The sweeping nature of Walras's discussion of consumption is in striking contrast with the abrupt introduction of his mathematical description of production. The entrepreneurs make sure that production takes place, as we saw in Chapter 7, but Walras is not very explicit about how they do so. A definition of such a thing as a firm is lacking. Without any introduction the so-called coefficients of production drop from the sky (*Eléments*, Section 203).

Walras introduced his fixed coefficients of production as a preliminary device (Section 204) but never realized a definitive generalization. Since he eventually wished to study the consequences of growth of the economy (more people disposing of more than proportionally more products) with a fixed quantity of land, the fiction of fixed coefficients of production could not be maintained. This means that the coefficients of production had to be replaced by variable coefficients. Walras never revised his formal mathematical models in this sense. He only studied marginal productivity and its dependence on the scale of production as an afterthought, in Part VII of the *Eléments*. Nevertheless, the topic is interesting enough to deal with.

FIXED COEFFICIENTS OF PRODUCTION

Walras was one of the first economists to use the notion of 'coefficient of production' in dealing with the production of goods (and services).[1] In introducing these coefficients he supposed them all to be fixed. Building a model of production in the way that Walras did – i.e. working with coefficients of production, whether fixed or not – is only meaningful in a context of constant returns to scale; only then are the coefficients of production independent of the quantities produced. It may be that in Walras's time, and in his domiciles, such an assumption was not in contradiction with reality.

The coefficients of production are indicated by the symbols a_t, a_p, a_k, $\ldots$, b_t, b_p, b_k, $\ldots$, c_t, c_p, c_k, $\ldots$, d_t, d_p, d_k, $\ldots$ and so on. The products are denoted by (A), (B), (C), (D), $\ldots$; their number is m. The production

49

factors, of the categories land, human capital and capital proper, are denoted by (T), (P), (K), ...;[2] their number is n. Hence there are mn coefficients of production. For example, by a_t Walras denoted the quantity of productive services of type (T) needed for the production of one unit of (A). The coefficients of production are assumed to be determined by the condition that the costs of production of the products be minimal, indicating efficiency of the production process.

By means of the coefficients of production Walras could make a direct link between quantities of products on the one hand and the needed quantities of the several categories of capital services on the other. Further, he could easily express in mathematical form his equilibrium condition of no losses and no benefits; for good (B), for instance, this becomes $p_b = b_t p_t + b_p p_p + b_k p_k + \ldots$, where the ps denote prices per unit.

Firms do not play an explicit role. There is no joint production and the firms produce without fixed costs. Further, Walras assumed, for convenience, that the firms operating in one and the same sector of production are of the same size and behave as price takers; the number of firms in a sector remains undetermined.

Raw materials (which also include unfinished products here) are supposed to be produced by combining productive services or by applying these services to other raw materials, which are in turn obtained by similar applications to still prior raw materials (*Eléments*, Section 205). They are considered to be incorporated in the production coefficients. Walras gave the following example. Suppose that producing one unit of (B) costs $p_b = \beta_t p_t + \beta_p p_p + \beta_k p_k + \ldots + \beta_m p_m$, where the βs are coefficients of production in which the use of raw materials has not been incorporated and p_m is the price of raw material (M). (M) itself is also a product, and hence $p_m = m_t p_t + m_p p_p + m_k p_k + \ldots$, where the ms are coefficients of production and (M) has been supposed to be produced without making use of other raw materials; then p_b can be rewritten as $p_b = b_t p_t + b_p p_p + b_k p_k + \ldots$, where $b_t = \beta_t + \beta_m m_t$, $b_p = \beta_p + \beta_m m_p$, ...

Walras apparently supposed that the raw materials which are needed for production of the 'final' goods in the period under consideration are produced simultaneously with these goods and are used up in the production processes in that same period. It is obviously a task for the entrepreneur to take care of efficient production and use of raw materials.[3]

As Jaffé (Walras 1954: Lesson 20, note 3) rightly remarked, fixed coefficients of production imply that capital services are limitational in the sense that given the quantity of only one type of capital service in the production of a certain good, the quantity of that good that can maximally be produced is determined irrespective of the quantities of the other services. Consequently, a severe restriction has been placed upon the growth of production once the quantity of any specific type of capital cannot be augmented.

FLEXIBLE COEFFICIENTS OF PRODUCTION[4]

This leads us to Walras's ideas on incorporating flexibility of these coefficients by allowing them to vary with the prices of the production factors such that minimization of production costs per unit of product is ensured. It will turn out that thereby he (unconsciously or not) abandoned the assumption of constant returns to scale.

In the first two editions of the *Eléments* (Walras 1877: 249) it is already asserted[5] that in reality the coefficients of production may, in fact, depend on the prices of the production factors:

> It would be easy to express these conditions [of minimal costs] by a system of as many equations as there are coefficients of production; *but as this [sub]system would be, in a sense, independent of the other [sub]systems we are considering*, we may abstract from it for the sake of simplicity....[6]

To support this view Walras proposed (1877: 314; 1990: Section 325) a so-called production equation for each product,[7] relating the coefficients of production to each other. For good (B), for example, the equation is

$$\phi(b_t, b_p, b_k, \dots) = 0, \tag{1}$$

where ϕ is such that each of its arguments can be written explicitly as a decreasing function of the other variables, i.e. all partial derivatives of ϕ (if they exist) have the same sign. Hence ϕ expresses the fact that using less (more) of some factor in the production of one unit of (B) requires more (less) of at least one of the other factors. Writing all these coefficients subsequently as a function of the other coefficients, i.e.

$$b_t = \theta(b_p, b_k, \dots), \qquad b_p = \psi(b_t, b_k, \dots),$$
$$b_k = \chi(b_t, b_p, \dots), \qquad \dots, \tag{2}$$

and given the prices of the production factors, we can determine all coefficients of production for (B) such that the costs of producing such a unit, or

$$p_t \theta(b_p, b_k, \dots) + p_p \psi(b_t, b_k, \dots) + p_k \chi(b_t, b_p, \dots) + \dots, \tag{3}$$

is minimized. The solution of this minimization problem yields just as many equations as there are unknown coefficients of production for this good. Likewise there are similar systems of n equations for the $m-1$ other goods produced. These mn equations determining all the coefficients of production contain only the n prices of the factors of production as variables and therefore form a subsystem that is 'in a sense' (as Walras says; see the quotation above) independent of the other subsystems of the model. This was as far as he went in the first two editions of the *Eléments*.

From the above exposition it becomes obvious that in the first instance Walras missed the opportunity to conclude at that time that the n equations for (B) are

$$\frac{\partial\phi/\partial b_t}{p_t} = \frac{\partial\phi/\partial b_p}{p_p} = \frac{\partial\phi/\partial b_k}{p_k} = \ldots, \tag{4a}$$

together with

$$\phi(b_t, b_p, b_k, \ldots) = 0, \tag{4b}$$

and that for the other goods similar equations hold.

MARGINAL PRODUCTIVITY

From the beginning of the 1890s, while preparing the third (1896a) and the fourth (1900) editions of his *Eléments*, Walras started reconsidering the issue of the coefficients of production. Several sources of inspiration for Walras's elaboration of the subject of marginal productivity can be distinguished. In a letter dated 6 January 1877 Walras's colleague H. Amstein (professor of mathematics at Lausanne) solved the above minimization problem, at Walras's request, using Lagrange multipliers;[8] Amstein arrived at equations like (4a) and (4b). Walras's poor mathematical education, however, prevented him at that time from fully grasping the enormous significance of Amstein's answer (Jaffé 1965: Letter 364). Jaffé's careful deciphering of Walras's scribbled notes attached to Amstein's letter revealed that after more than seventeen years Walras began to grasp the mathematics involved, in particular the use of Lagrange multipliers. This took place at about the same time that Walras became acquainted with Wicksteed's booklet *An Essay on the Co-ordination of the Laws of Distribution* (1894). With regard to this essay Walras rightly understood that its thesis is that cost minimization implies that each production factor is paid its marginal product, the whole production being exactly exhausted without surplus or deficit. (Wicksteed based his analysis on the assumption of constant returns to scale.)

The result of this appeared in Appendix III of the third edition of the *Eléments*, entitled 'Note sur la réfutation de la théorie anglaise du fermage de M. Wicksteed'.[9] It is only from the third edition of the *Eléments* (Section 362) onwards that Walras asserted:

> The marginal productivities are taken into account ... for the determination of the coefficients of production.

From the fourth edition onwards this appendix was removed and instead the text itself was enlarged with a passage on marginal productivity. This passage is Section 326, considerably rewritten in the fifth edition.

Barone (1895)[10] apparently revealed to Walras the consequences of the homogeneity of degree one of the latter's and Wicksteed's production functions. Barone and Walras both referred to Pareto,[11] who proposed to generalize the production equation (1) to

$$\chi_b(b_t, b_p, b_k, \ldots, Q) = 0, \tag{5}$$

where Q is the quantity of the good to be produced (here (B)) and where χ_b is such that its partial derivatives with respect to b_t, b_p, b_k, ... have the same sign, which expresses the same features as relation (1). If $\partial\chi_b/\partial Q$ always has the opposite (same) sign with respect to the above partial derivatives, then the production process displays ever decreasing (increasing) returns to scale over the whole range of production. Defining T, P, K, ... as the quantities of the factors (T), (P), (K), ... producing a quantity Q of good (B), we can rewrite (5) as

$$\chi_b\left(\frac{T}{Q}, \frac{P}{Q}, \frac{K}{Q}, \ldots, Q\right) = 0. \tag{6}$$

From (6) we can derive the following production function for (B), in Walras's notation:

$$Q = \phi(T, P, K, \ldots), \tag{7}$$

which is in general not homogeneous of degree one.

Under conditions of free competition, i.e. when prices p_t, p_p, p_k, ... as well as p_b are given and are such that the entrepreneurs make neither profits nor losses, Walras derived the following conditions for cost minimization on the basis of (7):

$$\frac{\partial\phi}{\partial T} = \frac{p_t}{p_b}, \qquad \frac{\partial\phi}{\partial P} = \frac{p_p}{p_b}, \qquad \frac{\partial\phi}{\partial K} = \frac{p_k}{p_b}, \qquad \ldots \tag{8}$$

Hence:

$$\frac{\partial\phi/\partial T}{p_t} = \frac{\partial\phi/\partial P}{p_p} = \frac{\partial\phi/\partial K}{p_k} = \ldots \tag{9}$$

(see also (2), (3) and (4) in Walras 1926: Section 326). Because of the zero-profit condition the solutions T, P, K, ..., given Q, of these equations fulfil the following relation:

$$Q = T\frac{\partial\phi}{\partial T} + P\frac{\partial\phi}{\partial P} + K\frac{\partial\phi}{\partial K} + \ldots \tag{10}$$

which means 'product exhaustion', but now only incidentally and not identically as in the case in which ϕ is homogeneous of degree one. We stress here that (10) is a consequence of Walras's presumption of zero profits.[12] This implies that the production functions cannot be homogeneous of a degree not equal to one because then (10) would *never* be fulfilled, as follows from Euler's theorem on homogeneous functions. It is a moot question whether Walras and his colleagues were aware of this.[13] The wavering way in which Walras inserted the matter in the last three editions of the *Eléments* might indicate that he sensed difficulties. In our view, Walras considered it as a kind of side issue not fitting within the framework of his models.[14]

9

WALRAS'S PRODUCTION MODEL

As we have set out above, there are two types of markets, namely markets for production factors and markets for products. Entrepreneurs play an important role in both types. In the markets for services, i.e. the production factors, the entrepreneurs are the demanders; they buy these services for production purposes. The land-owners, labourers and capitalists are the suppliers. The rents, wages and interest are the prices of the services, as has been set out in the preceding chapters. The entrepreneurs need not be the only buyers in the markets for services. There may be land-owners, labourers or capitalists who wish to buy services for direct consumption purposes.

In the product markets the entrepreneurs are the sellers, whereas the land-owners, labourers and capitalists, in their capacity of consumers, are the buyers of the products. In both types of market a *numéraire* is used as a unit of measurement and free competition is assumed to prevail. There must also be a medium of exchange. Let us take the *numéraire* for this. A labourer, say, sells his labour for *numéraire* on a labour market and uses the acquired quantity of this *numéraire* to buy products on the products market; in both cases he will find an entrepreneur as his opponent. We postpone the discussion on how payments are actually made until Chapters 14 onwards.

According to Walras, equilibrium in production can now be characterized by the following three conditions.

1 There are prices for each productive service such that at these prices effective demand and effective supply for each service are equal.
2 There are also selling prices of the products such that in all product markets effective demand equals effective supply.
3 The selling price mentioned in 2 of each product is equal to the cost of the productive services, calculated by means of the factor prices mentioned in 1, that are needed for the production of one unit of that product.

Just as in the case of pure exchange, the land-owners, labourers and

55

capitalists are impelled by their desire to maximize utility to enter the markets for services and products.

The entrepreneurs strive for maximum profits. Walras did not analyse the entrepreneurs' profit maximization procedures in the same detail as he did with respect to the consumers' utility maximization process. Instead, he modelled the final outcome in equilibrium which amounted in his linear world to the famous assertion that in a state of equilibrium the entrepreneurs make '*ni bénifice, ni perte*' ('neither profit, nor loss').[1]

INDIVIDUAL DEMAND AND SUPPLY

Suppose that an individual (1) has at his disposal quantities q_t, q_p, q_k, ...[2] of services of n production factors (T), (P), (K), ... The individual offers quantities o_t, o_p, o_k, ... of these services in exchange for quantities d_a, d_b, d_c, d_d, ... of m goods (products) (A), (B), (C), (D), ... The quantities satisfy the following budget equation:

$$o_t p_t + o_p p_p + o_k p_k + \ldots = d_a + d_b p_b + d_c p_c + d_d p_d + \ldots, \qquad (1)$$

where the ps denote prices and the price of good (A), being the *numéraire*, is set equal to 1. The quantities $q_t - o_t$, $q_p - o_p$, $q_k - o_k$, ..., that are retained and consumed,[3] and the quantities d_a, d_b, d_c, d_d, ..., that are demanded and consumed, yield utility for the individual. Let the individual's *rareté* functions be denoted by ϕ_t, ϕ_p, ϕ_k, ..., ϕ_a, ϕ_b, ϕ_c, ..., all functions of only one variable, namely the quantities of, respectively, (T), (P), (K), ..., (A), (B), (C), ... Since Walras supposed utility to be additive in amounts of goods and services, the *rareté* functions have only one argument. Note, however, that the reasoning remains valid for more general utility functions.[4] In the same way as in Chapter 5 on exchange we arrive at the following set of first-order conditions for utility maximization:

$$\phi_t(q_t - o_t) = p_t \phi_a(d_a),$$
$$\phi_p(q_p - o_p) = p_p \phi_a(d_a),$$
$$\phi_k(q_k - o_k) = p_k \phi_a(d_a), \qquad (2)$$
$$\vdots$$

and

$$\phi_b(d_b) = p_b \phi_a(d_a),$$
$$\phi_c(d_c) = p_c \phi_a(d_a),$$
$$\phi_d(d_d) = p_d \phi_a(d_a), \qquad (3)$$
$$\vdots$$

56

From equations (1), (2) and (3) the following individual demand and supply equations can be derived:

$$o_t = f_t(p_t, p_p, p_k, \ldots, p_b, p_c, p_d, \ldots),$$
$$o_p = f_p(p_t, p_p, p_k, \ldots, p_b, p_c, p_d, \ldots),$$
$$o_k = f_k(p_t, p_p, p_k, \ldots, p_b, p_c, p_d, \ldots), \tag{4}$$
$$\vdots$$

and

$$d_b = f_b(p_t, p_p, p_k, \ldots, p_b, p_c, p_d, \ldots),$$
$$d_c = f_c(p_t, p_p, p_k, \ldots, p_b, p_c, p_d, \ldots),$$
$$d_d = f_d(p_t, p_p, p_k, \ldots, p_b, p_c, p_d, \ldots),$$
$$\vdots$$

$$d_a = o_t p_t + o_p p_p + o_k p_k + \ldots - (d_b p_b + d_c p_c + d_d p_d + \ldots). \tag{5}$$

THE MODEL

Walras postulated that all individuals behave in a similar manner with respect to consumption. Consequently, systems of equations like (4) and (5) may de derived for all individuals. This, however, does not imply that Walras's individuals have to be considered as pure 'clones'. Since the ϕ functions may differ between individuals and, moreover, the individual endowments may differ, the demand and supply equations may differ per individual.[5]

For each factor and for each commodity all the demand and supply functions are aggregated over the individuals:

Now, let O_t, O_p, O_k, ... designate the sum *total* of the several offers of services, i.e. the excess of the positive o_t, o_p, o_k, ...'s over the negative o_t, o_p, o_k, ...'s; let D_a, D_b, D_c, D_d, ... designate the sum *total* of the several demands for products; and let F_t, F_p, F_k, ..., F_b, F_c, F_d, ... designate the sums of the several functions f_t, f_p, f_k, ..., f_b, f_c, f_d, ... [Then] we have, at once, the following system of n equations of total offer of services:

$$O_t = F_t(p_t, p_p, p_k, \ldots, p_b, p_c, p_d, \ldots),$$
$$O_p = F_p(p_t, p_p, p_k, \ldots, p_b, p_c, p_d, \ldots),$$
$$O_k = F_k(p_t, p_p, p_k, \ldots, p_b, p_c, p_d, \ldots), \tag{6}$$
$$\vdots$$

and the following system of m equations of the *total* demand for the products:

$$D_b = F_b(p_t, p_p, p_k, \ldots, p_b, p_c, p_d, \ldots),$$
$$D_c = F_c(p_t, p_p, p_k, \ldots, p_b, p_c, p_d, \ldots),$$
$$D_d = F_d(p_t, p_p, p_k, \ldots, p_b, p_c, p_d, \ldots),$$
$$\vdots$$
$$D_a = O_t p_t + O_p p_p + O_k p_k + \ldots$$
$$- (D_b p_b + D_c p_c + D_d p_d + \ldots); \qquad (7)$$

in all $n + m$ equations required for the determination of our unknowns.

(*Eléments*, Section 202; emphasis added; the numbering is ours)

This is the consumption side of Walras's production model. The reader of the *Eléments* would expect some comments on this bold example of aggregation, but throughout the *Eléments* no such comment is present. Apparently Walras saw no problem in arriving at equations (6) and (7). From aggregation theory, however, it is well known that consistent aggregation of micro functions is only possible under very restrictive conditions.[6]

Immediately after the passage quoted above the coefficients of production are introduced (*Eléments*, Section 203), indicated by the symbols a_p, a_k, a_t, $\ldots$, b_p, b_k, b_t, $\ldots$, c_p, c_k, c_t, $\ldots$, d_p, d_k, d_t, $\ldots$ and so on (see Chapter 8). We then get the n equations of the third subsystem ((6) and (7) being the first two subsystems):

$$a_t D_a + b_t D_b + c_t D_c + d_t D_d + \ldots = O_t,$$
$$a_p D_a + b_p D_b + c_p D_c + d_p D_d + \ldots = O_p,$$
$$a_k D_a + b_k D_b + c_k D_c + d_k D_d + \ldots = O_k, \qquad (8)$$
$$\vdots$$

'expressing the fact that *the quantities of productive services used* [and effectively demanded by the entrepreneurs] *are equal to the quantities effectively offered* [by the land-owners, labourers and capitalists]' (Walras's italics). We shall denote these equations as the 'transformation equations' for reasons that will become clear below.

Market clearing has been brought into the model by simply using the symbols D_a, D_b, D_c, D_d, $\ldots$, O_t, O_p, O_k, $\ldots$ with a double significance: in (7) the Ds are quantities demanded by households[7] while in (8) they are quantities produced and supplied by entrepreneurs; in (6) the Os are quantities offered by households and in (8) these variables are quantities demanded by entrepreneurs.

The fourth and last subsystem of equations of Walras's production model brings into expression the benefit position in equilibrium of the entrepreneurs: the price of each of the goods is equal to the cost of the productive services involved in producing one unit of that good. This results in the following m equations:

$$a_t p_t + a_p p_p + a_k p_k + \ldots = 1$$
$$b_t p_t + b_p p_p + b_k p_k + \ldots = p_b$$
$$c_t p_t + c_p p_p + c_k p_k + \ldots = p_c$$
$$d_t p_t + d_p p_p + d_k p_k + \ldots = p_d \tag{9}$$
$$\vdots$$

We shall denote these equations the 'price equations'.
So we have

1   the supply equations for services (6),
2   the demand equations for products (7),
3   the transformation equations (8) and
4   the price equations (9).

These $2(m + n)$ equations together form Walras's production model. They are not independent of each other, however, because one can derive the last equation of (7) from the subsystems (8) and (9).[8] Hence we have $2m + 2n - 1$ independent equations in the $2m + 2n - 1$ variables of the whole system: n quantities of services, m quantities of products and $n + m - 1$ prices.

DISCUSSION

A solution of this model consists of a set of aggregates, i.e. totals over the whole economy. As can be inferred, Walras developed his theory for the households such that, in equilibrium, the total quantities of goods demanded and of factors supplied can be exactly disaggregated over the households in optimal quantities. These optimal quantities are micro quantities that maximize individual utility subject to the budget constraint determined by the household's initial endowments.

The production side is elaborated in much less detail. A consequence of this is a certain degree of indeterminateness of the model's microstructure. In fact, one can hardly state that production has been modelled by Walras, certainly not in the same comprehensive way as he modelled consumption. In his verbal passages he spoke of many (small) identical production units operating under a regime of fixed coefficients of production, such that the results may be combined into system (8). Hence with respect to the production side the model strictly speaking is a macro model. For each of

the goods (A), (B), (C), ... there is, so to say, one economy-wide production unit, whose technology is expressed by the fixed coefficients of
production.

Despite the fact that Walras himself speaks of 'production equations',
equations (8) can hardly be considered as production functions in the sense
of modern theory. They only express that the entrepreneurs buy services
and that these services are transformed into consumption goods. This is in
accordance with the circumstance that Walras's first concern was always
exchange. We shall therefore use the term 'transformation equations' when
dealing with equations like equations (8).

As a conclusion of this chapter we can say that the resulting system of
equations (6)–(9) displays all the features of a general economic equilibrium model in the present sense: in equilibrium consumers obtain
maximum utility given their budget constraints, producers produce at
minimum costs and earn zero profits, and markets clear.

10

THE RATE OF NET INCOME
AND THE FUTURE

In the production model the capital goods themselves are not subjects of trade. The individual endowments of capital are considered to be given and capital is supposed to be indestructible. Therefore the initial endowments of capital will not change. The services of capital (i.e. the means of production) are considered to be used either for own consumption directly or for the production of consumption goods. A further step in the direction of more realism is the introduction of a third way of using these services, namely for the production of capital goods proper. This brings with it five new aspects that have to be incorporated into the model: (i) the prices of the capital goods themselves, in addition to those of their services, (ii) depreciation and insurance, (iii) returns to capital (the rate of interest), (iv) savings, needed to finance new capital goods, and (v) the individuals' motivation to save. These points will be dealt with in this chapter. In the subsequent chapter they will be synthesized into the equation system of Walras's model of capital formation.

PRICES, DEPRECIATION AND RETURNS
TO CAPITAL

Because the new capital goods are to be traded in a market for capital goods, they will have a price. Just as in the case of consumption goods, the equilibrium selling price per unit of a capital good proper is equal to the cost of producing that unit (again, neither benefit nor loss); this yields for each capital good proper a price equation similar to equations (9) of the preceding chapter.

For convenience Walras chose his units of measurement such that one unit of each capital good will yield one unit of the corresponding service per period. Just as in Chapter 9 there are n different types of capital goods; l of them are capital goods proper, denoted by (K), (K'), (K''), ... Again, each of the n capital goods may in principle yield both consumers' services to satisfy individuals' wants and productive services. The latter services, however, may now be used to produce consumption goods or new capital goods proper. The new capital goods proper are assumed to be productive from the period subsequent to their production onwards. This assumption was stated explicitly by Walras for the first time in the fourth edition of the *Eléments* (Section 251), but it was already made implicitly in the first three editions, as can be inferred from the transformation equations: only the services of existing capital goods enter in the production of goods.[1]

In Walras's models of capital formation it is supposed that capitalists may set aside a certain amount of the returns per unit of capital good proper to neutralize losses of capital due to wear and accidental destruction. These amounts were taken as deductions from gross income and supposed to be proportional to the prices of capital P_k, $P_{k'}$, $P_{k''}$, ...: for each capital good (K) a depreciation rate μ_k per unit as well as an insurance rate ν_k per unit are introduced.[2] Together with the prices p_k and P_k this leads to the following definition of *net income* π_k per unit of capital:[3]

$$\pi_k = p_k - (\mu_k + \nu_k)P_k. \tag{1}$$

π_k is considered to be non-negative.

It is stated by Walras that in equilibrium for each capital good (K) the ratio of its net income π_k to its selling price P_k is the same for all capital goods. This ratio is called by Walras the *rate of net income* and is denoted by the symbol i. For all l capital goods proper (K), (K'), (K''), ... we therefore have

$$\frac{\pi_k}{P_k} = \frac{\pi_{k'}}{P_{k'}} = \frac{\pi_{k''}}{P_{k''}} = \ldots = i. \tag{2}$$

Combining this with (1) we obtain l expressions of the form

$$P_k = \frac{p_k}{i + \mu_k + \nu_k} \tag{3}$$

for the capital goods' prices in equilibrium.

There is abundant evidence that Walras attached much value to his achievements with respect to the theory of capital formation. He considered the proportionality of the goods' *raretés* and their prices[4] as the 'basis' of his models of general economic equilibrium and the proportionality (2) above as their 'crowning'. The latter proportionality, according to Walras, was a necessary condition for the optimality of the formation of new capital goods:

> The theorem of maximum utility of new capital goods is the crowning of the entire pure political economy. Would it not be possible to give an elementary proof of it by means of a geometric representation of the total increments of the utility of the products and the partial increments of the utility of the productive services involved in the output of the products?

YES

under the condition that we may generalize the formula for maximum satisfaction.[5]

The above theorem states that the proportionality of net incomes and selling prices per unit of capital goods (see (2)) has to hold good if the services of the newly produced capital goods, bought by the consumers-capitalists by means of their savings, are such that they procure as much utility as possible (*Eléments*, Section 261). By linking this proportionality to utility maximization, Walras made clear that he wished to do more than simply posit the condition of the proportionality of net incomes and prices of the capital goods as an equilibrium condition. In fact, he wished to prove it. As will be set out in Chapter 12, it is at this point that he has gone too far.

SAVINGS

After having dealt with production as described in the preceding chapter, in the first three editions of the *Eléments* Walras introduced so-called 'empirical savings equations'. These equations described savings as functions of prices and the rate of interest, without discussing the underlying motives of the individuals other than stating that they could be derived from utility maximization. As he himself explained, he preferred not to venture on the problems that would arise by introducing *future utility*, and therefore he simply posited the savings equations. At the time he was of the opinion that for properly treating savings and capital formation it would be necessary to set up a 'dynamic' system of equations, i.e. a system of equations in which variables relating to future periods play a role.

The approach to the problem of how to incorporate savings into his model of general economic equilibrium based on these empirical savings functions differed distinctly from the one in the last two editions. We shall therefore refer to Walras's model of savings and capital formation as exposed in the first three editions of the *Eléments* as the 'nineteenth-century model';[6] the model of the fourth (1900) and fifth editions will be called his 'twentieth-century model'. In the remainder of this chapter and in the next chapter we shall occupy ourselves with Walras's twentieth-century approach to savings; we shall see thereby how he found a way of treating savings explicitly within the framework of utility maximization whilst remaining within the realm of statics, but bringing himself 'as close as possible to the dynamic point of view' (*Eléments*, 4th edition, Section 272).

Each individual is supposed to own, at the outset of the period under consideration, quantities $q_t, \ldots, q_p, \ldots, q_k, q_{k'}, q_{k''}, \ldots$ of, respectively, (T), $\ldots$, (P), $\ldots$, (K) (K') (K''), $\ldots$. The individual is supposed to offer in the markets for services certain quantities of capital services $o_t, \ldots, o_p, \ldots, o_k,$ $o_{k'}, o_{k''}, \ldots$ and thus to keep for his own use the quantities $q_t - o_t, \ldots,$ $q_p - o_p, \ldots, q_k - o_k, q_{k'} - o_{k'}, q_{k''} - o_{k''}, \ldots$ of the services of these capital goods.[7]

This is the same as in the model of production. The difference, however, is that now a consumer's income, i.e. the value of his supply of services, may be unequal to the value of his demand for consumption goods. This difference, denoted e, is called his *gross savings*. In formulae,

$$e = o_t p_t + \ldots + o_p p_p + \ldots + o_k p_k + o_{k'} p_{k'} + o_{k''} p_{k''}$$
$$+ \ldots - (d_a + d_b p_b + d_c p_c + d_d p_d + \ldots). \tag{4}$$

The amount e may be either positive, zero or negative.

The motivation for saving is related to expectations regarding the future. However, instead of introducing magnitudes relating to future periods, and thus introducing dynamics into his equation system, Walras introduced in the fourth edition of the *Eléments* the notion of *present utility of the expectation of future additional income*. This idea was given concrete form by devising a new 'good', denoted (E), in which future additional income is embodied and to which the individuals are assumed to attach utility. For convenience we consider the individuals to have their quantities of (E) embodied in the capital goods they have in their possession and not in the form of certificates or such like.[8] In this way the capital goods are indirectly linked to Walras's concept of utility.

Buying one unit of this commodity (E) warrants a *net* income of one unit of *numéraire* per period for all periods subsequent to the current one. Quantities of (E) are measured in units of *numéraire* per period, of price p_e (4th and 5th editions, Section 242). Consequently, we have[9]

$$p_e = \frac{1}{i}. \tag{5}$$

The quantity q_e of (E) in the possession of any individual at the outset of a given period depends on the quantities of capital owned at the beginning of that period:

$$q_e = q_t p_t + \ldots + q_p \pi_p + \ldots + q_k \pi_k + q_{k'} \pi_{k'} + q_{k''} \pi_{k''} + \ldots \tag{6}$$

In this equation π_p denotes net income per unit of human capital (P). This does not mean that there actually exists a price P_p for which human capital can be bought or sold, but it reflects the consideration that for keeping intact a certain quantity q_p of human capital (P) one has to deduct a part from its income $q_p p_p$ to be spent on, say, health and education. Below, in equation (8), this part will be denoted by the symbol η_p. Land is supposed to be indestructible; in other words, $p_t = \pi_t$ and $P_t = p_t / i$.

As with any other good or service in the model, good (E) can be exchanged. An individual's *net* demand for (E) is denoted d_e. The expression 'net demand for (E)' means the amount of (E) demanded above the amount needed to maintain the individual's total stock of (E) at its initial level q_e, which can be positive, zero or negative.[10] Consequently, the amount $d_e p_e$ is by definition his demand for *net savings*. The magnitude of d_e will be determined such that the quantity $q_e + d_e$ of commodity (E), together with the quantities of the other goods and services consumed, maximize the individual's utility subject to a budget constraint. The utility function of the preceding chapter should therefore be extended by one argument, namely the quantity of (E); in other words, an additional *rareté* function appears, denoted by ϕ_e.

The individual's budget equation, as presented by Walras, is

$$o_t p_t + \ldots + o_p p_p + \ldots + o_k p_k + o_{k'} p_{k'} + o_{k''} p_{k''} + \ldots$$
$$= d_a + d_b p_b + d_c p_c + d_d p_d + \ldots + d_e p_e \qquad (7)$$

(4th and 5th editions, Section 242). This budget restriction reflects equation (4) above with $d_e p_e$ substituted for *e*. However, strictly speaking the budget restriction is erroneous because, as can be readily seen, $d_e p_e$ is the amount of gross savings whereas it should be the amount of net savings.[11]

The error can easily be removed, however, by introducing into the budget restriction a term σ_e denoting the difference between an individual's gross and net savings, in other words the amount of *numéraire* needed for maintaining his q_e at its initial level:

$$\sigma_e = \eta_p q_p p_p + (\mu_k + \nu_k) q_k P_k + (\mu_{k'} + \nu_{k'}) q_{k'} P_{k'}$$
$$+ (\mu_{k''} + \nu_{k''}) q_{k''} P_{k''} + \ldots \qquad (8)$$

The budget restriction then becomes

$$\underbrace{o_t p_t + \ldots + o_p p_p + \ldots + o_k p_k + o_{k'} p_{k'} + o_{k''} p_{k''} + \ldots}_{\text{income}}$$

$$= \underbrace{d_a + d_b p_b + d_c p_c + \ldots}_{\text{consumption}} + \underbrace{d_e p_e + \sigma_e}_{\text{gross savings}} \qquad (9)$$

It is this type of budget restriction with which we shall work in the remainder of this book.

The individual is supposed to maximize the utility function under the budget restriction (9). This yields the demand and supply functions on which Walras's twentieth-century model of capital formation has been based.

The utility function is extended compared with that of the preceding chapter in the sense that now the total quantity $q_e + d_e$ of (E) is also an argument.

Jaffé summarizes as follows:[12]

What the individual is purchasing when he buys a perpetual annuity share [i.e. a unit of (E)] is *betterment*. And in Walras's static system betterment is a commodity which can be bought and sold like any other commodity ...[13] for which an individual is presumed to have a desire or utility function. The price of a unit of betterment (the reciprocal of the rate of capitalization) is thus determined in the same way as all other prices.

In the next chapter we shall see how these prices will come out.

11

WALRAS'S MODEL OF
CAPITAL FORMATION

In this chapter we shall discuss Walras's twentieth-century model of capital formation. Like the preceding model of the chain (the production model), it is a macro model of which the demand equations for goods and the supply equations of capital services are the result of aggregating individual demand and supply equations. These individual demand and supply equations will be discussed first.

THE INDIVIDUAL DEMAND AND SUPPLY EQUATIONS

The optimal amounts d_e, $q_t - o_t$, ..., $q_p - o_p$, ..., $q_k - o_k$, $q_{k'} - o_{k'}$, $q_{k'} - o_{k'}$, ..., d_a, d_b, d_c, d_d, ... can be found from

$$\phi_e(q_e + d_e) = p_e\phi_a(d_a),$$

$$\phi_t(q_t - o_t) = p_t\phi_a(d_a),$$

$$\vdots$$

$$\phi_p(q_p - o_p) = p_p\phi_a(d_a),$$

$$\vdots$$

$$\phi_k(q_k - o_k) = p_k\phi_a(d_a),$$

$$\phi_{k'}(q_{k'} - o_{k'}) = p_{k'}\phi_a(d_a),$$

$$\phi_{k'}(q_{k'} - o_{k'}) = p_{k'}\phi_a(d_a),$$

$$\vdots$$

$$\phi_b(d_b) = p_b\phi_a(d_a),$$

$$\phi_c(d_c) = p_c\phi_a(d_a),$$

$$\phi_d(d_d) = p_d\phi_a(d_a),$$ (1)

$$\vdots$$

together with

$$o_t p_t + \ldots + o_p p_p + \ldots + o_k p_k + o_{k'} p_{k'} + o_{k''} p_{k''} + \ldots$$
$$= d_a + d_b p_b + d_c p_c + \ldots + d_e p_e + \sigma_e \qquad (2)$$

where

$$\sigma_e = \eta_p q_p p_p + (\mu_k + \nu_k) q_k P_k + (\mu_{k'} + \nu_{k'}) q_{k'} P_{k'}$$
$$+ (\mu_{k''} + \nu_{k''}) q_{k''} P_{k''} + \ldots \qquad (3)$$

The functions ϕ are Walras's *rareté* functions, i.e. the marginal utility functions; note that a new *rareté* function has been introduced, namely that of good (E). Equation (2) is the individual's budget restriction, with the correction term σ_e explained in the preceding chapter.

From the above equations we get the n individual supply equations for the services of the capital goods,

$$o_t = f_t(p_t, \ldots, p_p, \ldots, p_k, p_{k'}, p_{k''}, \ldots, p_b, p_c, p_d, \ldots, p_e),$$
$$\vdots$$
$$o_p = f_p(p_t, \ldots, p_p, \ldots, p_k, p_{k'}, p_{k''}, \ldots, p_b, p_c, p_d, \ldots, p_e),$$
$$\vdots$$
$$o_k = f_k(p_t, \ldots, p_p, \ldots, p_k, p_{k'}, p_{k''}, \ldots, p_b, p_c, p_d, \ldots, p_e),$$
$$o_{k'} = f_{k'}(p_t, \ldots, p_p, \ldots, p_k, p_{k'}, p_{k''}, \ldots, p_b, p_c, p_d, \ldots, p_e),$$
$$o_{k''} = f_{k''}(p_t, \ldots, p_p, \ldots, p_k, p_{k'}, p_{k''}, \ldots, p_b, p_c, p_d, \ldots, p_e), \qquad (4)$$
$$\vdots$$

and the m demand equations for consumption goods,

$$d_b = f_b(p_t, \ldots, p_p, \ldots, p_k, p_{k'}, p_{k''}, \ldots, p_b, p_c, p_d, \ldots, p_e),$$
$$d_c = f_c(p_t, \ldots, p_p, \ldots, p_k, p_{k'}, p_{k''}, \ldots, p_b, p_c, p_d, \ldots, p_e),$$
$$d_d = f_d(p_t, \ldots, p_p, \ldots, p_k, p_{k'}, p_{k''}, \ldots, p_b, p_c, p_d, \ldots, p_e),$$
$$\vdots$$
$$d_a = o_t p_t + \ldots + o_p p_p + \ldots + o_k p_k + o_{k'} p_{k'} + o_{k''} p_{k''}$$
$$+ \ldots - (d_b p_b + d_c p_c + d_d p_d + \ldots + d_e p_e + \sigma_e), \qquad (5)$$

and, finally, the demand equation for (E):

$$d_e = f_e(p_t, \ldots, p_p, \ldots, p_k, p_{k'}, p_{k''}, \ldots, p_b, p_c, p_d, \ldots, p_e). \qquad (6)$$

Note that, because σ_e can be written in terms of prices, the appearance of σ_e in the budget restriction does not further increase the number of arguments of these demand and supply functions.

THE TWENTIETH-CENTURY MODEL OF CAPITAL FORMATION

We now can formulate the equations of the twentieth-century model of capital formation.

For each household Walras assumed that demand and supply equations exist of the type mentioned above. These equations yield, when aggregated over all households, $m + n + 1$ macro relations. The macro relations together with other equations to be discussed below form nine subsystems of equations which constitute the model.

The n equations describing total supply of the capital services form subsystem I:[1]

$$O_t = F_t(p_t, \ldots, p_p, \ldots, p_k, p_{k'}, p_{k''}, \ldots, p_b, p_c, p_d, \ldots, p_e),$$
$$\vdots$$

$$O_p = F_p(p_t, \ldots, p_p, \ldots, p_k, p_{k'}, p_{k''}, \ldots, p_b, p_c, p_d, \ldots, p_e),$$
$$\vdots$$

$$O_k = F_k(p_t, \ldots, p_p, \ldots, p_k, p_{k'}, p_{k''}, \ldots, p_b, p_c, p_d, \ldots, p_e),$$
$$O_{k'} = F_{k'}(p_t, \ldots, p_p, \ldots, p_k, p_{k'}, p_{k''}, \ldots, p_b, p_c, p_d, \ldots, p_e),$$
$$O_{k''} = F_{k''}(p_t, \ldots, p_p, \ldots, p_k, p_{k'}, p_{k''}, \ldots, p_b, p_c, p_d, \ldots, p_e), \tag{7}$$
$$\vdots$$

Total demands for the m consumption goods are described in subsystem II:

$$D_b = F_b(p_t, \ldots, p_p, \ldots, p_k, p_{k'}, p_{k''}, \ldots, p_b, p_c, p_d, \ldots, p_e),$$
$$D_c = F_c(p_t, \ldots, p_p, \ldots, p_k, p_{k'}, p_{k''}, \ldots, p_b, p_c, p_d, \ldots, p_e),$$
$$D_d = F_d(p_t, \ldots, p_p, \ldots, p_k, p_{k'}, p_{k''}, \ldots, p_b, p_c, p_d, \ldots, p_e),$$
$$\vdots$$

$$D_a = O_t p_t + \ldots + O_p p_p + \ldots + O_k p_k + O_{k'} p_{k'} + O_{k''} p_{k''} + \ldots$$
$$- (D_b p_b + D_c p_c + D_d p_d + \ldots + E), \tag{8}$$

where E is defined by $E = D_e p_e + \Sigma_e$ and explained in subsystem III:[2]

$$E = F_e(p_t, \ldots, p_p, \ldots, p_k, p_{k'}, p_{k''}, \ldots, p_b, p_c, p_d, \ldots, i). \tag{9}$$

Further, there are n transformation equations relating the quantities of services demanded by the entrepreneurs and offered by households to the quantities of consumption goods and capital goods produced, offered by entrepreneurs and demanded by the households. Here new magnitudes D_k, $D_{k'}$, $D_{k''}$, ... appear on the scene, denoting the quantities of the l capital goods proper newly produced and offered.[3] The n transformation equations form subsystem IV:

$$a_t D_a + b_t D_b + c_t D_c + d_t D_d + \ldots + k_t D_k + k'_t D_{k'} + k''_t D_{k''} + \ldots$$
$$= O_t,$$

$$\vdots$$

$$a_p D_a + b_p D_b + c_p D_c + d_p D_d + \ldots + k_p D_k + k'_p D_{k'} + k''_p D_{k''} + \ldots$$
$$= O_p,$$

$$\vdots$$

$$a_k D_a + b_k D_b + c_k D_c + d_k D_d + \ldots + k_k D_k + k'_k D_{k'} + k''_k D_{k''} + \ldots$$
$$= O_k,$$

$$a_{k'} D_a + b_{k'} D_b + c_{k'} D_c + d_{k'} D_d + \ldots + k_{k'} D_k + k'_{k'} D_{k'} + k''_{k'} D_{k''} + \ldots$$
$$= O_{k'},$$

$$a_{k''} D_a + b_{k''} D_b + c_{k''} D_c + d_{k''} D_d + \ldots + k_{k''} D_k + k'_{k''} D_{k'} + k''_{k''} D_{k''} + \ldots$$
$$= O_{k''}, \tag{10}$$

$$\vdots$$

Note that the Os denote quantities of services provided by existing capital goods, expressing the fact that the newly produced capital goods proper are not yet productive during the period of their construction.

There are $m + l$ price equations expressing mathematically that in equilibrium the entrepreneurs make neither benefits nor losses. This can be written in the following m equations of subsystem V,

$$a_t p_t + \ldots + a_p p_p + \ldots + a_k p_k + a_{k'} p_{k'} + a_{k''} p_{k''} + \ldots = 1,$$
$$b_t p_t + \ldots + b_p p_p + \ldots + b_k p_k + b_{k'} p_{k'} + b_{k''} p_{k''} + \ldots = p_b,$$
$$c_t p_t + \ldots + c_p p_p + \ldots + c_k p_k + c_{k'} p_{k'} + c_{k''} p_{k''} + \ldots = p_c,$$
$$d_t p_t + \ldots + d_p p_p + \ldots + d_k p_k + d_{k'} p_{k'} + d_{k''} p_{k''} + \ldots = p_d, \tag{11}$$
$$\vdots$$

and in the l equations of subsystem VI:

$$k_t p_t + \ldots + k_p p_p + \ldots + k_k p_k + k_{k'} p_{k'} + k_{k''} p_{k''} + \ldots = P_k,$$
$$k'_t p_t + \ldots + k'_p p_p + \ldots + k'_k p_k + k'_{k'} p_{k'} + k'_{k''} p_{k''} + \ldots = P_{k'},$$
$$k''_t p_t + \ldots + k''_p p_p + \ldots + k''_k p_k + k''_{k'} p_{k'} + k''_{k''} p_{k''} + \ldots = P_{k''}, \tag{12}$$
$$\vdots$$

In the next equation Walras expressed the equilibrium condition that the value of the quantities of new capital goods proper, produced during the current period and demanded by capital owners, just absorbs gross savings.

70

This condition is subsystem VII:

$$D_k P_k + D_{k'} P_{k'} + D_{k''} P_{k''} + \ldots = E. \tag{13}$$

The model is completed by the equations already developed in Chapter 10, which comprise subsystem VIII,

$$P_k = \frac{p_k}{i + \mu_k + \nu_k},$$

$$P_{k'} = \frac{p_{k'}}{i + \mu_{k'} + \nu_{k'}},$$

$$P_{k''} = \frac{p_{k''}}{i + \mu_{k''} + \nu_{k''}}, \tag{14}$$

$$\vdots$$

and subsystem IX,

$$p_e = \frac{1}{i}. \tag{15}$$

We therefore have the following number of equations:

in subsystem I	n equations
in subsystem II	m equations
in subsystem III	1 equation
in subsystem IV	n equations
in subsystem V	m equations
in subsystem VI	l equations
in subsystem VII	1 equation
in subsystem VIII	l equations
in subsystem IX	1 equation

In total there are $2m + 2n + 2l + 3$ equations. There is a dependence, however, and this makes the number of independent equations equal to $2m + 2n + 2l + 2$. This can be explained as follows: multiply both sides of the equations of subsystem IV by $p_t, \ldots, p_p, \ldots, p_k, p_{k'}, p_{k''}, \ldots$, respectively, and add the results; multiply both sides of the equations of subsystems V and VI by $D_a, D_b, D_c, D_d, \ldots, D_k, D_{k'}, D_{k''}, \ldots$, respectively, and add likewise. Comparing the results will lead to the conclusion that

$$O_t p_t + \ldots + O_p p_p + \ldots + O_k p_k + O_{k'} p_{k'} + O_{k''} p_{k''} + \ldots$$
$$= D_a + D_b p_b + D_c p_c + D_d p_d + \ldots + D_k P_k + D_{k'} P_{k'}$$
$$+ D_{k''} P_{k''} + \ldots. \tag{16}$$

From this we can derive subsystem VII by substituting the right-hand side of the last equation of subsystem II for D_a.

71

There are also $2m + 2n + 2l + 2$ unknown variables:

n variables $O_t, \ldots, O_p, \ldots O_k, O_{k'}, O_{k''}, \ldots$
n prices $p_t, \ldots, p_p, \ldots p_k, p_{k'}, p_{k''}, \ldots$
m variables $D_a, D_b, D_c, D_d, \ldots$
$m - 1$ prices $p_b, p_c, p_d, \ldots$
1 variable E
1 price p_e
1 rate of net income i
l variables $D_k, D_{k'}, D_{k''}, \ldots$
l prices $P_k, P_{k'}, P_{k''}, \ldots$

According to the mathematical standards of his time, the equality of the number of unknown variables on the one hand and the number of independent equations on the other was enough for Walras to conclude that the whole system had a solution; in other words, given the individuals' initial endowments q and their preferences laid down in their *rareté* functions ϕ, given the production structure in the form of the coefficients of production, and given the depreciation charges and the insurance premiums, the equilibrium prices follow from the model. These prices are such that, if all agents take them as guidelines, their actions in the form of quantities of goods demanded and of services supplied are such that all markets clear and all individual quantities are optimal in terms of utility.

OPTIMAL ALLOCATION OF CAPITAL

The role of the proportionality (14) above, or, for that matter, equation (2) of Chapter 10, and that of good (E) can be illustrated by the following consideration.

Suppose there exists a situation of equilibrium as described by the twentieth-century model. This means that there is an individually optimal allocation of goods and services of which the aggregates over the individual consumers obey the equations of the nine subsystems of the preceding section.

Consider any individual in this economy and suppose that his (individual) equilibrium amounts are $o_t, \ldots, o_p, \ldots, o_k, o_{k'}, o_{k''}, \ldots, d_e, d_a, d_b, d_c, d_d, \ldots$. Although being 'in equilibrium', he may investigate what to do in the hypothetical situation in which a small additional amount of, say, one unit of *numéraire* is at his disposal. Let us, for short, call this unit a *franc*. He may keep the franc in the form of a unit of (A) and gain additional utility $\phi_a(d_a)$. He may equally well buy $1/p_b$ units of (B) with a utility gain of $\phi(d_b)/p_b$, or some of (C) or (D) or any other consumption good; because of (1) above, all the quantities of additional utility are the same. He may also buy some additional services, for instance services of capital good (K); the additional utility will then be equal to $\phi_k(q_k - o_k)/p_k$, which, again because of (1), is equal to the utility gain yielded by spending the franc on any consumption good. However, he could also spend the franc on buying a quantity of a (new) capital good proper, say (K). One unit of (K) will give him (the expectation of) π_k units of *numéraire* income during all the periods subsequent to the current one; for one franc he can buy $1/P_k$ units of (K), which yields him the expectation of $\pi_k/P_k = i$ units of *numéraire* additional income per subsequent period. Consequently, buying some (K) for one franc is equivalent to buying i units of (E). The additional utility is then $i\phi_e(d_e)$, which is equal to $\phi_e(d_e)/p_e$ and, from (1), to $\phi_a(d_a)$. Hence the marginal utility of spending an additional franc on whatever good or service is the same, and is equal to the marginal utility of buying whatever capital good proper. Clearly, this marginal utility is also equal to the loss of utility as a result of spending one franc less on whatever good or service. Consequently, the above allocation is such that no other allocation can yield him more utility, because reshuffling his budget cannot increase his total effective utility. In other words, the allocation $o_t, \ldots, o_p, \ldots o_k$, $o_{k'}, o_{k'}, \ldots, d_e, d_a, d_b, d_c, d_d, \ldots$ is, indeed, optimal to him in terms of utility maximization under the restriction of a budget equation.

DYNAMICS AND UNCERTAINTY

Walras's twentieth-century model of capital formation displays a remarkable architectural unity. Nevertheless, his contemporaries did not pay serious attention to the fourth edition of the *Eléments*; neither Wicksell nor Edgeworth, Böhm-Bawerk, Marshall or Pareto ever referred to passages from that edition. The attention to his work ended mostly at the model of production. The capital model, when mentioned at all, did not find much recognition in the first instance. This may partly explain the misunderstanding that Walras only studied the economic process as having an outcome that is known with certainty from its very beginning. The misunderstanding has been further enhanced by the work of Arrow and Debreu and that of their followers. Arrow and Debreu's (1954) model is indeed a model in which the outcome of the economic process is known with certainty. It has been presented by its authors, however, as typically Walrasian.[4]

From the fourth edition of the *Eléments* onwards, Walras's theory of capital clearly refutes the widespread opinion that he only studied the economic process as having an outcome that is known with certainty from its very beginning.[5] In the first instance Walras stylized the economic process as a sequence of subsequent periods of time to each of which his model of capital formation applies. During each period production and trade take place as determined by the solution of the equations of the model, given the quantities of capital existing at the outset of the period, the technology (the coefficients of production) and the preferences of the consumers; a somewhat naïve assumption here is that the agents do not expect price changes between the current and the next period.[6] The result is a new collection of capital at the beginning of the next period. It is assumed that technology and preferences may change exogenously at the beginning of each period. A new equilibrium emerges and this goes on for following periods. Hence, although there is no trace of multi-period optimization in Walras's models, there is clearly a dynamic element in his theory as a whole, just as there is an element of uncertainty.[7]

THE ROLE OF THE ENTREPRENEUR IN CAPITAL FORMATION

We wish here to point to a flaw concerning the role of the entrepreneur in the capital goods market. As we already indicated above, Walras expressed market clearing for goods and services by using the symbols O and D in a twofold sense.[8]

Likewise we may distinguish between quantities of new capital proper demanded and supplied and between amounts of savings demanded and supplied. E in subsystem III is to be interpreted as the demand for capital in an unspecific form. Walras speaks in this connection of *numéraire capital* (*Eléments*, Section 235). At the same time it is supplied in order to be converted into capital proper of the various types. The conversion is expressed in subsystem VII; hence E in subsystem VII has to be considered as a quantity supplied and therefore the quantities of new capital proper in this subsystem are quantities demanded. Finally, the quantities of new capital proper in subsystem IV are quantities produced and offered by entrepreneurs.

So, as a result of the simple production side of the model and its static character, we have the rather strange circumstance that it is not the entrepreneur who is demanding new capital goods proper but the capital-owner. This is not what Walras wants us to believe, however. In the second to fifth editions of the *Eléments* we read:

> Instead of supposing, as we have done hitherto, that the creators of excesses of income over consumption go in person to the market of capital goods to buy new capital goods which they then rent in the market for services to entrepreneurs engaged in industry, let us now suppose that savers lend all or part of the value of these capital goods in *numéraire* to the manufacturers who go in place of the savers to the market for capital goods and buy the new capital good they want directly. Nothing will be changed in the latter market except that the demand for new capital goods will come from the entrepreneurs and not from the creators of excesses of income over consumption.
>
> (*Eléments*, Section 255; italics in original)

In all editions, with inconsequential difference in wording, Walras asserts:

> In reality, only land and personal faculties are always hired in kind; capital proper is usually hired in the form of money in the market for services. The capitalist accumulates his savings in money and lends this money to the entrepreneur who, at the expiration of the loan, repays the money. This operation is known as *credit*. Hence the demand for new capital goods comes from entrepreneurs who manufacture products and not from capitalists who create savings.
>
> (*Eléments*, Section 235; italics in original.)[9]

In our opinion, Walras is putting the reader on the wrong track. Clearly, he is speaking of something that is not in the model. The entrepreneur of the model is only interested in the profit of the current period.[10] Walras did not put any other entrepreneurial motive into the model. Since new capital is unproductive during the current period, it can only contribute to this period's profit in the same way as does, for instance, bread, because for the entrepreneurs new capital is only merchandise. Therefore, entrepreneurs are only interested in new capital because individuals attach utility to it.[11] Nobody is buying new capital goods as an entrepreneur. Anyone who is buying capital goods is doing so as a capital-owner. The entrepreneur in the above citations changes his role and becomes a capitalist himself as soon as he enters the market for new capital goods as a demander; by borrowing money and buying new capital goods he simply changes the 'composition' of his quantity q_e (see Chapter 10, equation (6)).

This is also in accordance with the following point. As we mentioned above, the amount E can be split into individual amounts $d_e p_e$ and σ_e. It is impossible in the model, however, to subdivide these amounts of *numéraire* capital over the different types of capital goods proper. In other words, although the macro amounts D_k, $D_{k'}$, $D_{k''}$, ... are mathematically well determined, we do not know how these quantities of new capital goods proper are eventually divided over the individual capital-owners; this indeterminacy does not occur if $l = 1$, i.e. in the unrealistic case that there exists only one type of capital proper.[12] The fact that there are no demand equations for each new capital good separately is a consequence of the fact that Walras did not (and should not) give each capital good a separate place in the individuals' utility functions. The individuals, being only interested in their quantities of good (E), are demanding unspecified *numéraire* capital and leave it to the entrepreneurs, the market mechanism and the technological circumstances to split this amount over the various types of capital goods.

But this does not take away that in this model it is the capitalists *as a group* who decide on investment. They decide on how much to save, i.e. on how much future income they wish to have in addition to what they already may expect. All this is a consequence of the fact that Walras did not introduce any investment equation into the model. This, however, would have made the model overdetermined. Moreover, the entrepreneurs' behaviour should have been remodelled. Compared with his production model Walras made his consumers less myopic in the twentieth-century model of capital formation, but his entrepreneurs remained as myopic as they were in the other models. From his verbal expositions one may infer that Walras did not realize that, as far as acting in the mathematical models, his entrepreneur, in fact, simply did not materialize. One of the basic entrepreneurial tasks, namely making decisions about investment, remained strictly reserved to the capitalists in his formal models.[13]

12

ON THE FUTILITY OF LESSONS 26 AND 27 OF THE *ÉLÉMENTS*

In all five editions of the *Eléments* Walras readdressed the issue of the optimality of capital formation. In the second edition he presented for the first time his 'Theorem of maximum utility of new capital goods', in which he asserted that the proportionality of the net incomes of the capital goods to their prices is a *necessary* condition for the optimality of capital formation. Apparently, Walras wished to do more than simply posit the condition of the proportionality of net incomes and prices of the capital goods as an equilibrium condition. He wished to prove it to be necessary.[1] The theorem is very important for understanding Walras's groping to the final version of his capital theory and is therefore discussed in this chapter, even though it will turn out to be erroneous. Since it is a typical product of the nineteenth-century model, we discuss this model first. We shall return to the twentieth-century model in the following chapters.

THE NINETEENTH-CENTURY MODEL OF CAPITAL FORMATION

The considerations on depreciation and insurance as exposed on page 62, from which follows the notion of net income of capital, can already be found in the second edition of the *Eléments*. The same can be said about the price equations and the transformation equations. So far there is no difference between what we called the nineteenth-century model and the twentieth-century model. The difference, however, relates to the treatment of savings, as we shall set out below.

An individual's amount of gross savings e in a certain period depends on the prices of all services and consumption goods as well as on the rate of net income i. In the nineteenth-century model Walras supposed e to be a function of prices and the rate of net income:

$$e = f_e(p_t, \ldots, p_p, \ldots, p_k, p_{k'}, p_{k''}, \ldots, p_b, p_c, p_d, \ldots, i). \tag{1}$$

He simply stated equation (1), without deducing it from theoretical premises. Relations stated in this way were denoted by Walras as 'empirical relations'. He expressed it as follows:

> We posit this savings function empirically .... Perhaps there are grounds for investigating the mathematical elements that constitute the savings function, just as we have investigated those of the function[s] of demand. For this we should obviously have to reconsider utility, viz. to distinguish *present* and *future* utility. We will not perform this research and we will let the savings function have its empirical character, without in any way pretending herewith that it were impossible to go back to its elements; such an operation, however, is not necessary for us for the moment.
>
> (1st edition, Section 279; 2nd and 3rd editions, Section 238; the italics are Walras's)

In the nineteenth-century model the quantities of capital services supplied and consumption goods demanded by the individual households are again derived from utility maximization while taking into account a budget restriction. Here, this budget restriction is of the form

$$e = o_t p_t + \ldots + o_p p_p + \ldots + o_k p_k + o_{k'} p_{k'} + o_{k''} p_{k''} + \ldots$$
$$- (d_a + d_b p_b + d_c p_c + d_d p_d + \ldots) \tag{2}$$

given equation (1). As a consequence, the supply and demand functions have i as an additional argument. Just as in the preceding models these equations are aggregated into macro supply and demand equations.

All the individuals are supposed to have savings functions like relation (1). Aggregating these over the individuals yields

$$E = F_e(p_t, \ldots, p_p, \ldots, p_k, p_{k'}, p_{k''}, \ldots, p_b, p_c, p_d, \ldots, i) \tag{3}$$

where E denotes total gross savings and $F_e(.)$ is the sum of all the individual saving functions $f_e(.)$. This amount, by definition, is invested in newly produced capital goods proper, which leads to the equilibrium equation

$$D_k P_k + D_{k'} P_{k'} + D_{k''} P_{k''} + \ldots = E, \tag{4}$$

where D_k, $D_{k'}$, $D_{k''}$ ... denote quantities of newly produced capital goods K, K', K'', ...[2] We shall not spell out all the equations of the system because they are similar to those of the twentieth-century model.

THE THEOREM ON THE OPTIMALITY OF CAPITAL FORMATION

Walras considered the model of capital formation as an optimization model with two stages. In the first stage the income of an individual is split into two parts: one part to be spent on consumption goods, the other (determined on the basis of (1)) to buy capital goods. The second stage of the optimization procedure consists of the optimal allocation of the consumption part of income to the various consumption goods on the one hand and, on the other hand, the optimal allocation of the savings part of income to the various types of capital goods. The first allocation problem of the second stage has been solved by the principle of marginal utility. With respect to the other allocation problem, Walras apparently was of the opinion that the proportionality of net incomes and prices of the capital goods is the necessary condition for the optimality of the formation of new capital.

Starting from a supposedly optimal situation of general economic equilibrium he developed a reasoning which led to the proportionality as a conclusion. In the situation supposed by Walras 'all capital services are employed as consumers' services and none as productive services' (*Eléments*, 2nd edition, Section 258, and 4th edition, Section 262). In fact, however, the situation considered was even more specific, as follows from the sequel of the citation:

And we shall let

$$D_k = \delta_{k,1} + \delta_{k,2} + \delta_{k,3} + \dots$$
$$D_{k'} = \delta_{k',1} + \delta_{k',2} + \delta_{k',3} + \dots$$
$$D_{k''} = \delta_{k'',1} + \delta_{k'',2} + \delta_{k'',3} + \dots$$
$$\vdots$$

define at one and the same time *quantities of {new} capital services* (K), (K'), (K''), ... consumed by parties [i.e. the individuals] (1), (2), (3), ..., respectively, at the prices p_k, $p_{k'}$, $p_{k''}$, ... of these capital-services in terms of (A), and the *quantities of new capital goods* (K), (K'), (K''), ... *manufactured.*

(Walras's italics)

The bracketed word *new*[3] appeared for the first time in the fourth edition, but it only causes confusion because it is just in that same edition that the explicit statement that new capital goods cannot be productive, nor be consumed during the period of their production, appeared for the first time. The word *new* has therefore to be ignored because preceding passages and the remainder of the text indicate that capital services from the existing stock are meant.

Starting from the above cited specific equilibrium situation, which was assumed to result from the equations of the model, Walras tried to prove the proportionality. Consequently, this 'proof' applies only to one specific situation of general economic equilibrium, namely a situation of general economic equilibrium in which the quantities of newly produced capital goods are just equal to that part of the quantities of capital goods existing at the beginning of the period of which the services are withheld by the consumer-capitalists themselves for own use, i.e. the quantities that are not sold at the market for services in order to be used for productive purposes.[4]

In the first and later versions of the galley proofs of Lesson 26 of the second edition of the *Eléments*[5] (Walras 1889), in Lesson 26 of the second and third editions, in Lesson 26 of the fourth and fifth editions and in various letters Walras presented many variants of his proof, sometimes with geometrical illustrations (for instance, in a letter to Foxwell;[6] see also the carnet cited in Chapter 10 above), all ending with the proportionality of net incomes and prices of capital goods as a conclusion. Note that all the 'proofs' were devised during the 1880s when Walras was preparing the second edition of the *Eléments*. At the time he was still working with his empirical savings functions, in a much more primitive model than that in the fourth edition. As we shall set out below, it is remarkable that Walras maintained the theorem until the last edition of the *Eléments*.

In essence the reasoning is always the same. In the specific case of equilibrium considered, Walras asserted that the total quantities of newly produced capital goods are allocated to individuals such that each individual receives of each type of new capital good a quantity that is just the same as the quantity of capital goods of which he takes the services for his own use. This follows from equations $[\zeta]$ and $[\eta]$ of Walras (1954: 299; 1988: 414); similar equations can be found in the second and third editions. In this specific case the allocation as such is possible, but the problem is that the individual has to finance his new capital goods by means of his savings. There is nothing in the model nor in the specificity of the case under study, however, that guarantees that for each individual the value of his savings is equal to the value of the capital goods of which he himself consumes the services. In other words, the individual budget restrictions do not hold.[7] This is a death-blow for the validity of the proof, but the remainder is interesting enough to deal with.

In equilibrium, Walras argues, the ratio between the marginal utility (*rareté* in Walras's terminology) of the service of some capital good and the price per unit of this service is the same for every individual, for each type of capital good; for ease of reasoning we call this proportionality 1. The new capital goods acquired by the individual are also assumed by Walras to yield utility, in spite of the fact that there is no room for the quantities of capital goods in his utility functions. But then, the reasoning continues, there must also exist proportionality between the *raretés* of the newly produced capital goods and their selling prices; this we call proportionality 2. This proportionality is untenable within the framework of the model, irrespective of the verbosity and the abundance of formulae Walras spent on it: there is nothing in the model (in whatever version) that justifies proportionality 2.

Walras went even further. He made the *faux pas* of considering the *raretés* of the services in proportionality 1 to be the same as those of the new capital goods of proportionality 2; presumably, he did so because every individual gets just as much new capital goods as the quantity of existing capital goods he retains for his own consumption. Combining these proportionalities, then, yields a third one (proportionality 3): between the prices of the services of the capital goods $(p_k, p_{k'}, p_{k''}, \ldots)$ and the selling prices of the capital goods themselves $(P_k, P_{k'}, P_{k''}, \ldots)$. Proving proportionality 3 for Walras was in the first instance the proof of his theorem when depreciation and insurance factors are the same for all capital goods. It was von Bortkiewicz who convinced Walras that this was not enough, and therefore a passage was added to the galley proofs of the second edition. In this passage Walras stated that in proportionality 2 the prices of the capital goods themselves have to be increased by the capitalized value of depreciation and insurance,[8] because only then will total 'production costs' be taken into account, he said. However obscure, the combination of the thus amended proportionality with proportionality 1 yields, after some mathematical operations, the proportionality between the net incomes of the capital goods and their prices (the π_ks and the P_ks).

In our opinion this result is purely accidental.

Strictly speaking, the proportionality derived is one relevant to individual consumers. The special 'reservation' (the 'constraint' mentioned in the citation above) now appears to be the condition that the proportionality holds for all individuals with the same factor of proportionality:

> Free competition in capital formation and credit results in maximum utility from capital goods, subject only to the condition that the ratio of net interest to capital is the same for all savers.
>
> (*Eléments*, 4th edition, Section 264)[9]

Because the numerators and the denominators of the ratios involved contain prices that, in Walras's world of free competition, are the same for all consumers, the condition is superfluous and therefore nonsensical.

For Walras the key to the reasoning was the direct relation, in this specific case, between newly produced capital and realized utility, namely that of the services withheld for own consumption.[10] It is obvious, however, that Walras must have forgotten his own assumption that the capital goods will only bear fruit from the period after their production onwards. Skipping this assumption for the time being does not save the reasoning, of course.

DISCUSSION

Our conclusion must be that this proof is not correct and therefore that Walras should have skipped his Lessons 26 and 27, certainly from the fourth edition onwards.

In our opinion Walras should have contented himself with the proportionality as a postulated equilibrium condition. He could have confined himself to a verbal explanation – just as he did with respect to his condition of 'no benefits, no losses' – as a part of his model. In addition, he could have justified his verbal explanation by pointing to the entry of entrepreneurs into sectors with a high rate of net return and their withdrawal from sectors where the rate is low, or to arbitration as a mechanism for equalizing the net rates of profits for all capital goods.

Another point is that Walras never tried to prove *in general* that the proportionality condition is necessary for optimal capital formation. He dealt with only two very specific cases of general economic equilibrium, as we have seen, for which he tried to prove the correctness of the proportionality. It is an unanswered question whether he was aware of this.[11]

For the model of the first three editions it is even impossible to prove optimality of capital formation; in other words his condition is not sufficient in the nineteenth-century model either. The reason for this impossibility is simply that what is not in the model cannot come out of it or, in other words, one cannot derive theoretical results from empirically stated relations. In the final model, from the fourth edition onwards, sufficiency can be simply proved, as we did on pages 72–3. Walras did not do this, however.

13

CIRCULATING CAPITAL

In the fourth edition of the *Eléments* Walras introduced two other major innovations. First, he introduced a new type of capital, *circulating capital*, consisting of products among which were consumption goods: certain quantities of the goods produced are kept by consumers because they attach utility to having these quantities available. Money was considered as a special type of circulating capital.[1] When he dealt with the production model, Walras had already announced the introduction of this kind of capital[2] because of the need to bridge possible lapses of time between the moments of consumption and of production of the goods. In addition, Walras assumed that the producers also need circulating capital and money for the production of goods. So he introduced separate coefficients of production for each kind of circulating capital and for money. This important generalization of the treatment of production did not attract much attention in the literature until now. Second, Walras introduced a completely new treatment of money with as a result a solid integration of money into the theory of general economic equilibrium.

These two innovations, together with the introduction of circulating capital, were dealt with by Walras in no more than the twelve pages of Lesson 29 of the fourth edition of the *Eléments*.[3] His exposition is so compendious that the average reader will expend much effort to evaluate the changes,[4] which are highly interesting refinements and improvements that deserve reflection. In this chapter we shall therefore only deal with the notion of circulating capital. We shall illustrate the functioning of circulating capital by extending the twentieth-century model of capital formation with this type of capital. Thus we create a new, intermediary, model in Walras's chain of equilibrium models.

THE NOTION OF CIRCULATING CAPITAL

In the fourth edition of the *Eléments* Walras's *tâtonnement* process was altered by his adopting the assumption that there can be no production unless there is equilibrium.[5] This entailed a problem for the suppliers of capital services: after having supplied their services they will have to wait until the first results of the production processes become available before they can be paid for these services; likewise a problem arises for the entrepreneurs. In the production model Walras resolved these problems 'simply by ignoring the time element at this point' (4th edition, Section 207). Circulating capital and money will be brought in in order to make the model more realistic, he said in the same section.

Indeed, in the fourth edition, Section 273, when extending the model of capital formation, he assumed that consumers are concerned that they have on hand a fund of circulating capital consisting of certain quantities of final products, which are mathematically determined by the attainment of maximum satisfaction in accordance with each consumer's initial quantities of these products and his utility or want functions of their services of availability. Likewise he assumed that producers are concerned that they have on hand a fund of circulating capital consisting, in this case, of certain quantities of raw materials held in stock for future use and certain quantities of finished products placed on display for sale, which are mathematically determined by the attainment of equality between selling price and cost of production.

In order to cope with this complication, Walras introduced a new type of capital: stocks of produced goods. He called this type of capital 'circulating capital'. The specific service rendered by this new type of capital is the *service of availability* and it is this service that makes circulating capital a useful good. That is why it is in the first instance these *services* that are traded. Walras materialized this by stating that selling one unit of services (say, (B′)) means that the individual puts one unit of his stock of circulating capital of the relevant type at the buyer's disposal during the period in question under the condition that the buyer pays the unit price of that service (p_b) as a reward for the service of that unit, and that he will return the unit *in kind* at the end of the period.

It was now supposed by Walras that each consumer and each producer has an idea of the magnitude of the stock of products that will be convenient to him during the period under consideration. The producers' demand for stocks is determined by their supply (= production) of goods and by the technical coefficients and can therefore be perfectly foreseen. The stocks that the consumers need during the period in question are also completely known given the demand for consumption goods and the supply of services. Nevertheless, Walras chose a set-up in which the individuals are supposed to attach utility to keeping some goods in stock and to determine this stock accordingly. This may result in optimal stocks that are different from those strictly needed and foreseeable.

Walras denoted by (A′), (B′), (C′), ..., (M′), ... the products (A), (B), (C), ... and the raw materials (M), ...,[6] respectively, considered as circulating capital, i.e. as rendering the *service of availability* when kept in stock.

Again, one unit of circulating capital delivers one unit of service during the period. The prices of the services of availability of these capital goods are denoted by, respectively, $p_{a'}$, $p_{b'}$, $p_{c'}$, ..., $p_{m'}$, ... and are determined as follows:

$$p_{a'} = i, \qquad p_{b'} = p_b i, \qquad p_{c'} = p_c i, \qquad ..., \qquad p_{m'} = p_m i, \qquad ...; (1)$$

good (A) is the *numéraire*. This is in accordance with the way in which the prices of the services of the other capital goods were derived in the model of capital formation; depreciation and accidental destruction of circulating capital are disregarded, however.[7]

THE MODEL OF CAPITAL FORMATION WITH CIRCULATING CAPITAL

In addition to the initial quantities of the capital goods (T), ..., (P), ..., (K), ..., the individuals are now also supposed to have initial stocks of circulating capital. Let $q_{a'}$, $q_{b'}$, $q_{c'}$, $q_{d'}$, ..., $q_{m'}$, ... be an individual's initial quantities of (A'), (B'), (C'), ..., (M'), ... The amounts of services of availability rendered by an individual's initial quantities $q_{a'}$, $q_{b'}$, $q_{c'}$, ... $q_{m'}$, ... of circulating capital are not necessarily optimal for his own use during the period under consideration. Therefore let $o_{a'}$, $o_{b'}$, $o_{c'}$, ..., $o_{m'}$, ... be quantities of *services*[8] of (A'), (B'), (C'), ..., (M'), ... that the individual offers in the market for services.[9] He will then have available for himself the quantities $q_{a'} - o_{a'}$, $q_{b'} - o_{b'}$, $q_{c'} - o_{c'}$, ..., $q_{m'} - o_{m'}$, ...; the quantities $o_{m'}$, ... are supposed to be equal to the initial quantities $q_{m'}$, ... because neither the raw materials themselves nor their services of availability are considered to be of (direct) use for the consumers.

The individual's collection of *rareté* functions (i.e. the marginal utility functions) is now extended by the *rareté* functions $\phi_{a'}$, $\phi_{b'}$, $\phi_{c'}$, $\phi_{d'}$, ..., $\phi_{m'}$, ... of the services of availability of the various kinds of circulating capital. The budget equation for the case of circulating capital is

$$o_t p_t + ... + o_p p_p + ... + o_k p_k + o_{k'} p_{k'} + ... + o_{a'} p_{a'} + o_{b'} p_{b'} + ...$$
$$+ q_{m'} p_{m'} + ...$$
$$= d_a + d_b p_b + d_c p_c + d_d p_d + ... + d_e p_e + \sigma_e. \qquad (2)$$

Note that in this equation Walras was expressing that it is *services* of circulating capital that the individual is offering on the pertinent markets and not quantities of circulating capital. Although the units offered will be returned at the end of the period, this does not mean that the levels of the individual stocks have to remain unchanged. Changing these levels, however, is a matter of buying new capital. The only difference with the situation of the preceding model is that an individual's gross savings $d_e + \sigma_e$ may now be used to buy both new capital goods (K), (K'), (K''),

..., and new circulating capital; see equation (10) below.

Maximization of utility will be ensured if (2) above and the first-order equations for the model of capital formation hold, together with the following new equations:

$$\phi_{a'}(q_{a'} - o_{a'}) = i\phi_a(d_a),$$

$$\phi_{b'}(q_{b'} - o_{b'}) = p_b i\phi_a(d_a),$$ (3)

$$\vdots$$

From these first-order conditions one obtains the supply equations for circulating capital:

$$o_{a'} = f_{a'}(p_t, \ldots, p_p, \ldots, p_k, p_{k'}, p_{k''}, \ldots, p_b, p_c, p_d, \ldots, p_m, \ldots, p_e),$$

$$o_{b'} = f_{b'}(p_t, \ldots, p_p, \ldots, p_k, p_{k'}, p_{k''}, \ldots, p_b, p_c, p_d, \ldots, p_m, \ldots, p_e),$$ (4)

$$\vdots$$

The other supply and demand equations are similar to those of the model of capital formation, amended in the sense that now prices p_m, ... of raw materials appear as additional arguments in the functions f. Note that the prices of the services of circulating capital do not appear directly as arguments in the functions f: according to (1) these prices can be expressed in terms of i ($= 1/p_e$) and the prices of the goods themselves; see equation (1).

The budget equation and the supply and demand equations of all the individuals are, as in all models, aggregated. The aggregate budget equation is

$$O_t p_t + \ldots + O_p p_p + \ldots + O_k p_k + O_{k'} p_{k'} + \ldots + O_{a'} p_{a'} + O_{b'} p_{b'} +$$

$$\ldots + Q_{m'} p_{m'} + \ldots$$

$$= D_a + D_b p_b + D_c p_c + D_d p_d + \ldots + E,$$ (5)

where $E = D_e p_e + \Sigma_e$, the aggregate of the individual terms $d_e p_e + o_e$. The aggregate supply equations of the services of circulating capital are

$$O_{a'} = F_{a'}(p_t, \ldots, p_p, \ldots, p_k, p_{k'}, p_{k''}, \ldots, p_b, p_c, p_d, \ldots, p_m, \ldots, p_e),$$

$$O_{b'} = F_{b'}(p_t, \ldots, p_p, \ldots, p_k, p_{k'}, p_{k''}, \ldots, p_b, p_c, p_d, \ldots, p_m, \ldots, p_e),$$ (6)

$$\vdots$$

Further, new transformation equations relating to the services of circulating capital appear. The demand for these services is exercised by the entrepreneurs and will, again, be expressed in technical relations (the transformation equations) with fixed coefficients of production. The aggregate supply of new circulating capital has therefore to be taken into account; this means that new variables $D_{a'}, D_{b'}, D_{c'}, \ldots, D_{m'}, \ldots$, i.e. the total supply of new circulating capital, appear in all transformation equations.[10] For (A'), (B'), ... we obtain as new equations

$$a_a \cdot (D_a + D_{a'}) + b_a \cdot (D_b + D_{b'}) + \ldots + m_a \cdot D_{m'} + \ldots + k_a \cdot D_k + k'_a \cdot D_{k'} + \ldots$$
$$= O_{a'},$$

$$a_b \cdot (D_a + D_{a'}) + b_b \cdot (D_b + D_{b'}) + \ldots + m_b \cdot D_{m'} + \ldots + k_b \cdot D_k + k'_b \cdot D_{k'} + \ldots$$
$$= O_{b'}, \tag{7}$$
$$\vdots$$

For raw materials as circulating capital we obtain the following new equations:

$$a_m \cdot (D_a + D_{a'}) + b_m \cdot (D_b + D_{b'}) + \ldots + m_m \cdot D_{m'} + \ldots + k_m \cdot D_k$$
$$+ k'_m \cdot D_{k'} + \ldots$$
$$= Q_{m'}. \tag{8}$$
$$\vdots$$

In addition to these new transformation equations, the transformation equations of Chapter 11 appear again, but everywhere D_a, D_b, ... should be replaced by $D_a + D_{a'}$, $D_b + D_{b'}$, ... Furthermore, terms relating to the production of $D_{m'}$, ... have to be added.[11] Note that in (7) and (8) the symbols $O_{a'}$, $O_{b'}$, ..., $Q_{m'}$, ... denote quantities of services of circulating capital, existing at the beginning of the period, demanded by the entrepreneurs, whereas $D_{a'}$, $D_{b'}$, ..., $D_{m'}$, ... are quantities of (A), (B), ..., (M), ... produced during the period under consideration in order to be added to the stock of circulating capital.

The price equations, expressing the equality between the cost of production of one unit of a product and the price per unit of that product, now also include those for raw materials. Further, all price equations have to be adapted to include the services of circulating capital needed in the production processes:

$$a_t p_t + a_p p_p + a_k p_k + \ldots + a_a \cdot p_{a'} + a_b \cdot p_{b'} + \ldots + a_m \cdot p_{m'} + \ldots = 1,$$

$$b_t p_t + b_p p_p + b_k p_k + \ldots + b_a \cdot p_{a'} + b_b \cdot p_{b'} + \ldots + b_m \cdot p_{m'} + \ldots = p_b,$$
$$\vdots$$

$$m_t p_t + m_p p_p + m_k p_k + \ldots + m_a \cdot p_{a'} + m_b \cdot p_{b'} + \ldots + m_m \cdot p_{m'} + \ldots$$
$$= p_m,$$
$$\vdots$$

$$k_t p_t + k_p p_p + k_k p_k + \ldots + k_a \cdot p_{a'} + k_b \cdot p_{b'} + \ldots + k_m \cdot p_{m'} + \ldots = P_k,$$
$$\vdots \tag{9}$$

Finally, the equation expressing equilibrium between savings and investment has to be changed in order to include the possibility that savings may also be spent on buying circulating capital:

$$D_k P_k + D_{k'} P_{k'} + D_{k'} \cdot P_{k'} + \ldots + D_{a'} + D_{b'} p_b + \ldots + D_{m'} p_m + \ldots$$
$$= E. \tag{10}$$

In this equation the symbols D denote aggregate demand by individuals for the various types of fixed and circulating capital.

In comparison with the model of capital formation of the preceding chapter we now have a model with $3m + 3s$ additional variables and equations, where s denotes the number of the various types of raw materials. The additional variables are m quantities $O_{a'}$, $O_{b'}$, $O_{c'}$, ... of services offered (and demanded), $m + s$ quantities $D_{a'}$, $D_{b'}$, $D_{c'}$, ..., $D_{m'}$, ... of newly produced circulating capital, the $m + s$ prices $p_{a'}$, $p_{b'}$, $p_{c'}$, $p_{d'}$, ..., $p_{m'}$, ..., and the s prices p_m, ... (included in (9)). The prices p_m, ... of the raw materials themselves now have to be considered explicitly as variables of the system because raw materials may be kept as circulating capital. The quantities of the services of raw materials as circulating capital offered by the individuals are fixed, as we saw above, because they are not supposed to keep any of these services for their own use.

The additional equations are the m equations (6), representing the supply of services of circulating capital (A'), (B'), (C'), (D'), ..., the $m + s$ equations (7) and (8) for the services of the availability of final products and of raw materials, the s price equations for p_m, ... in (9)[12] and the $m + s$ equations (1) expressing the prices of the services of circulating capital in terms of the prices of the goods themselves and i.

For ease of exposition, this model will be interpolated between the model of capital formation of Chapter 11 and Walras's general economic equilibrium models with money to be introduced in Chapters 15 and 16. Before that, however, in the next chapter we shall present some introductory considerations on Walras's monetary ideas.

14

A PRELUDE TO THE
MONEY MODELS

All three services of money, i.e. as an accounting unit, a means of payment and a store of value, find a place somewhere in Walras's work. The unit of measurement we have already encountered in the form of the *numéraire*, in the models of the preceding chapters. These models may be considered as relating to situations in which paying is supposedly costless. Money, then, need not to be taken into consideration if one is only interested in the (relative) prices in equilibrium and the related quantities of goods and services.

As an elaboration of the preceding models, money is introduced as a means of payment. In the two subsequent chapters we shall deal with Walras's definitive treatment of money within the framework of a general equilibrium model. Money, then, is considered as a special kind of circulating capital, which provides the service that it is available as a means of payment; making use of this service costs money. This conception of money, however, is the result of an elaborate process of changes and refinements and we shall therefore briefly review these developments first.

DEVELOPMENTS IN MONETARY THOUGHT

Walras's theory of money has been subjected to more changes and refinements than any other topic dealt with by him. This is probably exhibited most clearly in the changes made in the consecutive editions of the *Eléments*. In the first edition money was directly linked to exchange, in a part entitled 'Du numéraire et de la monnaie'. It turns out that as early as 1874 Walras developed a pure, flawless quantity theory of money including notions such as the 'velocity of money', better known in the version of Fisher some decades later.[1] The institutional framework within which the actual exchange would take place was left open by Walras. In his first-edition money model, the quantity and value of money as a medium of exchange were explained by what was called the 'circulation à desservir par la monnaie' (circulation [of goods] to be sustained by money) and what may be recognized as a reflection of the banking principle.

Walras specified, and modified, this position in his *Théorie de la monnaie* (1886),[2] where the treatment of money was centred around the individuals' so-called *encaisses désirées* (desired cash balances). The desired cash balances were based on the idea that consumers and producers appreciate cash holdings because the money reserves give them the possibility of acquiring any bundle of goods corresponding to the amount of money.

In the second and third editions of the *Eléments* we find a similar exposition of the desired cash balances approach, but rather different in form from the earlier attempts. An important change, in comparison with the first edition of the *Eléments*, is that in these editions the treatment of money is preceded by a discussion of exchange, production and capital formation respectively. The capital formation model was then enlarged by equations relating to the circulation of money, thus completing his 'chain' of cumulative models.

In the fourth and fifth editions the basis of the demand for money was further elaborated by deriving the consumers' cash balances from the maximization of utility.[3]

THE NINETEENTH-CENTURY CASH BALANCES APPROACH

Let (U) be money and let Q_u be the total amount of money that is present in the economy. Money is in first instance considered to have no value in exchange:

> For pure theory it is obviously advantageous to investigate [first] how something gets value when it becomes money, before exploring how this value as money has to be combined with value as a merchandise.
> (*Eléments*, 2nd and 3rd editions, Section 320; Walras 1988: 452)

This quotation clearly illustrates that Walras considered the analysis of fiduciary money as a pedagogical expedient only.

Taking (B) as the *numéraire*[4] – in order to leave open the possibility to take (A) as money at a later stage – Walras introduced empirical consumers' cash balances, just as he introduced the empirical savings functions earlier.[5] Individuals and entrepreneurs need money for transactions and for saving; the amounts depend on the present situation, including the preferences of the people. In the second edition of the *Eléments*, the total cash balance evaluated in *numéraire* was simply posited as

$$ap_a + b + cp_c + dp_d + \ldots + TP_t + \ldots + PP_p + \ldots + KP_k + K'P_{k'}$$
$$+ K''P_{k''} + \ldots + tp_t + \ldots + pp_p + \ldots + kp_k + k'p_{k'} + k''p_{k''}$$
$$+ \ldots + mp_m + \ldots$$
$$= H. \tag{1}$$

The quantities $a, b, c, \ldots, T, \ldots, P, \ldots, K, K', K'', \ldots, t, \ldots, p, \ldots, k, k',$ $k'', \ldots, m, \ldots$ are the total quantities of the respective goods and services for which the parties to the exchange wish to have available the value in money (2nd and 3rd editions, Section 321); these quantities have to be considered as given parameters of the model. The amount H on the right-hand side of (1) is the total value in *numéraire* of the money that the agents need either for their transactions or for other purposes. The price of money, p_u, then simply follows from

$$Q_u p_u = H. \tag{2}$$

The money prices of the goods and services may now be found by dividing by p_u all prices in terms of the *numéraire* (B). Walras's nineteenth-century money model of general economic equilibrium, then, consists of his nine-teenth-century model of capital formation supplemented by equations (1) and (2) above. H can be found from equation (1) once the prices of the goods and services are obtained from the equations of the model of capital formation. The price of money p_u then simply follows from (2). We can conclude that the model displays what we now call a monetary dichotomy.

This inspired Walras to propose what we would like to call his 'macro money model'.

WALRAS'S MACRO MONEY MODEL

In order to explore how the value of money has to be combined with the exchange value of merchandise, Walras considered the money good (U) to be the same as (A). In Walras's macro money model, then, good (A) is both money and a commodity. A total quantity Q_a of this good is supposed to exist, of which a part Q'_a is in the commodity form and the other part $Q''_a = Q_a - Q'_a$ is in the form of money. Walras stated the relation between the quantity Q''_a of the monetized good (A) and the cash balance H as similar to (2) above:

$$Q''_a P_a = H. \tag{3}$$

P_a is the price of (A) measured in *numéraire* (B). If (A) were the *numéraire*, it would be impossible to study the effect of changes in the price of money. P_a is written as a capital letter in order to emphasize its different content, with respect to the price p_a, as a consequence of making (A) the money-good. H was considered by Walras as 'predetermined' (*Eléments*, Section 283), i.e. independent of P_a.[6]

Walras further simplified the reasoning by considering only two goods, namely (A) and (B). We assume that the buyers and sellers, knowing the prices of (C), (D), ... in *numéraire* (B), always buy or sell (A) against (B).[7] This means that there is a demand curve $A_q A_p$ in the (p, q) plane with equation

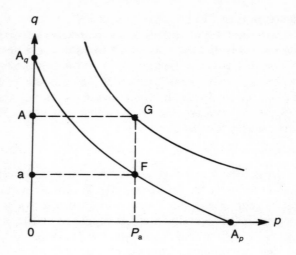

Figure 14.1

$$q = F_a(p),$$ (4)

which displays for each price p of (A) in (B) the quantity q of (A) as a commodity that buyers demand if p is the prevailing price.

The orthogonal hyperbola

$$q = \frac{H}{p}$$ (5)

displays the combinations of quantities q of (A) used as money, on the one hand, and the corresponding prices p of (A) on the other; see, for instance, equation (3). We may further analyse this by means of Figure 14.1.

In this figure the curve $A_q A_p$ describes the demand for (A) as a commodity (equation (4)). The curve through point G is the graph of the equation

$$q = F_a(p) + \frac{H}{p}.$$ (6)

This relation describes the total demand for (A) as a function of its price p in (B). Let the length 0A represent the total amount Q_a of good (A). The horizontal line through A intersects the graph of total demand for (A) at G. The vertical through G gives us the price P_a of (A) in (B). One can clearly observe what the price of (A) would have been if all of (A) were taken as a commodity. Furthermore, one can easily see how the amount Q_a is divided into the amounts $Q_a' = 0a$ and $Q_a'' = aA$. This is what Walras called his

92

geometric solution of the problem of the determination of: (1) the price of the money-commodity (A); (2) the quantity of (A) in commodity use; and (3) the quantity of (A) in monetary use.

(*Eléments*, Section 283)

He even goes so far as to add that this solution is 'precisely the solution which is reached in the real world'.

Walras maintained this macro money model throughout his whole career; it can be found in all editions of the *Eléments*, irrespective of the considerable changes of his assumptions with respect to underlying motives of monetary behaviour of the agents in his general economic equilibrium models.[8] He used this model as a basis for important questions of both a theoretical and an applied nature. We mention his study on bank notes,[9] his theory of bimetallism[10] and his ideas on price stabilization in a regime with gold as the principal money-commodity.[11] On all these occasions Walras revealed himself as a 'dichotomist'.

In the next two chapters we shall deal with Walras's general economic equilibrium models of money. We start, in Chapter 15, with a model with fiat-money as a prelude to Walras's commodity-money model in Chapter 16. We shall see that, in comparison with the models of the first three editions of the *Eléments*, one of the consequences of Walras's further integration of money into his models of general economic equilibrium was the disappearance of the dichotomy. It is a moot question whether Walras, or his contemporaries, were fully aware of this.

15

WALRAS'S EQUILIBRIUM MODEL WITH FIAT-MONEY

In the general equilibrium models of Walras's chain dealt with so far, the *numéraire* served as a standard of value. As we already said in the previous chapter, money *as a medium of exchange* did not play any role. One might conceive of this situation as one in which money (or some clearing-house) exists but paying is costless. In equilibrium all consumers' budget restrictions hold, the entrepreneurs make neither profits nor losses and the markets clear. Hence every consumer spends all the money he received for the services he offered and every entrepreneur receives back all the money he paid for the services he bought; in the end there is just as much money for transaction purposes as there was at the beginning of the period. One may think of various ways of solving the technical problem of how to organize the payments in the economy in question. If payments are supposed to be costless, however, then it does not matter how they are organized.

In this chapter money, to be denoted (U), is supposed to be so-called fiat-money, i.e. it is money because it is so decided by law or other arrangements. Consequently, in this chapter money and the *numéraire* good (A) are two different things. Our starting point is the model with circulating capital of Chapter 13 and we investigate how this model has to be supplemented and adapted when fiat-money is introduced.

THE INDIVIDUALS' CASH BALANCES

Fiat-money is circulating capital *in optima forma*. The money stuff (pieces of printed paper, for instance) has no utility as such;[1] it is its service that is useful. These services are measured such that one unit of money renders one unit of money service. The price in *numéraire* of its service of availability, $p_{u'}$, is the quantity of *numéraire* that has to be paid for the use, or the availability, of one unit of money during one period. Each individual is assumed to have in stock at the outset of the period under consideration a quantity q_u of money. The aggregate Q_u of all the quantities q_u is the total quantity of money considered by Walras to exist in the economy in ques-

94

tion. In his fiat-money model Walras apparently supposed that the individual quantities q_u of money at the outset of a period do not change from period to period.[2] Consequently, in this model only the price of the service of money plays a role. We shall therefore denote this price by $p_{u'}$ (not p_u); in the next chapter the price of money itself comes into play.

Walras's budget equation for an individual consumer, with the correction term σ_e, is

$$o_t p_t + \ldots + o_p p_p + \ldots + o_k p_k + o_{k'} p_{k'} + o_{k''} p_{k''} + \ldots$$
$$+ o_a p_{a'} + o_b p_{b'} + \ldots + q_m p_{m'} + \ldots + o_u p_{u'}$$
$$= d_a + d_b p_b + d_c p_c + d_d p_d + \ldots + d_e p_e + \sigma_e. \tag{1}$$

A term $o_u p_{u'}$ is included in addition to the terms of the budget equation (2) (Chapter 13) of the model of circulating capital. This means that the individual is willing to offer a quantity o_u of money as circulating capital, i.e. to lend that amount to entrepreneurs for the duration of the period. Consequently, he will keep for himself the availability of an amount $q_u - o_u$; this amount is determined on the basis of utility maximization and will henceforth be called the individual's *cash balance.*

THE SUPPLY OF MONEY

According to Walras, the usefulness of money is not the availability of the money itself, but the circumstance that it provides its possessor with purchasing power. The individual has an idea both about what stocks of circulating capital he wishes to retain (see Chapter 13) and about 'what cash-balances he ought to have, not only to replenish these stocks [of circulating capital] and make current purchases of consumers' goods and services for daily consumption while waiting to receive rents, wages and interest payable at fixed future dates, but also in order to acquire new capital goods' (4th and 5th editions, Section 273).

Walras therefore assumed that the individual wishes to have quantities α, β, γ, δ, $\ldots$, ε of, respectively, (A), (B), (C), (D), $\ldots$, (E) available *in the form of money.* From this it follows that Walras should have included these extra expenses in his budget equation, as follows:[3]

$$o_t p_t + \ldots + o_p p_p + \ldots + o_k p_k + o_{k'} p_{k'} + o_{k''} p_{k''} + \ldots$$
$$+ o_a p_{a'} + o_b p_{b'} + \ldots + q_m p_{m'} + \ldots + q_u p_{u'}$$
$$= d_a + d_b p_b + d_c p_c + d_d p_d + \ldots + d_e p_e + \sigma_e + \alpha p_{a'} + \beta p_{b'}$$
$$+ \gamma p_{c'} + \delta p_{d'} + \ldots + \varepsilon. \tag{2}$$

Further, he extended the individual's utility function such that there are now also *rareté* functions ϕ_α, ϕ_β, ϕ_γ, ϕ_δ, $\ldots$, ϕ_ε, denoting the intensive utility of the availability of goods (A), (B), (C), (D), ..., (E), *in money* rather than in kind.[4] The first-order conditions for utility maximization are those we met already in Chapter 13, supplemented by[5]

$$\phi_a(\alpha) = p_a \cdot \phi_a(d_a),$$
$$\phi_\beta(\beta) = p_b \cdot \phi_a(d_a),$$
$$\vdots$$
$$\phi_\epsilon(\epsilon) = \phi_a(d_a). \tag{3}$$

In addition to the demand and supply equations for the non-monetary goods and services, we then get the following equations of the desire for services of circulating capital (A'), (B'), ..., (E') in the form of money:

$$\alpha = f_a(p_t, \ldots, p_p, \ldots, p_k, p_{k'}, p_{k''}, \ldots, p_b, p_c, p_d, \ldots, p_{m'}, \ldots, p_e, p_{u'}),$$
$$\beta = f_\beta(p_t, \ldots, p_p, \ldots, p_k, p_{k'}, p_{k''}, \ldots, p_b, p_c, p_d, \ldots, p_{m'}, \ldots, p_e, p_{u'}),$$
$$\vdots$$
$$\epsilon = f_\epsilon(p_t, \ldots, p_p, \ldots, p_k, p_{k'}, p_{k''}, \ldots, p_b, p_c, p_d, \ldots, p_{m'}, \ldots, p_e, p_{u'}). \tag{4}$$

Note that the price $p_{u'}$ also has to be added to the list of arguments of the individual's demand functions for consumption goods and supply functions of fixed-capital services.

The value in *numéraire* of the availability of the quantities $\alpha, \beta, \gamma, \ldots, \epsilon$ is $\alpha p_{a'} + \beta p_{b'} + \ldots + \epsilon$; its amount $(\alpha p_{a'} + \beta p_{b'} + \ldots + \epsilon)/p_{u'}$ in money is the individual's cash balance. Hence the *quantity* of money effectively offered by the individual, i.e. the amount put available to entrepreneurs or other capitalists for the duration of the period, is equal to the individual's quantity of money at the outset of the period minus his desired cash balance:[6]

$$o_u = q_u - \frac{\alpha p_{a'} + \beta p_{b'} + \gamma p_{c'} + \delta p_{d'} + \ldots + \epsilon}{p_{u'}}. \tag{5}$$

Just as Walras has done for all the demand and supply equations until now, he could have written (5) in the form

$$o_u = f_u(p_t, \ldots, p_p, \ldots, p_k, p_{k'}, p_{k''}, \ldots, p_b, p_c, p_d, \ldots, p_{m'}, \ldots, p_e, p_{u'}). \tag{6}$$

Aggregating (5) yields the first additional equation:

$$O_u = Q_u - \frac{d_\alpha p_{a'} + d_\beta p_{b'} + d_\gamma p_{c'} + d_\delta p_{d'} + \ldots + d_\epsilon}{p_{u'}}, \tag{7}$$

where $d_\alpha, d_\beta, d_\gamma, d_\delta, \ldots, d_\epsilon$ are the aggregates of $\alpha, \beta, \gamma, \delta, \ldots, \epsilon$. Relation (6) is aggregated into[7]

$$O_u = F_u(p_t, \ldots, p_p, \ldots, p_k, p_{k'}, p_{k''}, \ldots, p_b, p_c, p_d, \ldots, p_{m'}, \ldots, p_e, p_{u'}). \tag{8}$$

The aggregate budget equation is

$$O_t p_t + \ldots + O_p p_p + \ldots + O_k p_k + O_{k'} p_{k'} + O_{k''} p_{k''} + \ldots$$
$$+ O_{a'} p_{a'} + O_{b'} p_{b'} + \ldots + Q_m p_{m'} + \ldots + O_u p_{u'}$$
$$= D_a + D_b p_b + D_c p_c + D_d p_d + \ldots + D_e p_e + \Sigma_e. \tag{9}$$

Relation (9) is the budget equation of the complete model. Note that it is not the strict aggregate of (2). Since O_u has been duly defined, we may indeed write the aggregate budget equation in the form (9).

The complete model with fiat-money has thus two additional variables compared with the model of capital formation with circulating capital of Chapter 13. These two new variables are the price $p_{u'}$ of the service of money and the aggregate supply O_u of (the service of) money offered by the individuals and demanded by the entrepreneurs.[8] Consequently, only two extra equations will be needed. The first equation, as we have seen, is the capitalists' aggregate supply of money services as a function of all prices. The second equation will be the one expressing equilibrium in the market for money services. For that we shall need to go into the demand for money first.

THE DEMAND FOR MONEY

The demand for money is exerted by the entrepreneurs, as we mentioned above. The entrepreneurs are supposed to need money in the production processes, in addition to a stock of the quantities of (A′), (B′), ..., (M′), ..., (E′) themselves. The entrepreneurs have an idea of what quantity of money they 'ought to have [available] for the replenishment of these stocks [i.e. the stocks of circulating capital] and for the purchase of productive services while waiting to be paid for the[ir] products' (4th and 5th editions, Section 273). The total quantities demanded of (A′), (B′), ..., (M′), ..., (K), ..., *in the form of money*, were denoted by Walras δ_a, δ_β, ..., δ_μ, ..., δ_κ, ...[9] They are determined by the following transformation equations:

$$\alpha_{a'}(D_a + D_{a'}) + \beta_{a'}(D_b + D_{b'}) + \ldots + \mu_{a'} D_{m'} + \ldots + \kappa_{a'} D_k + \ldots$$
$$= \delta_a,$$
$$\alpha_{b'}(D_a + D_{a'}) + \beta_{b'}(D_b + D_{b'}) + \ldots + \mu_{b'} D_{m'} + \ldots + \kappa_{b'} D_k + \ldots$$
$$= \delta_\beta,$$
$$\vdots$$
$$\alpha_{m'}(D_a + D_{a'}) + \beta_{m'}(D_b + D_{b'}) + \ldots + \mu_{m'} D_{m'} + \ldots + \kappa_{m'} D_k + \ldots$$
$$= \delta_\mu,$$
$$\vdots$$

97

$$\alpha_k(D_a + D_{a'}) + \beta_k(D_b + D_{b'}) + \ldots + \mu_k D_{m'} + \ldots + \kappa_k D_k + \ldots$$
$$= \delta_\kappa,$$
$$\vdots$$
(10)

where $\alpha_{a'}$ is the quantity of (A') in money necessary for the production of one unit of (A), $\beta_{a'}$ is the quantity of (A') in money necessary for the production of one unit of (B), and so forth. Here we see that already at the end of the nineteenth century[10] Walras had 'production equations' with money as arguments. Writing a_u, b_u, $\ldots$, m_u, $\ldots$, k_u, $\ldots$ for the total quantities of money, evaluated in *numéraire*, the availability of which the entrepreneurs are believed to need for the production of one unit of (A), (B), $\ldots$, (M), $\ldots$, (K), $\ldots$, respectively, we get

$$a_u = \alpha_{a'} p_{a'} + \alpha_{b'} p_{b'} + \ldots + \alpha_{m'} p_{m'} + \ldots + \alpha_k p_k + \ldots,$$
$$b_u = \beta_{a'} p_{a'} + \beta_{b'} p_{b'} + \ldots + \beta_{m'} p_{m'} + \ldots + \beta_k p_k + \ldots,$$
$$\vdots$$
$$m_u = \mu_{a'} p_{a'} + \mu_{b'} p_{b'} + \ldots + \mu_{m'} p_{m'} + \ldots + \mu_k p_k + \ldots,$$
$$\vdots$$
$$k_u = \kappa_{a'} p_{a'} + \kappa_{b'} p_{b'} + \ldots + \kappa_{m'} p_{m'} + \ldots + \kappa_k p_k + \ldots,$$
$$\vdots$$
(11)

From this we may derive the total amount of the *services* of availability of money demanded by the entrepreneurs, measured in *numéraire*, as follows:

$$\delta_\alpha p_{a'} + \delta_\beta p_{b'} + \ldots + \delta_\mu p_{m'} + \ldots + \delta_\kappa p_k + \ldots$$
$$= a_u(D_a + D_{a'}) + b_u(D_b + D_{b'}) + \ldots + m_u D_{m'} + \ldots + k_u D_k$$
$$+ \ldots$$
(12)

Hence the total quantity of money demanded is

$$\frac{\delta_\alpha p_{a'} + \delta_\beta p_{b'} + \ldots + \delta_\mu p_{m'} + \ldots + \delta_\kappa p_k + \ldots}{p_{u'}}.$$
(13)

EQUILIBRIUM IN THE MARKET FOR MONEY SERVICES

The second additional equation is

$$\frac{\delta_\alpha p_{a'} + \delta_\beta p_{b'} + \ldots + \delta_\mu p_{m'} + \ldots + \delta_\kappa p_k + \ldots}{p_{u'}} = O_u,$$
(14)

'expressing equality between the demand and offer of the service of money (U)' (*Eléments*, Section 276).

THE PRICE EQUATIONS

The equations expressing the equality between the price of a product and the cost of production of one unit of that product become in this complete model

$$a_t p_t + a_p p_p + a_k p_k + \ldots + a_{a'} p_{a'} + a_{b'} p_{b'} + \ldots + a_{m'} p_{m'} + \ldots + a_u$$
$$= 1,$$

$$b_t p_t + b_p p_p + b_k p_k + \ldots + b_{a'} p_{a'} + b_{b'} p_{b'} + \ldots + b_{m'} p_{m'} + \ldots + b_u$$
$$= p_b,$$

$$\vdots$$

$$m_t p_t + m_p p_p + m_k p_k + \ldots + m_{a'} p_{a'} + m_{b'} p_{b'} + \ldots + m_{m'} p_{m'} + \ldots$$
$$+ m_u = p_m,$$

$$\vdots$$

$$k_t p_t + k_p p_p + k_k p_k + \ldots + k_{a'} p_{a'} + k_{b'} p_{b'} + \ldots + k_{m'} p_{m'} + \ldots + k_u$$
$$= P_k, \tag{15}$$

$$\vdots$$

In equations (15) Walras wrote $p_{u'} a_u, p_{u'} b_u, \ldots, p_{u'} m_u, \ldots, p_{u'} k_u$ instead of $a_u, b_u, \ldots, m_u, \ldots, k_u, \ldots$, respectively.[11] The mistake is obvious, because $p_{u'} a_u, \ldots$ have *numéraire* squared as dimension, whereas the rest of the terms on the left-hand sides simply have *numéraire* as dimension.

Above we have seen that Walras's model of general economic equilibrium with fiat-money consists of $(2m + 2n + 2l + 2) + (3m + 3s) + 2 = 5m + 2n + 2l + 3s + 4$ equations and variables. We have also seen that the two monetary variables, namely the price $p_{u'}$ of the money services and the quantity O_u supplied (and demanded) of these money services, have been solidly anchored to the $5m + 2n + 2l + 3s + 2$ non-monetary variables. This interdependence should be kept in mind when judging Walras's considerations which follow below.

WALRAS'S QUANTITY THEORY OF MONEY

Inserting (7) into (14) yields

$$Q_u = \frac{d_a p_{a'} + d_\beta p_{b'} + \ldots + d_\epsilon}{p_{u'}} +$$

$$+ \frac{\delta_a p_{a'} + \delta_\beta p_{b'} + \ldots + \delta_\mu p_{m'} + \ldots + \delta_x p_k + \ldots}{p_{u'}}$$

$$= \frac{H_a}{p_{u'}}, \tag{16}$$

where H_a denotes the sum of the two numerators on the right-hand side of (16). H_a may be considered as the total value in *numéraire* of all the money services that individuals and entrepreneurs need for their cash balances in equilibrium. Walras referred to (16) as the 'single equation of monetary circulation' (*Eléments*, Section 278). The ds (and the δs) will depend, as he argued, indirectly and very weakly on $p_{u'}$, since this price appears only in the budget equation.[12] This brings him to the conclusion:

> The equation of monetary circulation [i.e. (16)], when money is not a commodity, comes very close, in reality, to falling outside the system of equations of economic equilibrium.
>
> > (*Eléments*, 4th edition, Section 278)

Walras meant that, if all other equations of the system are holding, the equality in (16) can simply be obtained by solving for $p_{u'}$. Hence, if Walras were right, the model with fiat-money appears to display monetary dichotomy in the sense that, given the initial endowments and the parameters of the model,

> *the value of the service of money is ... inversely proportional to its quantity.*
>
> > (*Eléments*, 4th edition, Section 279; italics in original)

Walras denoted the considerations above as his 'quantity theory'. His indefensible assertion that in (16) H_a is approximately independent of $p_{u'}$ has certainly contributed to the opinion that in neoclassical economics 'money is a veil'.

PAYMENTS IN THE FIAT-MONEY MODEL

What Walras neglected to do was to set out how payments could actually take place in the fiat-money model, i.e. to explain how much had to be paid in units of money for a unit of a good or a service. We shall speculate on this now.

The amount $1/p_{u'}$ is the price of one unit of *numéraire* measured in units of money services; multiplying this by i makes it the 'price' of a unit of *numéraire* in money itself and so we obtain a kind of virtual money-price P for the *numéraire*:

$$P = \frac{i}{p_{u'}}. \tag{17}$$

Hence we can conceive of P as the quantity of money *needed for paying* one unit of *numéraire* (A). From this it follows that amounts $p_b P$, $p_c P$, $p_d P$, ... are *needed for paying* one unit of (B), (C), (D), ..., respectively.

Furthermore, let G be the total value, measured in *numéraire*, of all the transactions described by the solution of the equations of the model:

$$G = O_t p_t + \ldots + O_p p_p + \ldots + O_k p_k + O_{k'} p_{k'} + O_{k''} p_{k''} + \ldots$$

$$+ O_{a'} p_{a'} + O_{b'} p_{b'} + \ldots + Q_{m'} p_{m'} + \ldots + O_u p_{u'}$$

$$+ D_a + D_b p_b + D_c p_c + D_d p_d + \ldots + D_e p_e + \Sigma_e. \tag{18}$$

The amount Gi is the value in *numéraire* of all money services actually provided during the period. Writing

$$Q_u = \frac{H_a}{p_{u'}} = \frac{H_a}{Gi p_{u'}} \, Gi = \frac{H_a}{Gi} \, G \, \frac{i}{p_{u'}} = \frac{1}{v} \, GP, \tag{19}$$

where we take

$$v = Gi / H_a, \tag{20}$$

we get

$$Q_u v = PG. \tag{21}$$

v denotes the average number of times that a unit of money is used for paying equilibrium transactions (inclusive of the units that remain possibly unused in the cash balances, kept for other motives). Relation (21) is of exactly the same form as Fisher's famous $MV = PT$, but here v, P and G are all interdependent.[13] The only thing Walras would have reached in continuing the analysis as we did above is an endogenous explanation of v.

16

WALRAS'S EQUILIBRIUM MODEL WITH COMMODITY-MONEY

In his *Théorie de la monnaie* Walras indicated four features that a commodity should have in order to be suitable for money. These features are homogeneity, great scarcity, divisibility and immutability. Nature, according to Walras, has supplied two commodities which appear to incorporate all these features, namely gold and silver. One of them, or both at the same time, may be taken as money. In this chapter we shall point out how the model of the preceding chapter changes when such a commodity is taken as money.

THE MODEL

Let us take (A) as the money-commodity and let us again take the model with circulating capital of Chapter 13 as a starting point. For (A) as the money-commodity there are three functions: it can be used as merchandise, as circulating capital and as money. The new material, in comparison with the first three editions, of Lesson 30 (Sections 278–82) in the fourth and fifth editions of the *Eléments* seems to deal in an obscure way with three applications, but does not fit with the remainder of the lesson nor with the other chapters on money. Walras seems to be aware of this because in Section 281 of the fourth edition he stated that 'the role of (A')' as circulating capital is generally overshadowed by its role as money', after which he disregarded (A') as circulating capital and came back again (Section 282) to the macro money model that we dealt with on pages 91–3.

There is another problem, however, relating to the three different applications. From a producer's point of view (U) and (A') are identical and distinguishing between them would lead to the problem that it is impossible to distinguish between the total quantities $D_{a'}$ demanded by capitalists of newly produced (A') in the form of circulating capital and the total quantity D_u of newly produced (A') in the form of money. This leads to the following mathematical problem.

Maintaining (A') together with (U) gives rise to the following two equations for the prices $p_{a'}$ and $p_{u'}$ of (A') and (U): $p_{a'} = p_{u'} = i$. Hence we would have one additional equation in comparison with the fiat-money model. There will be also one additional variable, namely D_u, the total quantity of (A) produced in order to be added to the total stock of money at the end of the period. The problem, however, is that $D_{a'}$ and D_u always go together in the model in the sense that only $D_{a'} + D_u$ appears in the equations: the variable $D_{a'}$ has to be replaced everywhere by $D_{a'} + D_u$. Hence, mathematically speaking, no new variable has appeared – only a change of name of a variable has taken place. The mathematical difficulty disappears when (A') is dropped as a separate good in the system. This seems to be the most obvious way to avoid the inconsistency. Another way to avoid it is to drop the assumption that (A) can be costlessly monetized and demonetized; in our view, however, this would lead us too far from the original model. Consequently, we shall now consider as a starting point the model of Chapter 13 without (A'), i.e. without the first of equations (6) and (7), without the variables $O_{a'}$ and $D_{a'}$ and without $p_{a'}$ and its pertinent equation in (1).

What has been said in Chapter 15 about the consumers' cash balances in the case of fiat-money applies equally to the case of commodity-based money. Suppose that an individual is endowed at the outset of the period with a quantity q_u of (commodity-based) money and suppose that he is willing to offer the services of an amount o_u of it, retaining for his own use an amount sufficient to buy the quantities $\beta, \gamma, \delta, \ldots, \varepsilon$ of (B'), (C'), (D'), $\ldots$, (E'). Hence the new budget equation for the individual becomes

$$o_t p_t + \ldots + o_p p_p + \ldots + o_k p_k + o_{k'} p_{k'} + o_{k'} p_{k'} + \ldots$$
$$+ o_{b'} p_{b'} + o_{c'} p_{c'} + \ldots + q_m p_{m'} + \ldots + q_u p_{u'}$$
$$= d_a + d_b p_b + d_c p_c + d_d p_d + \ldots + d_e p_e + o_e + \beta p_{b'} + \gamma p_{c'}$$
$$+ \delta p_{d'} + \ldots + \varepsilon. \tag{1}$$

Note that $p_{u'} = i, p_{b'} = p_b i, p_{c'} = p_c i, p_{d'} = p_d i, \ldots$. The variable α does not appear in this equation. Maximization of the individual's utility under the restriction of (1) yields first-order conditions similar to those of the preceding chapter. From these the demand and supply equations for all goods and services can be derived, including those for $\beta, \gamma, \delta, \ldots, \varepsilon$. The total value in *numéraire* of these quantities is equal to $\beta p_{b'} + \gamma p_{c'} + \delta p_{d'} + \ldots + \varepsilon$, and consequently the quantity of money offered by the individual is

$$o_u = q_u - \frac{\beta p_{b'} + \gamma p_{c'} + \delta p_{d'} + \ldots + \varepsilon}{p_{u'}}. \tag{2}$$

Aggregating this over all individuals yields

$$O_u = Q_u - \frac{d_\beta p_{b'} + d_\gamma p_{c'} + d_\delta p_{d'} + \ldots + d_\varepsilon}{p_{u'}}, \tag{3}$$

where d_β, d_γ, d_δ, ..., d_ε are the aggregates of β, γ, δ, ..., ε. Equation (3) may be written as

$$O_u = F_u(p_t, \ldots, p_p, \ldots, p_k, p_{k'}, p_{k''}, \ldots, p_b, p_c, \ldots, p_{m'}, \ldots, p_e, p_{u'}), \quad (4)$$

where, as we already stated,

$$p_{u'} = i. \tag{5}$$

The demand for money, again, is exerted by the entrepreneurs and is modelled in the same way as in Chapter 15, albeit that some adaptations have to be made. δ_a has to be dropped as a variable, which implies that the first of equations (10) has to be deleted and that in each of equations (11) the first term of the right-hand member has to be deleted. The transformation equations change in the sense that everywhere $D_a + D_{a'}$ is replaced by $D_a + D_u$, where D_u denotes the total amount of (A) produced, and offered by the entrepreneurs, to be added to the stock of money. Equation (12) of Chapter 15 then becomes[1]

$$a_u(D_a + D_u) + b_u(D_b + D_{b'}) + \ldots + m_u D_{m'} + \ldots + k_u D_k + \ldots$$
$$= \delta_\beta p_{b'} + \delta_\gamma p_{b'} + \ldots + \delta_\mu p_{m'} + \ldots + \delta_\kappa p_k + \ldots \tag{6}$$

Equation (14) becomes

$$\frac{\delta_\beta p_{b'} + \delta_\gamma p_{c'} + \ldots + \delta_\mu p_{m'} + \ldots + \delta_\kappa p_k + \ldots}{p_{u'}} = O_u. \tag{7}$$

The 'savings equals investment' equation has to be changed to

$$D_k P_k + D_{k'} P_{k'} + D_{k''} P_{k''} + \ldots + D_u + D_{b'} p_b + \ldots + D_{m'} p_m + \ldots$$
$$= E \tag{8}$$

where D_u now denotes the total amount demanded by individuals of newly produced (A) to be kept as money. Note that equations (15) of Chapter 15 change in the sense that everywhere the terms with a' as an index disappear. Note also that Walras's notation has as a consequence that O_u and D_u are not supply and demand of some good in the same market but magnitudes that relate to different markets. O_u is a quantity of money services, whereas D_u is an amount of money.

Compared with the model of circulating capital without (A') the complete model with commodity-based money has $p_{u'}$, O_u and D_u as additional variables and (3), (5) and (7) as additional equations. Consequently, the total number of independent equations, and of variables, turns out to be $(2m + 2n + 2l + 2) + (3m + 3s - 3) + 3 = 5m + 2n + 2l + 3s + 2$. It is obvious that in this model the monetary variables are even more connected to non-monetary ones than in the model with fiat-money. Nevertheless, even for this model Walras adhered to the reasoning that led him to his macro money model.

DISCUSSION

Walras merged his ideas on circulating capital and on fiat-money and commodity-money directly into one model (Lesson 29 of the *Eléments*). The result was a nearly incomprehensible mass of formulae. Above we have tried to clear this up by formulating three separate models: a model of capital formation with circulating capital, a model of capital formation with circulating capital and fiat-money, and a model of capital formation with circulating capital and commodity-based money. An unfortunate consequence of Walras's confusing exposition was that neither Walras himself nor any of his contemporaries was able to use the results of Lesson 29 for further analysis of monetary phenomena.[2]

What Walras, unintentionally, did from the fourth edition of the *Eléments* onwards was devise a comprehensive economic theory in which the dichotomy between the real and the monetary sector *does not exist at all.* The considerations on his quantity theory within the framework of the model with fiat-money appear at least questionable because there is much more interdependence between the monetary and the real variables than Walras seems to suggest; a quick glance at the equations will convince the reader (see Appendix IV). In the commodity-money model the interdependence between the monetary variables and the real variables is even stronger, as can easily be inferred from the equations. The quantity of money itself has become endogenous in this model which removes the last ground for a quantity theory in the sense of pages 99–101 above.[3]

In fact, Walras has succeeded in devising a complete model of general economic equilibrium, in which money is incorporated in all of its aspects. We shall deal with this in the next section.

ON THE NATURE OF MONEY IN WALRAS'S MODELS

Money has three well-known functions: it serves as a means of measurement, as a medium of exchange and as a store of value. These tasks can only be fulfilled if there is confidence, felt by all or most of the economic actors, that the general circumstances in which the money is functioning will continue to exist in the future, and therefore that the money will more or less maintain its value; it is only factual circumstances that may change (gradually). It is obvious that in particular the use of money as a store of value depends on confidence. At the same time, of course, there should be confidence that the economy as a whole will continue to function normally, as it did before.[4] We shall consider the money in Walras's models in the light of these considerations.

In both the fiat-money model and the model with commodity-based money it is clear that the functions of money as a means of measurement

105

of (relative) value and as a means of payment are well developed. The twentieth-century models also demonstrate that cost of payments may be modelled elegantly in a convincing way. In the fiat-money model, however, the individual quantities of money are given and are not supposed to change from period to period. This means that it is difficult to maintain that Walras's fiat-money is a store of value in an active sense; this is not altered by the, implicit, assumption that the money that the individuals get back from the entrepreneurs at the end of the period will again have value in the subsequent period. It is impossible in this model, however, for an individual to increase or decrease his initial quantities of money. In our opinion this is the reason why Walras's fiat-money is not money because it does not fulfil all the above three functions; it only is an artificial device in a pedagogical set-up.

This shortcoming does not apply to the case of commodity-based money. Commodity-based money serves as a means of measurement, a medium of exchange and a store of value which can be changed at will by its owner. Therefore, one may say that this kind of money fulfils all three functions.

Walras's assumptions about the absence of uncertainty only apply to the period in question. Between successive periods there is uncertainty about exogenous changes; tastes and habits of the consumers may change, their number may change, technological changes may occur and so on. Since money has become an integral part of his model of general economic equilibrium, Walras's theory *as a whole* contains the potential to describe and explain what happens during a sequence of periods.[5] The agents in Walras's theory do not know with certainty the outcomes of the economic process when more than one period is considered. Hence there must be the tacit assumption that there exists confidence that the money of today will also have value tomorrow. In this chapter we have argued that Walras's theory allows for such an assumption.[6]

Part III

EXTENSION

La conception des courbes de besoin ou
d'utilité des produits ou services d'intérêt
public serait indispensable pour compléter
la théorie mathématique de l'équilibre
économique.

Léon Walras
(*EES*, p. 433)

17

REALITY AND REALISTIC UTOPIAS

In this part we shall speculate on a possible extension of Walras's mathematical general economic equilibrium models by including additional features of the envisaged ideal. These features are market conditions other than perfectly free competition, public goods, the ownership of land and the abolition of taxation.

An economic model is viewed as a simplified reflection of reality. A similar conception of an economic model seems applicable to Walras's models, as discussed in the previous chapters. Compared with twentieth-century ideas, however, Walras's conception of 'a simplified reflection', on the one hand, and of 'a reflection of reality', on the other, is slightly different and to some extent confusing. In particular, these differences in conceptualization relate to differences in the 'art' of model building and choice of variables. Simultaneously, then, the intent of Walras's models may well be of a different nature from modern contemporary economic models.

The nature of Walras's models has been discussed extensively by William Jaffé and Donald Walker in the economic literature.[1] The discussion concentrates on the degree of normativity of Walras's (pure) economic models which, in our view, may be conflated with the degree of reality reflected by the model.[2] Prior to a discussion of the degree of reality, however, one may discuss the degree of 'simplification' of reality. To this we now turn.

SIMPLIFICATION OR GENERALIZATION?

Walras's theory of general economic equilibrium has been praised by many writers for its architecture and monumentality. Many of these authors, however, used and developed the theory for their own purposes, neglecting or ignoring the initial purpose for which Walras himself has devised it. From the very beginning of his career Walras aimed at contributing to the realization of a 'social ideal', as we indicated on pages 8–10. His economics and notably his models of general economic equilibrium were his instruments to indicate this ideal and to analyse its characteristics. This implies that the models of general economic equilibrium have to be supplemented by matters outside the realm of free competition.

As we observed above,[3] Walras's conception of an exchange mechanism was predominantly inspired by the exchange mechanism at the Paris Stock Exchange at the time. Although the Paris Stock Exchange could not be considered as an exact representation of each and every market, Walras considered that it fulfilled the conditions of an effective market to a large degree:

> The markets which are best organized from the competitive stand-point are those in which purchases and sales are made by auction, through the instrumentality of stockbrokers, commercial brokers or criers acting as agents who centralize transactions in such a way that the terms of every exchange are openly announced and an opportunity is given to sellers to lower their prices and to buyers to raise their bids. This is the way business is done in the stock exchange, commercial markets, grain markets, fish markets, etc.
>
> (*Eléments*, Section 41)

It therefore comes as no surprise that in Walras's free-competition models 'purchases' and 'sales' are openly made by auction, 'transactions' are centralized by criers, and sellers and buyers adjust their bids in the *tâtonnement* process. In this respect, Walras's models not only bear resemblance to the actual exchange mechanism at a stock exchange but are, in fact, modelled to reflect this mechanism.

This does not imply that Walras's models have been devised in order to reflect the exchange mechanism at the stock exchange. Although it implies that it is the process of exchange which is modelled, Walras considered the stock exchange mechanism as a class of transactions that take place under a regime of free competition. As such, the exchange mechanism at the stock exchange became a general type of exchange process which may be applicable in a more general context. In Walras's terminology this type of exchange process is a 'real-type concept' of exchange.[4]

These observations from experience, or real-type concepts, are taken as the building-blocks from which the models are constructed. In theory, however, these real-type concepts are translated into abstract 'ideal-type concepts'; the latter concepts seem to lose touch with the details of reality although they enable, according to Walras, further reasoning:

> Following this same procedure, the pure theory of economics ought to take over from experience certain type concepts, like those of exchange, supply, demand, market, capital, income, productive services and products. From these real-type concepts the pure science of economics should then abstract and define ideal-type concepts in

terms of which it carries on its reasoning.... Thus in an ideal market
we have ideal prices which stand in an exact relation to an ideal
demand and supply.

(*Eléments*, Section 30)

The procedure followed by Walras in constructing the models is therefore one in which reality is stripped of each and every specific detail and
retains the essences of the mechanism. The models are believed to be
generic and therefore not a simplified reflection of reality but rather the
reflection of the nature of reality. In this light, Walras may speak of
essences and (general) laws, i.e. 'the aggregate of necessary relations which
follow from the nature of things'.[5]

Although Walras's models seem to elevate themselves from everyday
life, the outcomes and conclusions are destined to solve (social) problems
in reality. This follows from the general character of the models and their
propositions, which, in Walras's view, can be applied to any specific
circumstance that reality seems to display:

Reality admits of a very wide and fruitful application of these propositions.

(*Eléments*, Section 30)

According to this line of argument, Walras's models do not describe
reality itself but are based upon the common features of the various modal-
ities of reality. This implies that a discussion of the degree of reality of
Walras's models should take place in the light of Walras's procedures to
construct his models. Simultaneously, it implies that the discussion should
also address the question of what the model does describe if it does not
describe reality as such. To this we shall turn next.

A UTOPIAN REALITY

From the sequence of models described in the previous chapters[6] it follows
that Walras tried to elaborate each previous model by including additional
'ideal-type concepts'. Although the additional concepts were included so as
to approach reality as closely as possible the models were never designed to
describe an actual situation. The question, then, is what the subsequently
enlarged models describe and for what purpose.

All models, as presented in the previous chapters, clearly describe an
equilibrium situation. The exchange model, the production model, the
model of capital formation and the money models assume that equilibrium
exists or will be attained. As such the models describe a hypothetical situation which may or may not be attained.[7] Although many subsequent
general equilibrium theorists have tried to demonstrate the existence,
stability or uniqueness of equilibrium, this seems to be of little concern to
Walras's intentions.

As we have set out in the previous section, the exchange mechanism in the models is expressed in ideal-type concepts. By describing an equilibrium situation in ideal-type concepts, Walras believed that he was able to formulate general principles and conditions for equilibrium. These general principles may be used, according to Walras, in a practical situation of economic policy. Hence, any attempt to attain equilibrium, or to prevent crises, may be guided by general principles formulated by Walras's theory. In this respect, neither the existence, stability nor uniqueness conditions for equilibrium are important in themselves but only in relation to a preconceived goal in reality.

This preconceived goal formulated by Walras related to what was known as 'the social question'.[8] The social question in nineteenth-century France was the outcome of entangled conflicts relating to social, political, economic and ideological matters. According to Walras, these conflicts resulted from a transition of the French economy from an agricultural stage to an industrial stage. This transition had put a strain on the economic relations within the existing social organization. Therefore, in Walras's view, the time had come to reform society by reformulating the economic relations.

By investigating the generic exchange process of free competition Walras believed that he was able to uncover one of the essential mechanisms in society. Stress on a regime of free competition, then, was motivated by the consideration that individual freedom within social constraints would effectuate an optimal situation, both in terms of self-interest and in terms of social justice. The description of an ideal-type model of the exchange process could thus serve as a basis for describing an ideal society. It is in this respect that Jaffé referred to 'a realistic utopia'.[9]

Walras's 'realistic utopia' was based on the idea that theory formulated the conditions of an abstract and ideal society founded on real premises. Although the conditions were formulated in abstract terms this did not imply that the ideal society could never be attained. In fact, Walras believed that in due time his scientific arguments might convince honest politicians who might introduce the delineation of the new society. The economic agents would subsequently converge voluntarily towards the new 'equilibrium situation'.[10] This is what we shall call Walras's 'general general economic equilibrium situation'.

The converging process of the economic agents towards the new equilibrium situation was never described by Walras, and, for that matter, this process seems hard to predict. The new conditions, or social constraints, for his 'utopian reality' were given ample attention by Walras. We shall first discuss these conditions before presenting the final 'general general economic equilibrium model'.

18

FREE COMPETITION REVISITED

The general equilibrium models, as developed in the previous chapters, were above all theoretical expressions of a free-competition situation. In reality, however, the production and consumption of goods and services displayed hybrid forms of organizations and did not always have the same characteristics as a regime of free competition. In this respect, the results obtained while assuming free competition were applicable to a restricted number of markets, i.e. those markets in which free competition prevailed.

As we stated above, the results of Walras's models were designed to describe an ideal situation. By implication, the ideal situation described by the models did not coincide with the practical situation. In Walras's view, however, this ideal situation could serve as a blueprint for practical improvements.[1] In other words, the 'imperfect' practical situation could be adjusted to conform to the 'perfect' ideal. It was according to the results of a free-competition situation that Walras tailored these improvements.

The question of where the limits of free competition lie, and thus of where these practical improvements may take place, remains. At the same time, a question arises of how these improvements can be shaped in order to comply with the prescribed results of free competition.

As we shall set out in this chapter, the limitations of free competition relate to different fields in Walras's work. In the first place, they relate to Walras's 'applied economics', as far as the organization of production is concerned.[2] In the second place, they relate to Walras's 'social economics', as far as the distribution of incomes is concerned.[3]

In discussing free competition the question arises as to the desirability of free competition and the optimality of the results. As such the matter of the optimality of *laissez-faire*, which we have seen in Chapter 2, re-emerges. In this chapter we shall review some of the considerations of desirability and optimality of free competition that will lead to a generalization of Walras's general equilibrium model in the next chapter. First, however, we shall briefly discuss *laissez-faire* and its relation to the optimality of free competition.

LAISSEZ-FAIRE AND FREE COMPETITION

In the *Eléments* any social organization is considered as an artificial construct. In this light, Walras believed that the system of *laissez-faire* was the result of a historical process of organizational progress in which each society selected its own social organization.

> In the production and distribution of wealth, and generally in all matters pertaining to social organization, man has the choice between better and worse and tends more and more to choose the better part. Thus man has progressed from a system of guilds, trade regulations and price fixing to a system of freedom of industry and trade.... The superiority of the later forms of organization over the earlier forms lies not in their greater naturalness ... but rather in their closer conformity with material well-being and justice. The proof of such conformity is the only justification for adhering to a policy of *laissez-faire, laissez-passer.*

(Eléments, Section 7)

By stressing the necessity of a proof of the conformity with material well-being and justice, Walras not only accentuated the arbitrariness of any social system but also implied that the proof of such conformity as far as *laissez-faire* concerns was not at all established in the economic theories of his days.

In order to study the consequences of *laissez-faire* on economic inter-actions, Walras elevated free competition to an indisputable doctrine in his pure theory. This did not imply that Walras propagated free competition as the one and only exchange regime:

> It seemed to me that you consider me as an adherent of absolute free competition (for the very reason that I study attentively and meticulously the effects of free competition). Whatever it may be, I would like you to know that, quite to the contrary, it is rather the desire to repudiate the ill-founded and unintelligible applications of free competition made by orthodox economists which has led me to study free competition in matters of exchange and production.[4]

Instead, by studying free competition, the limitations set by the assumptions of this regime would necessarily be exposed. At the same time, free competition, as defined in Chapter 2, could be drawn away from the realm of *laissez-faire* and supplemented by prescriptions of state intervention.

Walras explicitly assumed that within the feasible area of free competition this regime would procure a relative maximum of utility. He believed that it could be concluded that 'the natural economic mechanism is, up to a certain extent, a self-moving and self-regulating mechanism'.[5] Although this implication was not proved by Walras, it led him to conclude that no other form of state intervention would be required in the case of free competition than those measures that guarantee its unhampered working.

There are three issues, however, which are beyond the feasibility area of free competition. The first concerns those goods of private industry in which the condition of equality between selling price and cost of production would not apply under a policy of strict *laissez-faire*.

> The principle of free competition is not generally applicable to the production of things which are within the province of natural and necessary monopolies.
>
> (*Eléments*, Section 223)

A second issue concerns public goods, which cannot be evaluated in terms of individual wants but can only be estimated jointly, by public wants.

> The principle of free competition, which is applicable to the production of things for private demand, is not applicable to the production of things where public interest is involved.
>
> (*Eléments*, Section 223)

Whereas the two issues just mentioned primarily relate to matters of utility, or well-being, there is a third issue outside the feasibility area of free competition which relates to matters of justice.

> Though our description of free competition emphasizes the problem of utility, it leaves the question of justice entirely to one side, since our sole object has been to show how a certain distribution of services gives rise to a certain distribution of products. The question of the [original] distribution of services remains open, however.
>
> (*Eléments*, Section 223)

From the very fact that the results of free competition do not apply to public goods or monopoly goods, nor to the issue of distribution, one may conclude that free competition cannot answer the question about *laissez-faire*'s 'closer conformity with well-being and justice'. In this light, Walras could neither provide nor dismiss the justification of *laissez-faire*. Instead, as we shall see in the next section, Walras provided an alternative approach to bring his own social ideal in closer conformity with well-being and justice.

THE ORGANIZATION OF PRODUCTION

The first reason to withdraw free competition from the realm of *laissez-faire* was motivated by Walras's observation that *laissez-faire* could neither institute nor maintain a regime of free competition. In fact, a policy of *laissez-faire*, i.e. leaving economic matters to the individuals' decisions,

115

could very well lead to a deterioration of free competition and give rise to a situation of monopoly:

> An industry, which starts out under free competition with a large number of small enterprises, tends to be divided among a smaller number of enterprises of medium size, and then among a still smaller number of large-scale enterprises – to end, finally, in a *monopoly first selling at cost of production and then selling at a price yielding a maximum profit*. This statement is confirmed by facts.
>
> (*Eléments*, Appendix I, Section 8, n. 1; Walras's italics)

This tendency towards a situation of monopoly may be explained by what might happen in the case of price fixing, as Walras argued. Hence, consider a price to be regulated, e.g. through agreement by individual entrepreneurs. In the case of a maximum price set below the market price, the cost of production per unit of product may be higher than the selling price. In terms of the price equations this implies for product (B) that

$$b_t p_t + b_p p_p + b_k p_k + \ldots > p_b. \tag{1}$$

Since the price for (B) is fixed, some entrepreneurs will make a loss and therefore stop producing (B) altogether by withdrawing from this branch of production. The remaining entrepreneurs, for whom this inequality does not hold, will continue their production at a maximum selling price equal to the cost of production. Assuming an unchanged demand for good (B), the remaining entrepreneurs may expand their production to compensate for the withdrawal of a part of the total production. Hence, the market is served by a smaller number of larger enterprises.[6]

In the case of a minimum price set above the market price, the selling price will exceed the cost of production, thus giving rise to a continuous profit. In terms of the price equations this may be expressed for good (B) as follows:

$$b_t p_t + b_p p_p + b_k p_k + \ldots < p_b. \tag{2}$$

Since the minimum price for (B) is above the free-competition market price, Walras assumed that demand will be reduced and that only a few entrepreneurs will be able to sell their product. This implies that some entrepreneurs may not be able to sell their product at this higher price and consequently will withdraw from this branch of production.[7] Again, the consequence of this type of price fixing is a tendency towards a smaller number of larger enterprises.

The tendency towards fewer enterprises in particular branches of production will finally result in a situation of a monopoly.[8] The level of production in a monopolistic situation in the *Eléments* is set so as to maximize net receipts.[9] Since this level of production need not coincide with the level of production that would procure the greatest possible satisfaction of the desires of the consumers, Walras concluded that a situation of monopoly was suboptimal compared with a situation of free competition.

In order to (re)establish an optimal market system, Walras concluded that maintaining free competition would require a framework of rules. Within this framework of rules the economic agents would interact in 'relative' freedom. Furthermore, in those situations in which free competition did not exist Walras suggested instituting, by means of a set of rules, a market system with results comparable with those of free competition. In this sense he extended the notion of free competition to regulated free competition.

The institution of this framework of rules was attributed by Walras to the community or the state. Hence, instead of a *laissez-faire* policy, free competition in Walras's work implied an active participation of the state:

Instituting and maintaining free competition in economics in a society is a matter of legislation, very complicated legislation, belonging to the State.

(*EPA*, p. 476)

These rules were, in fact, restrictions placed upon price manipulations and monopolies. As such, price manipulations, either price fixing or price discrimination, were suggested to be regulated by the state to ensure the equality of selling price and cost of production. Similarly, monopolies should be regulated in the sense that they are allowed to exist under the condition that they sell at the cost of production and therefore at one single price.

The latter restriction on monopolies was also utilized by Walras to formulate a criterion for state monopolies. As we observed above, some goods and services could not be estimated by individual wants but only by collective or public wants. In this respect, one could think of matters such as national defence, infrastructure or the administration of law. For those goods and services production would not take place by private initiative. Walras suggested that the state should engage in its production:

Because of social interest the State should undertake the production of the public goods and services that cannot be produced by individual initiatives.

(*EPA*, p. 268)

Since the state, by definition, would be the sole producer, Walras defined this type of production as a 'moral monopoly'. As in the case of the 'economic monopolies',[10] the state should sell its goods and services at the cost of production.

In these respects, free competition not only gave freedom to the economic agents but also required a certain degree of organization of production to restrict the tendencies that could oppress this freedom of competition.

THE DISTRIBUTION OF INCOME

Whereas the rules of the organization of production, as discussed in the previous section, primarily relate to the 'optimality' of free competition, questions concerning the distribution of incomes address the matter of the *desirability* of the outcome of free competition. In other words, the question is whether the outcome of the exchange process in a system of free competition would also be a just outcome.

The analysis of exchange in the models in the previous chapters was based on the increments of utility for the individuals obtained through economic interaction in the market. As such, questions of justice or (in)equality fall outside this analysis, as we observed above.

In his *Etudes d'économie sociale* (1896b), Walras dealt with matters of justice and equality. In this context, the question whether the outcome of the exchange process is considered to be 'just' depended on two circumstances:[11] the individuals' efforts during the exchange compared with their 'rewards', and the initial distribution of capital prior to the exchange. Since exchange was assumed to take place in a system of free competition, Walras stated that individual rewards would increase with individual efforts.[12] Hence, the outcomes of free competition would by definition be just if the first circumstance prevailed.

The question of a just initial distribution of capital was above all a question of property:

> Justice consists in rendering to each what is properly his....
>
> (*Eléments*, Section 38)

To determine what one's property is, Walras relied on what he called 'the good old natural law', but which in fact was a very specific natural law conception developed by his father, Auguste Walras.[13] In the *EES* the natural law concept was effectuated through the allocation of capital, i.e. land, human capital and capital goods proper, to potential proprietors, i.e. the individuals and the state. As such, Walras argued that individuals should be the 'natural' proprietors of their own human capital. Simultaneously, the community is the 'natural' proprietor of the land, i.e. the state should be the owner of its national territory. Since capital goods proper is an 'artificial' capital made up of either land, human capital or both land and human capital, Walras argued that capital goods proper should be owned by those who produced it.

This allocation of capital to either individuals or the state is clearly an arbitrary classification based on simple beliefs of what is 'natural'. Nevertheless, Walras attached great importance to this strict division of property which not only implied the nationalization of land by the state but also the abolition of taxes. In this type of economy, the state would obtain an income through the rents of the land instead of taxing individuals' labour or capital. On the other hand, the individual would obtain an income through his own labour and should not rely on the state for additional income.

Thus, Walras believed that he had created an equal initial situation which through exchange would reward each individual in proportion to his efforts. Free competition, in this respect, was a necessary condition, but not a sufficient condition, to guarantee justice. Justice could only be achieved in Walras's view through a different organization of society. In this respect, only the state could pursue these changes by buying the land from individuals and abolishing taxes. As such a *laissez-faire* policy, i.e. no active participation of the state in economic affairs, was suboptimal not only in terms of well-being but also in terms of justice.

19

WALRAS'S 'GENERAL GENERAL EQUILIBRIUM MODEL'[1]

Of all formal mathematical models of general economic equilibrium, Walras's final model[2] is of such a richness and depth of ideas and of such a wideness of scope that it has often been taken to represent reality. Nevertheless, Walras was at all times aware of the incompleteness of his models and therefore he expressed the desirability of enlarging the system of general economic equilibrium. The extended model should also be suited to dealing with exceptions to free competition and should incorporate, in addition, public goods and services. Further, aspects of a just distribution of wealth should be taken up. The model would thus reflect principles of economic efficiency as well as of social justice. Much of Walras's work may be considered as aimed at the completion of his models in this sense. Although he provided all the building-blocks of such a model of 'general general economic equilibrium', Walras did not arrive at a full synthesis of them. This is the more remarkable because this synthesis appears to be a fundamental issue of the Walrasian legacy.[3]

A discussion of such a synthesis may, for simplicity, take place within the framework of the model with exchange and production of consumption goods only. This will be the subject of this chapter. It will become clear to the reader that the whole reasoning likewise applies to Walras's more inclusive models.

SYNTHESIS: WALRAS'S UTOPIAN REALITY

In this section we shall show that Walras's ideal can be described by a model of general economic equilibrium expressed in equations similar to those of Walras's other models, with the same optimality properties.

We try to follow as much as possible Walras's system of notation in his production model:

    (A), (B), (C), ... are private consumption goods produced by freely competing industries; their number is m'.

    (M), (N), (O), ... are private consumption goods produced under regulated monopoly in the sense of our Chapter 18; their number is m''.

(G), (H), (I), ... are public goods produced in a situation of moral monopoly; their number is m'''.

The total number of the above goods is $m' + m'' + m''' = m$. The prices of all these goods are $1, p_b, p_c, \ldots, p_m, p_n, p_o, \ldots, p_g, p_h, p_i, \ldots$; good (A) is the *numéraire.*

In the production model capital is supposed to exist in fixed, invariable quantities. Therefore the quantity of services that can be supplied during a certain period by each type of each of the three categories of capital is also given and invariable; it is these services that play a role here:

(T), ... denote the services of the various types of land; the number of types is n'.

(P), ... denote the services of human capital; there are n'' different types of this kind of services, i.e. of labour.

(K), ... denote the services of capital proper; there are n''' types of these capital services.

In total there are $n = n' + n'' + n'''$ types of capital (services). The prices of the services of capital are denoted by $p_t, \ldots, p_p, \ldots, p_k, \ldots$.

An individual's demand equations for consumption goods and for land services are as follows:

$$d_a = o_p p_p + \ldots + o_k p_k + \ldots - (d_b p_b + d_c p_c + \ldots + d_m p_m + d_n p_n$$
$$+ d_o p_o + \ldots + d_t p_t),$$
$$d_b = f_b(p_t, p_p, p_k, \ldots, p_b, p_c, \ldots, p_m, p_n, p_o, \ldots),$$
$$d_c = f_c(p_t, p_p, p_k, \ldots, p_b, p_c, \ldots, p_m, p_n, p_o, \ldots),$$
$$\vdots$$
$$d_m = f_m(p_t, p_p, p_k, \ldots, p_b, p_c, \ldots, p_m, p_n, p_o, \ldots),$$
$$d_n = f_n(p_t, p_p, p_k, \ldots, p_b, p_c, \ldots, p_m, p_n, p_o, \ldots),$$
$$d_o = f_o(p_t, p_p, p_k, \ldots, p_b, p_c, \ldots, p_m, p_n, p_o, \ldots),$$
$$\vdots$$
$$d_t = f_t(p_t, p_p, p_k, \ldots, p_b, p_c, \ldots, p_m, p_n, p_o, \ldots), \tag{1}$$
$$\vdots$$

His supply equations of labour and services of capital proper are

$$o_p = f_p(p_t, p_p, p_k, \ldots, p_b, p_c, \ldots, p_m, p_n, p_o, \ldots),$$
$$\vdots$$

$$o_k = f_k(p_t, p_p, p_k, \ldots, p_b, p_c, \ldots, p_m, p_n, p_o, \ldots), \tag{2}$$
$$\vdots$$

The ds denote the quantities demanded of the various goods and services; the os denote quantities of services offered. Equations (1) and (2) result from the maximization of the individual's utility function:

$$u = u(q_p - o_p, \ldots, q_k - o_k, \ldots, d_a, d_b, d_c, \ldots, d_m, d_n, d_o, \ldots, d_t, \ldots) \tag{3}$$

under the restriction of his budget constraint, given his initial endowments $q_p, \ldots, q_k, \ldots$ of the services of capital and given the prices of the consumption goods and of the services of capital;[4] he retains quantities $q_p - o_p, \ldots, q_k - o_k, \ldots$ for his own use. The first equation of system (1) is the budget restriction solved for d_a. Contrary to the original production model of Lesson 20 of the *Eléments* the individual is now demanding land services, which the state supplies; see the last of equations (1) and the last arguments of (3).

We now introduce the assumption that it is the community as a whole that is demanding the public goods. We assume as it were a community utility function with the quantities of these goods as arguments:

> Want curves, or utility curves, of products and services of public interest would be indispensable for completing the mathematical theory of economic equilibrium.
>
> (*EES*, p. 433, n. 1)

The state's 'demand equations' for public goods are

$$D_g = F_g(p_t, \ldots, p_g, p_h, p_i, \ldots),$$
$$D_h = F_h(p_t, \ldots, p_g, p_h, p_i, \ldots),$$
$$D_i = F_i(p_t, \ldots, p_g, p_h, p_i, \ldots), \tag{4}$$
$$\vdots$$

Its supply equations of the various types of land services are

$$S_t = F_t(p_t, \ldots, p_g, p_h, p_i, \ldots), \tag{5}$$
$$\vdots$$

Equations (4) and (5) obey the budget constraint

$$S_t p_t + \ldots = D_g p_g + D_h p_h + D_i p_i + \ldots. \tag{6}$$

The Ds denote quantities of the various public goods and services demanded and the Ss are the quantities supplied of the various types of land services; the use of capital letters indicates that these quantities are aggregate quantities. They result from maximizing the state's utility function, the 'welfare function' that Walras hinted at,

$$U_s = U_s(D_g, D_h, D_i, \ldots, Q_t - S_t, \ldots),\tag{7}$$

while taking account of (6), given the total quantities $Q_t, \ldots$ available and given the prices.

For all individuals there are supposedly equations like those of systems (1) and (2). Aggregating all these equations over all individuals yields the following systems of macro equations:

$$D_a = O_p p_p + \ldots + O_k p_k + \ldots - (D_b p_b + D_c p_c + \ldots + D_m p_m +$$
$$D_n p_n + D_o p_o + \ldots + D_t p_t),$$

$$D_b = F_b(p_t, p_p, p_k, \ldots, p_b, p_c, \ldots, p_m, p_n, p_o, \ldots),$$

$$D_c = F_c(p_t, p_p, p_k, \ldots, p_b, p_c, \ldots, p_m, p_n, p_o, \ldots),$$

$$\vdots$$

$$D_m = F_m(p_t, p_p, p_k, \ldots, p_b, p_c, \ldots, p_m, p_n, p_o, \ldots),$$

$$D_n = F_n(p_t, p_p, p_k, \ldots, p_b, p_c, \ldots, p_m, p_n, p_o, \ldots),$$

$$D_o = F_o(p_t, p_p, p_k, \ldots, p_b, p_c, \ldots, p_m, p_n, p_o, \ldots),$$

$$\vdots$$

$$D_t = F_t(p_t, p_p, p_k, \ldots, p_b, p_c, \ldots, p_m, p_n, p_o, \ldots),\tag{8}$$

$$\vdots$$

and

$$O_p = F_p(p_t, p_p, p_k, \ldots, p_b, p_c, \ldots, p_m, p_n, p_o, \ldots),$$

$$\vdots$$

$$O_k = F_k(p_t, p_p, p_k, \ldots, p_b, p_c, \ldots, p_m, p_n, p_o, \ldots),\tag{9}$$

$$\vdots$$

Equations (8) and (9), relating to the individual consumers, and equations (5) and (6), relating to the state as a consumer, are combined into the aggregate demand and supply equations of the 'consumption sector' of the economy in question. This sector's budget equation follows from (6) and the first of equations (8):

$$D_a = O_t p_t + \ldots + O_p p_p + \ldots + O_k p_k + \ldots$$
$$- (D_b p_b + D_c p_c + \ldots + D_m p_m + D_n p_n + D_o p_o + \ldots + D_g p_g$$
$$+ D_h p_h + D_i p_i + \ldots),\tag{10}$$

where $O_t = S_t - D_t, \ldots$, i.e. the net supplies of land services to be offered to the entrepreneurs, including the state itself as an entrepreneur.

The sector's demand equations for the goods (B), (C), ..., (M), (N),

$(O), \ldots, (G), (H), (I), \ldots$ are repeated below for exposition purposes:

$$D_b = F_b(p_t, p_p, p_k, \ldots, p_b, p_c, \ldots, p_m, p_n, p_o, \ldots),$$

$$D_c = F_c(p_t, p_p, p_k, \ldots, p_b, p_c, \ldots, p_m, p_n, p_o, \ldots),$$

$$\vdots$$

$$D_m = F_m(p_t, p_p, p_k, \ldots, p_b, p_c, \ldots, p_m, p_n, p_o, \ldots),$$

$$D_n = F_n(p_t, p_p, p_k, \ldots, p_b, p_c, \ldots, p_m, p_n, p_o, \ldots),$$

$$D_o = F_o(p_t, p_p, p_k, \ldots, p_b, p_c, \ldots, p_m, p_n, p_o, \ldots),$$

$$\vdots$$

$$D_g = F_g(p_t, p_p, p_k, \ldots, p_b, p_c, \ldots, p_m, p_n, p_o, \ldots),$$

$$D_h = F_h(p_t, p_p, p_k, \ldots, p_b, p_c, \ldots, p_m, p_n, p_o, \ldots),$$

$$D_i = F_i(p_t, p_p, p_k, \ldots, p_b, p_c, \ldots, p_m, p_n, p_o, \ldots), \tag{11}$$

$$\vdots$$

Similarly the equations for $D_t, \ldots,$ of (8), $O_p, \ldots, O_k, \ldots$ of (9), and $S_t, \ldots$ of (5) are combined:

$$O_t = F_t(p_t, p_p, p_k, \ldots, p_b, p_c, \ldots, p_m, p_n, p_o, \ldots, p_g, p_h, p_i, \ldots),$$

$$\vdots$$

$$O_p = F_p(p_t, p_p, p_k, \ldots, p_b, p_c, \ldots, p_m, p_n, p_o, \ldots),$$

$$\vdots$$

$$O_k = F_k(p_t, p_p, p_k, \ldots, p_b, p_c, \ldots, p_m, p_n, p_o, \ldots), \tag{12}$$

$$\vdots$$

Equations (10) and (11) are the m macro demand equations of private and public goods and equations (12) are the n supply equations of the services of capital.

In equilibrium the total supply of services by private persons (labour and the services of capital proper) and by the state (land services net of the demand by individuals) must be equal to the demand for those services by both entrepreneurs in the private-goods sector and the producers of public goods. This demand for services can be expressed in the total quantities to be produced of the various private goods and public goods. The latter quantities must be equal to the quantities demanded by the individuals and the state. This gives rise to the following equations, the n transformation equations:

$$a_t D_a + b_t D_b + c_t D_c + \ldots + m_t D_m + n_t D_n + o_t D_o + \ldots + g_t D_g$$
$$+ h_t D_h + i_t D_i + \ldots$$

$$= O_t$$

$$\vdots$$

$$a_p D_a + b_p D_b + c_p D_c + \ldots + m_p D_m + n_p D_n + o_p D_o + \ldots + g_p D_g$$
$$+ h_p D_h + i_p D_i + \ldots$$
$$= O_p$$

$$\vdots$$

$$a_k D_a + b_k D_b + c_k D_c + \ldots + m_k D_m + n_k D_n + o_k D_o + \ldots + g_k D_g$$
$$+ h_k D_h + i_k D_i + \ldots$$
$$= O_k \tag{13}$$

$$\vdots$$

The coefficients of the Ds are, again, the production coefficients.

In equilibrium there are neither profits nor losses for the entrepreneurs producing under conditions of free competition; the monopolists' prices are stipulated to be equal to the costs per unit product and the same applies to the public goods. This gives rise to the following system of m price equations:

$$a_t p_t + \ldots + a_p p_p + \ldots + a_k p_k + \ldots = 1$$
$$b_t p_t + \ldots + b_p p_p + \ldots + b_k p_k + \ldots = p_b$$
$$c_t p_t + \ldots + c_p p_p + \ldots + c_k p_k + \ldots = p_c$$
$$\vdots$$
$$m_t p_t + \ldots + m_p p_p + \ldots + m_k p_k + \ldots = p_m$$
$$n_t p_t + \ldots + n_p p_p + \ldots + n_k p_k + \ldots = p_n$$
$$o_t p_t + \ldots + o_p p_p + \ldots + o_k p_k + \ldots = p_o$$
$$\vdots$$
$$g_t p_t + \ldots + g_p p_p + \ldots + g_k p_k + \ldots = p_g$$
$$h_t p_t + \ldots + h_p p_p + \ldots + h_k p_k + \ldots = p_h$$
$$i_t p_t + \ldots + i_p p_p + \ldots + i_k p_k + \ldots = p_i \tag{14}$$
$$\vdots$$

The $2m + 2n$ equations (10)–(14) together form Walras's 'general general equilibrium model' of production. Because good (A) is the *numéraire* there are $2m + 2n - 1$ variables in the model. However, there are also $2m + 2n - 1$ independent equations in the model because the macro budget equation (10) can be derived from equations (13) and (14).

DISCUSSION

The 'general general equilibrium model' (10)–(14), indeed, has the same mathematical structure as the production model of Lesson 20 of the *Eléments*. From the way the extended model has been constructed it is immediately clear that the more sophisticated models, with capital formation (Chapter 11) and circulating capital and money (Chapters 15 and 16), may be extended similarly.

The mathematical structure of the equations, however, is not the most important point. More important are the optimality properties of the model. These, too, are the same for the extended models in comparison with the corresponding original models. Again, a solution of an extended model is Pareto optimal, as can easily be demonstrated. This circumstance leans heavily on two features of the extended models. First, because of the constant returns to scale, expressed by the fixed coefficients of production, the marginal costs and the average costs will always coincide. This means that Lipsey and Lancaster's second-best theorem (1956) – which states that when some conditions for general economic equilibrium are not fulfilled, it is not guaranteed that imposing the remaining conditions will lead to a 'second-best' situation – does not apply in this case. The condition which is not fully fulfilled in this case is that of free competition. The linear production structure, however, together with the stipulation that prices per unit of each monopoly product should equal costs per unit, guarantees that the extended model here does not differ from the original one. Therefore the second-best theorem is irrelevant here.

Second, the abolition of taxation combined with ownership of the land by the state and the fiction of the social welfare function have the effect that the state has a real budget constraint and plays a role that, in fact, is not different from that of an individual. Hence, with respect to optimality, the solution of the extended model does not differ from those of the original Walrasian models.

There is yet another important similarity between the extended model and its original. The *tâtonnement* procedure of the original model is applicable in both types of models. The only amendment that has to be made is the slight and harmless supposition that the producers in the sectors where free competition does not prevail do not withdraw when costs per unit are higher than their selling price (mostly they are the sole producer of the product concerned) but instead decrease their supply, and that, when their prices are higher than unit costs, no entrance will take place but instead the incumbent producer(s) will increase supply.

As a conclusion we may state that the ideal situation envisaged by Walras is a feasible one with the optimality properties he considered desirable. We may therefore claim that Léon Walras's equilibrium economics indeed describes his own utopian reality.

APPENDICES

I

A LIFE SKETCH OF LÉON WALRAS

THE ANTECEDENTS

If anything could be said about the origins of the name 'Walras', it is certainly not that it is a typically French name. To some extent, this accounts for the existing confusion regarding the pronunciation of Léon Walras's surname, both in his own day and at the present time. The non-French 'W' as well as the sounding 's' at the end of the name[1] reveal the non-French origin of the Walras family.

Léon Walras's great-grandfather was an immigrant from the Low Countries who arrived in Montpellier in the middle of the eighteenth century.[2] Born in 1724 at Arcen, now in the south of the Netherlands, as Andraeas Walravens, son of Jacob Walravens and Anna van Dalen, Léon Walras's great-grandfather started a new life as a journeyman tailor in pre-revolutionary France. In 1752 Andraeas Walras, whose name had been 'latinized' by this time, married the daughter of a Monsieur Levat, a master tailor. Andraeas Walras and Anne Levat had seven children, among whom the last but one was Léon Walras's grandfather, Louis Auguste.

Louis Auguste Walras was born in 1765 in Montpellier and grew up to become an administrator of the local government. As a bookkeeper in the collector's office of the Préfecture of the Département de l'Hérault and later as a businessman, Louis Auguste may have improved the social status of the Walras family although they remained, as Léon Walras described them, 'petits bourgeois, très honorables, très catholiques et très royalistes'.[3] At the age of 33, Léon Walras's grandfather married Léon's grandmother-to-be, Marie Esprit Tricou. Louis Auguste and Marie Esprit had eight children of whom two died at an early age. Léon Walras's father was the third child from this marriage, born on 1 February 1801 in Montpellier and baptized as Antoine-Auguste.

About Léon Walras's maternal family little is known. His mother, Louise Aline de Sainte-Beuve, came from an old Norman family in the Loire area. Léon Walras's maternal grandfather was a notary at Evreux and therefore belonged to the notables of this small provincial town in the

Département de l'Eure. Monsieur de Sainte-Beuve and his wife[4] had six children among whom was Louise Aline.

Antoine-Auguste Walras married Louise Aline de Sainte-Beuve at the age of 33, thereby following his father's example of marrying at a more advanced age. The couple settled in Evreux, where Antoine-Auguste had accepted the job of Principal of the Collège of Evreux. Nine months after their wedding their first child was born on 16 December 1834 and was named Marie Esprit Léon after his paternal grandmother. Of their three following children, Henri, Jeanne Isadore Louis ('Jenny') and Louis Auguste, only Jenny survived the epidemics that struck the Walras family.

LIKE FATHER, LIKE SON

Léon Walras's childhood years were mainly shaped by the changes in his environment and the places to which the Walras family moved. After two years at Evreux, Auguste Walras's position at the Collège d'Evreux appeared to be untenable and the family moved to Paris in 1836. In Paris, Auguste Walras resumed his studies in order to obtain his *aggrégation*. In 1839 he was assigned a teaching post for one year at the Collège Royal de Lille although immediately after having passed the *aggrégation* he was appointed as a professor of philosophy at the Collège Royal de Caen. From 1840 to 1847 the Walrases seemed to enjoy a happy life in which the family reached completion with the birth of Louis Auguste.

During these early years, Léon Walras had his father as his teacher, an experience which continued until Auguste's death in 1866. As a 3-year-old boy, Léon Walras started teaching himself to read and further learning was stimulated by his parents in the years to come. At the Collège Royal de Caen, Léon and his brother Henri figured among the best students of the class, excelling in grammar, mathematics and reading. In 1847, bad fortune struck the Walras family: Léon Walras's brother Henri died at the age of 11. At the same time, Auguste Walras's publications had outraged his superiors and led to a downgrading of his position at the Collège. Although Auguste Walras was 'exiled' to Nancy and later to Cahors as an Inspecteur d'Académie, he was able with the help of his in-laws to stay at Caen. Finally, however, he had to give in and accepted a position in the South of France at Pau.

From 1850, Léon Walras had left the warmth and care of the family home to enter the lycée at Douai. A year later he was awarded the degree of bachelier-ès-lettres and in 1853 he graduated from the lycée as a bachelier-ès-sciences. At Douai, Léon Walras seems to have fostered his social attitude and temperament with respect to the succession of revolutions which flooded across France. In this process of social maturing, Léon Walras was guided by his father's outbursts of social indignation, which materialized in carefully concealed writings on what was believed to be the social truth and how problems could be solved. Although these writings were never published during Auguste Walras's lifetime, the germ was planted in his son and would soon bear fruit.

After his education at the lycée at Douai, Léon Walras presumably moved to Paris in 1853 to apply for admission to the Ecole Polytechnique. Failing to pass the examination of the Polytechnique twice, because of insufficient or irrelevant preparation, Léon Walras applied for admission to the Ecole des Mines and entered the Ecole in 1854 as *élève externe*. The reformist ideas which slowly matured in Léon Walras's mind, however, did not go together with the strict education of a mining engineer. It seems that the 'Salons' in Paris and the intellectual discussions on how to reform society had a fiercer attraction for the young Walras than the conservative and practical engineering ambience. Four years after his first enrolment at the Ecole des Mines, Léon Walras had achieved very little that reflected a serious study of mining engineering. Instead, he had tried to express his social ideas in a novel called *Francis Sauveur* (1858) and in ambitious plans for art criticism. In the summer of 1858, Auguste Walras felt obliged to summon Léon to Pau and to redirect his libertine son. The occasion was later nostalgically described as follows:

> In front of the entry of an estate called *Les Roseaux*, I promised him to let literature and art criticism be and to devote myself entirely to the continuation of his work.[5]

THE BEGINNING OF A CAREER

After his return to Paris, Léon Walras immediately started working on economic subjects. It appears from the intensive correspondence with his father that the subjects varied from practical matters such as the question of copyright laws, which was much in vogue at the time, to a philosophy of science. The first economic articles[6] were published in the *Journal des Economistes*, and the remuneration from them supplied him with some income to live on. At the same time Walras worked on a larger essay on the refutation of the theory of Proudhon.[7] The latter book reveals the considerable influence of Auguste Walras on the beginning of his son's career in the late 1850s and early 1860s. The existing correspondence of this time from father to son clearly shows the one-way direction of the ideas and theories.

During this same period, Léon Walras met his future wife Célestine Aline Ferbach (1835–79) through a common friend in Paris.[8] Mademoiselle Ferbach, who had been left with the care of her son Jean Gabriel Georges, aroused the sympathy of Léon Walras and, though quite contrary to the family's liking, Léon Walras decided to live together with Aline Ferbach in the Parisian suburb St Mandé.[9]

In June 1860, Léon Walras had a major breakthrough when he joined the newspaper *La Presse*. In his newspaper articles, however, he expressed himself explicitly on reformist subject matters, to the dislike of the owners of the newspaper. At the same time, he presented his *Théorie critique de l'impôt* at an international conference on taxation at Lausanne. This essay on tax reforms had been written in a short period of time and was only made possible by the ideas and text keenly supplied in many letters by his father. Although his essay made some impression on the jury in Lausanne, the conservative economists in his home country clearly repudiated its socialist content. It seems that his position at *La Presse* therefore also came under fire. His contract lasted less than a year, when he was eventually expelled for being unwilling to conform to the standards.

In April 1862 Walras accepted an administrative position with the railway company Chemin de fer du Nord. Although the position did not give him much intellectual challenge, nor sufficient time to work extensively on his 'scientific' articles, it did supply him with desperately needed financial support. His spare time was spent on theoretical and practical considerations regarding producers' and consumers' co-operations.

In January 1865 Walras resigned from the railway company to accept a hazardous position as managerial secretary of a newly founded Caisse d'escompte des Associations populaires, a bank which was set up to discount bills offered by co-operations and mutual credit unions. Walras's responsibility was to manage the bills department and a section of the general administration. He also figured among the editors of *Le Travail*, a journal for the co-operative movement. Both the Caisse and the journal were short-lived. In 1868 the Caisse had lost all its capital. In its liquidation many lost their money, including the Banque de France, Walras himself, and Walras's sister and his mother. In the same year the journal, too, closed down.

In great debt and without a job, Léon Walras was quite fortunate to be invited to work in the office of one of the former commissioners of the Caisse, Mr Hollander, who was a banker himself. He stayed in Mr Hollander's office for a year and a half, when he was saved from oblivion by Mr Ruchonnet, a Swiss government representative in charge of reorganizing the Academy of Lausanne. Léon Walras would arrive in Lausanne in December 1870.

PROFESSOR AT LAUSANNE

At Lausanne, Walras was in the first instance only appointed for one academic year (1870–1), as 'professeur extraordinaire', because of some reservations among nominating committee members about Walras's supposed socialist points of view. In 1871, however, he was appointed 'professeur ordinaire'.

Walras devoted his research during his Lausanne period almost exclusively to pure economics. This was justified by the fact that his pure economics was the basis for his applied and social economics and at the time the former was the least developed. During the first year in Lausanne Walras sought, and found, mathematical expressions for his economic theory.

The idea of a mathematical representation of exchange had been inspired according to Walras by the attempts made by Cournot. Walras had read Cournot's *Recherches sur les principes mathématiques de la théorie des richesses* (1838) in the 1850s. For Léon Walras the authority and scientific nature of mathematics seemed to provide an acceptable means with which to prove the soundness of the 'Walrasian' social reform scheme.

Because of some severe criticism of this mathematical approach to political economy, he found himself in a rather vulnerable position from the start. Just before the publication of the *Eléments* in 1874, Walras wrote to one of his correspondents:

> *My father and I have devoted our lives to the elaboration of a political and social economy which is quite different from the mainstream views, both with respect to its foundations as well as with respect to its conclusions, either economic or ethic.* The moment has come to produce the results and, since these results are purely scientific and hardly of a very popular character, I need to search for even a very limited audience, both readers and judges, far and wide.
>
> (Jaffé (1965), Letter 250 to Edouard Pfeiffer,
> 12 March 1874; Walras's italics)

To this end, Walras carefully selected an international network of potentially interested economists from all over the world. With great dedication he exchanged names and addresses, thereby bringing students of economics, who resembled each other in their shared anxiety not to miss 'something new' rather than in their ideas, into contact with one another. The fact that Walras's correspondents eventually included every major economist of his day reflects the recognition from abroad.

When Walras arrived in Lausanne in 1870, his concern was not only to discharge his academic duties but, besides that, to satisfy his pecuniary wants. Because of the insufficiency of his ordinary remuneration Walras embarked on several activities which could fill this gap. In 1872 he gave a number of lectures in Geneva entitled 'Système des Phénomènes Economiques'. These lectures expounded his early ideas on pure economics. The lectures were followed in the same year by a new series of lectures entitled 'Exposition et Conciliation des Doctrines Sociales',[10] and from 1874 Walras found some supplementary employment as consulting actuary for the life insurance company La Suisse. In 1875 he was elected Recteur de l'Academie, a post which he held for two years, and in 1878 he accepted a visiting chair at the Academy at Neuchâtel for several months. All in all, the plethora of activities was burning him out from the very start.

In June 1879, his sickly wife Célestine Aline died. Five years later Walras married Léonide Désirée Mailly, a spinster in her late fifties with a British–French upbringing. Unfortunately, this second marriage only lasted for sixteen years, when Walras's second wife died.

During the 1880s, teaching at the Academy/University of Lausanne[11] became increasingly detrimental to his (mental) health. After several years of ill health, Walras went into untimely retirement in July 1893, which freed him from his educational burden and would offer him the opportunity for further research.

THE YEARS OF REST

Soon after his retirement Walras realized that he was running out of time if he was to achieve his initial plan: the publication of his *Elements of Social Economics* and his *Elements of Applied Economics*. Instead, Walras decided to compile a collection of previously published and unpublished material. Eventually, the *Etudes d'économie sociale* (*EES*) appeared in November 1896, and the *Etudes d'économie politique appliquée* (*EPA*) in August 1898. New ideas and thoughts developed after his retirement were included in a fourth edition of the *Eléments*. These new ideas mainly relate to the models of capital formation and of money circulation, as we have seen in Part II. These fortunate extensions clearly exhibit a final upswing of Walras's research activities.

After the death of his second wife Léon Walras and his daughter Aline moved to Clarens, near Montreux. During the last years in Clarens, Walras spent his time classifying and revising his pamphlets, papers and books, since he was sure of the eventual publication of his collected works and those of his father.

On 10 June 1909, Walras's jubilee was celebrated at the University of Lausanne. A marble commemorative tablet was presented on this occasion; it bore the inscription

À LÉON WALRAS – NÉ À EVREUX
Professeur à l'Académie et à l'Université de Lausanne
qui le premier a établi les conditions générales
de l'équilibre économique – fondant ainsi
L'ÉCOLE DE LAUSANNE
POUR HONORER 50 ANS DE TRAVAIL DÉSINTÉRESSÉ[12]

Léon Walras died on 5 January 1910 at the age of seventy-five and was buried in the cemetery at Clarens in the municipality of Montreux-Chatelard, Vaud, Switzerland, on 7 January 1910.

II

ON WALRAS'S WORKS

In 1906 Walras composed a bibliography of his economic writings. The manuscript is preserved in the Fonds Walras of Lausanne in Carton 7 of Section IVa. Together with the biography in Appendix I it gives a good overview of Walras's activities as a scientist. We shall present this autobibliography below. Prior to the bibliography, however, we shall describe the various attempts to publish Walras's complete economic works and those of his father.

PUBLISHING THE COMPLETE ECONOMIC WORKS

Walras himself already envisaged a publication of his father's and his own complete economic works. Since the 1890s he had set up a number of schemes for such a publication; see the general introduction to A. Walras (1990). For a number of reasons none of these plans was much of a success.

Some months after his death Léon Walras's children donated all his personal library, his archives and his own and his father's manuscripts to the University of Lausanne with the stipulation that the University would promote a publication of the complete economic works of Léon and Auguste Walras. Unfortunately, it cannot be said that, at the time, the University of Lausanne took this moral obligation seriously.[1]

It was Walras's daughter Aline in particular who was much concerned by this attitude of (some persons of) her father's university. Consequently, she and some of her friends took the initiative to try to bring out such a publication themselves. In 1924 she conveyed a part of her father's papers and books to the University of Lyon on the basis of which the publication of an important part of the economic works of her father and her grandfather could be achieved. It was Etienne Antonelli, at the time professor of economics in the University of Lyon, who had taken upon himself the task of editing the twofold work. Unfortunately, illness and, later, political engagements prevented Antonelli from starting the project seriously. Having recourse to other friends (in particular Gaston Leduc), however,

Aline Walras finally succeeded in having published the fifth edition of the *Eléments* (1926, the so-called édition définitive) and the second editions of the *EES* and the *EPA* (1936). Further, Léon Walras's *Abrégé des éléments d'économie politique pure* was brought out (1938). The latter book was a previously unpublished, simplified version of the *Eléments*, finished in 1903.

Aline Walras died during the Second World War and from then the attempts to publish the remaining works ceased for many decades. The Lyon archives fell into oblivion until 1984 when they were rediscovered under a thick cover of dust at the bottom of a bookcase in one of the university buildings. This discovery was a reminder that there was a task still unfinished. Therefore, it was decided that the University of Lyon would, eventually, finish Antonelli's task. To that end the University of Lyon 2 founded the Centre Auguste and Léon Walras, in which a team of economists was grouped to start the activities which would lead to the publication. After making a first inventory and creating a data bank with respect to the two authors they decided on the following set-up in fourteen volumes (the volumes that have already appeared are indicated by the year of publication).

AUGUSTE ET LÉON WALRAS
OEUVRES ÉCONOMIQUES COMPLÈTES

AUGUSTE WALRAS
I   *Richesse, liberté et société* (1990)
II   *La vérité sociale*
III *Cours et pièces diverses*
IV   *Correspondance*

LÉON WALRAS
V   *L'économie politique et la justice*
VI   *Les associations populaires coopératives* (1990)
VII   *Mélanges d'économie politique et sociale* (1987)[2]
VIII *Eléments d'économie politique pure ou théorie de la richesse sociale* (1988; variorum edition)
IX   *Etudes d'économie sociale: théorie de la répartition de la richesse sociale* (1990)
X   *Etudes d'économie politique appliquée: théorie de la production de la richesse sociale* (1992)
XI   *Théorie mathématique de la richesse sociale (et autres écrits mathématiques et d'économie pure)* (1993)
XII   *Cours d'économie sociale et d'économie politique appliquée*
XIII *Oeuvres diverses*
XIV   *Tables et index*

So far seven volumes have been brought out by the publishing house Economica in Paris; four volumes are in some stage of printing. The remaining volumes are in such a state of preparation that we may safely presume that within some years the Walrases will finally have the publication of their complete economic works.

LÉON WALRAS'S ECONOMIC AUTOBIBLIOGRAPHY

Below we represent as faithfully as possible Léon Walras's handwritten autobibliography.[3] At the end of each entry we indicate in roman numbers between square brackets the number of the volume of the *Complete Economic Works*, mentioned above, in which it is published.[4,5]

Bibliographie économique
(Léon Walras)

1859

1   De la propriété intellectuelle. Position de la question économique. (*Journal des Economistes*, décembre) [V]

1860

2   *L'Economie politique et la Justice. Examen critique et réfutation des doctrines économiques de M. P.-J. Proudhon, précédés d'une Introduction à l'étude de la question sociale.* 8°, LXIV, 258 pp. Paris [V]
3   Des octrois, à propos de la loi belge. (*La Presse*, 12 et 22 juillet et 3 août) [VII]
4   De la mise en valeur des biens communaux. (*La Presse*, 20, 21 et 23 septembre) [VII]
5   De la cherté des loyers à Paris. (*La Presse*, 19, 26 et 29 octobre et 6 novembre) [VII]
6   La Bourse et le développement du capital. (*La Presse*, 25 et 26 décembre) [VII]
7   Paradoxes économiques I – Que le sens commun n'est point le critérium de la science en général, ni en particulier, celui de l'économie politique. (*Journal des Economistes*, décembre) [VII]

1861

8   De l'élévation du taux de l'escompte. (*La Presse*, 23 et 26 janvier) [VII]
9   A. M. Félix Solar, rédacteur en chef de *La Presse*. (*La Presse*, 15 février) [VII]

10   *Théorie critique de l'impôt, précédée de Souvenirs du Congrès de Lausanne.* 8°, XXXVI, 124 pp. Paris [V]

11   *De l'impôt dans le canton de Vaud. Mémoire auquel un quatrième accessit a été décerné ensuite du concours ouvert par le Conseil d'Etat du canton de Vaud sur les questions relatives à l'impôt.* 8°, 100 pp. [Lausanne] [V]

–   L'industrie moderne et l'économie politique. (Inédit) [VII]

1863

12   *Principe de la théorie des richesses,* par M. Cournot. (*L'Indépendent de la Moselle,* 13 juillet) [VII]

13   *La crise cotonnière et les textiles indigènes,* par I.-E. Horn. (*L'Indépendent de la Moselle,* 27 juillet) [XIII]

14   *De l'esprit communal et de la routine administrative,* par M. de Labry. (*L'Indépendent de la Moselle,* 19 août) [VII]

15   *De la constitution de la propriété en Algérie.* (*L'Indépendent de la Moselle,* 2 et 21 septembre et 12 octobre) [VII]

1864

16   *L'atmosphère est un engrais complet,* par M. le Dr Schneider. (*L'Indépendent de la Moselle,* 13 et 16 janvier) [XIII]

–   De l'enseignement de l'économie politique dans les Facultés de Droit. (Inédit) [VII]

1865

17   *Les associations populaires de consommation, de production et de crédit. Leçons publiques faites à Paris en janvier et février 1865.* 12°, XXIV, 228 pp. Paris [VI]

18   Les Sociétés coopératives et la législation. Lettre au rédacteur de *La Presse.* (*La Presse,* 20 avril) [VI]

19   *Le Crédit et les Finances,* par Victor Bonnet. (*Journal des Economistes,* décembre) [XIII]

1866

20   Des opérations de la Caisse d'escompte des Associations populaires. Leçon publique faite à Paris en mars 1866. 8°, 24 pp. Paris [VI]

21   Le mouvement d'association et la politique libérale. (*La Presse,* 2 avril) [VI]

22   L'association à la française. (*La Presse,* 20 avril) [VI]

23   Programme économique et politique. (*Le Travail,* juillet) [VI]

24 Société coopérative immobilière. (*Le Travail*, août et septembre) [VI]
25 De la cherté du pain et de l'établissement de boulangeries coopératives. (*Le Travail*, octobre) [VI]
26 Socialisme et libéralisme. [Lettres à M. Ed. Scherer.] ([*Le Travail*], octobre et décembre 1866, février 1867) [IX]
27 A propos d'un article de M. Horn. (*Le Travail*, octobre) [VI]
28 Discussion sur les associations coopératives à la Société d'économie politique du Paris. (*Le Travail*, novembre) [VI]
29 Des doctrines en matière d'association coopérative. (*Le Travail*, décembre) [VI]

1867

30 Enoncé des principes relatifs aux associations populaires coopératives. (*Le Travail*, janvier) [VI]
31 Le crédit gratuit réciproque. (*Le Travail*, janvier) [VI]
32 La liberté des sociétés. (*Le Travail*, février) [VI]
33 Le futur parti. (*Le Travail*, février) [VI]
34 De la gratuité par la réciprocité dans les banques d'échange (*Le Travail*, mars) [VI]
35 Les sociétés de résistance. (*Le Travail*, mars) [VI]
36 Discussion sur les coalitions et les grèves à la société d'économie politique de Paris. (*Le Travail*, avril) [VI]
37 Le projet de loi sur les sociétés à capital variable. (*Le Travail*, mai) [VI]
38 Les erreurs du système monétaire français. (*Le Travail*, mai) [XIII]
39 La discussion du corps législatif sur les sociétés à capital variable. (*Le Travail*, juin) [VI]
40 Syndicat du crédit à Paris. (*Le Travail*, juin) [VI]
41 La Bourse et le crédit à Paris. (*Paris Guide*) [VII]
42 Congrès international coopératif. (*Le Travail*, août) [VI]
43 Société d'économie politique de Paris. (*Le Travail*, septembre) [VI]
44 Les syndicats de garantie mutuelle. (*Le Travail*, septembre) [VI]
45 De l'éducation des filles. (*Le Travail*, novembre) [VI]
46 La science et le socialisme. (*Le Travail*, décembre) [VI]
47 La sécurité générale. (*Le Travail*, décembre) [VI]

1868

48 Le socialisme scientifique. (*Le Travail*, janvier) [VI]
49 Le mouvement d'instruction populaire. (*Le Travail*, mars) [VI]
50 De la spéculation, étude d'économie financière. (*Le Travail*, avril et juin) [XIII]

51 Les réunions publiques. (*Le Travail,* juin) [VI]
52 *Recherche de l'idéal social. Leçons publiques faites à Paris. Première Série (1867–8). Théorie générale de la société.* 8°, XXXII, 192 pp. Paris [IX]

1871

53 Des billets de banque en Suisse. (*Bibliothèque Universelle,* juillet) [XIII]
54 Discours d'installation en qualité de professeur ordinaire d'économie politique à l'Académie de Lausanne, prononcé dans la séance académique du 20 octobre 1871. [Académie de Lausanne] [VII]
–   Système des phénomènes économiques (10 leçons publiques faites à Genève, 1871/72). (Inédit) [XI]
–   Exposition et conciliation des doctrines sociales (6 leçons publiques faites à Genève, 1872/73). (Inédit) [XIII]

1873

55 Sur la théorie mathématique de l'échange. Lettre à M. Paul Piccard lue dans la séance du 5 novembre 1873 de la Société Vaudoise des Sciences Naturelles. (*Bulletin [de la Société Vaudoise des Sciences Naturelles],* vol. XII) [XI]
56 Le cadastre et l'impôt foncier. (*Bibliothèque Universelle,* novembre et décembre) [IX]

1874

57 Principes d'une théorie mathématique de l'échange. Mémoire lu à l'Académie des Sciences Morales et Politiques, à Paris, dans les séances des 16 et 23 août 1873. (*Séances et travaux de l'Académie,* janvier) (A été reproduit par le *Journal des Economistes* d'avril) [VII], [XI]
58 Correspondance entre M. Jevons, professeur à Manchester, et M. Walras, professeur à Lausanne. (*Journal des Economistes,* juin) [VII], [XI]
59 De l'influence de la communication des marchés sur la situation des populations agricoles. Mémoire lu à la Société Vaudoise d'utilité publique dans la séance du [29 avril 1874]. (*Journal de la Société [Vaudoise d'Utilité Publique],* mai et juin) [X]
60 *Eléments d'économie politique pure ou Théorie de la richesse sociale,* 1re partie. 8°, VIII, 208 pp. Lausanne, Paris et Bâle [VIII]
–   Examen critique de la doctrine de Cournot. (inédit) [XIII]
61 *Eléments d'économie politique pure,* par Léon Walras. (*Théologie et Philosophie,* octobre) [XI]

62 *L'Italia industriale. – Le nuove istituzione economiche nel Secolo XIX.* – di Alberto Errera. (*Journal des Economistes*, novembre) [XIII]

1875

63 Economie politique. (*La Revue*, 9 janvier) [XI]
64 La loi fédérale sur l'émission et le remboursement des billets de banque. (*Gazette des Tribunaux Suisses*, 12 août) [VII]
65 *Biblioteca dell'Economista*, diretta dal Professore Gerolamo Boccardo. (*Journal des Economistes*, octobre) [XI]
– Rapport sur le calcul des réserves de la Compagnie *La Suisse* au 31 décembre 1874. (Inédit) [XIII]

1876

66 Le loi fédérale sur le travail dans les fabriques. (*Gazette des Tribunaux Suisses*, 10 février) [VII]
67 Une branche nouvelle de la mathématique. De l'application des mathématiques à l'économie politique. (Inédit en français; a paru en italien dans le *Giornale degli Economisti* d'avril) [VII]
68 Equations de l'échange. 69. Equations de la production. Mémoires lus à la Société Vaudoise des Sciences Naturelles à Lausanne dans les séances des 1er et 15 décembre 1875 et des 19 janvier et 16 février 1876. (*Bulletin* [*de la Société Vaudoise des Sciences Naturelles*], vol. XIV) [XI]
– Note sur l'impôt progressif. (Inédit) [IX]
70 Note sur le 15¹/₂ légal. (*Journal des Economistes*, décembre) [XI]

1877

71 Equations de la capitalisation et du crédit. Mémoire lu à la Société Vaudoise des Sciences Naturelles à Lausanne dans la séance du 5 juillet 1876. (*Bulletin* [*de la Société Vaudoise des Sciences Naturelles*], vol. XIV) [XI]
72 *Eléments d'économie politique pure ou Théorie de la richesse sociale*, 2e partie. 8°, 200 pp. Lausanne, Paris et Bâle [VIII]

1878

73 Bibliographie des ouvrages relatifs à l'application des mathématiques à l'économie politique, en collaboration avec le Prof. Jevons. (*Journal des Economistes*, décembre) [XI]

1879

74 De l'assurance sur la vie. (*Almanach de la Suisse*) [VII]

75 De la culture et de l'enseignement des sciences morales et politiques. (*Bibliothèque Universelle*, juillet et août) [VII]

– Note sur l'organisation de l'enseignement de l'économie politique à l'Ecole des Hautes-Etudes, remise à M. Albert Dumont. (Inédit) [VII]

76 De l'émission des billets de banques. (*Gazette de Lausanne*, 2 et 3 décembre) [XIII]

1880

77 La Bourse, la spéculation et l'agiotage. (*Bibliothèque Universelle*, mars et avril) [X]

– De l'enseignement de l'économie politique en France. (Inédit) [VII]

78 Théorie mathématique du billet de banque. Mémoire lu à la Société Vaudoise des Sciences Naturelles à Lausanne, séance du 19 novembre 1879. (*Bulletin* [*de la Société Vaudoise des Sciences Naturelles*], vol. XVI) [X], [XI]

79 De la propriété intellectuelle. (*Gazette de Lausanne*, 10, 11 et 12 juin) [IX]

– Défense des salaires. (Conférence faite à Lausanne) (Inédit) [X[6]]

80 Théorie mathématique du bimétallisme. (*Journal des Economistes*, mai) [XI]

81 Théorie mathématique du prix des terres et de leur rachat par l'Etat. Mémoire lu à la Société Vaudoise des Sciences Naturelles à Lausanne dans la séance du 17 novembre 1880. (*Bulletin* [*de la Société Vaudoise des Sciences Naturelles*], vol. XVII) [IX], [XI]

1882

82 De la fixité de valeur de l'étalon monétaire. (*Journal des Economistes*, octobre) [XI]

1883

83 *Théorie mathématique de la richesse sociale.* 4°, 256 pp. Lausanne, Paris, Rome et Leipzig
Recueil des travaux suivants: Principe d'une théorie mathématique de l'échange. – Correspondance entre M. Jevons et M. Walras. – Equations de l'échange. – Equations de la production. – Equations de la capitalisation et du crédit. – Note sur le $15^1/_2$ légal. – Théorie mathématique du bimétallisme. – De la fixité de valeur de l'étalon

monetaire. – Théorie mathématique du billet de banque. – Théorie mathématique du prix de terre et de leur rachat par l'Etat.

Les cinq premiers ont été traduits en italien sous le titre *Teoria matematica della ricchezza sociale*, Biblioteca dell' Economista, seria terza, vol. II [Turin, 1878]; et en allemand sous le titre *Mathematische Theorie der Preisbestimmung der wirtschaftlichen Güter*. 1881, Stuttgart [XI]

84   À M. le Rédacteur du *Figaro*. (*Figaro*, 17 juin) (A été reproduit par le *Journal des Débats* du 18 juin) [VI]

1884

85   Monnaie d'or avec billon d'argent régulateur. Principes proposés à la conférence monétaire pour la prorogation de l'Union latine. (*Revue du Droit International* [*et de la Législation comparée*], 1er décembre) [X]

1885

86   Un système rationel de monnaie. (*Gazette de Lausanne*, 12 janvier) [XIII]

87   Un économiste inconnu: H.-H. Gossen. (*Journal des Economistes*, avril et mai) [IX]
     À M. le Rédacteur du *Journal des Economistes* (*Journal des Economistes*, mai) [IX⁷]

88   D'une méthode de régularisation de la variation de valeur de la monnaie. Mémoire lu à la Société Vaudoise des Sciences Naturelles à Lausanne dans la séance du 6 mai 1885. (*Bulletin* [*de la Société Vaudoise des Sciences Naturelles*], vol. XXI) [X]

89   Contribution à l'étude des variations des prix depuis la suspension de la frappe des écus d'argent, en collaboration avec M. Alfred Simon. Mémoire lu à la Société Vaudoise des Sciences Naturelles à Lausanne dans la séance du 3 juin 1885. (*Bulletin* [*de la Société Vaudoise des Sciences Naturelles*], vol. XXI) [X]

90   *Primi elementi di economia politica. – Primi elementi di scienza della Finanze.* – Del dottore Luigi Cossa. (*Bibliothèque Universelle* [août]) [XIII]

1886

91   Théorie de la monnaie. (*Revue Scientifique*, 10 et 17 avril) [X]
92   *Théorie de la monnaie.* 8°, XII, 124 pp. Lausanne, Paris, Rome et Leipzig (Les 1ère et 2ème parties avaient paru dans la *Revue Scientifique* des 10 et 17 avril) [X]

93   *La question sociale,* par. Ch. Secrétan. (*Gazette de Lausanne,* 22 juillet) [IX]

1887

94   *Théorie de la monnaie,* par Léon Walras. (*Revue d'Economie Politique,* janvier–février) [X^8]
95   Note sur la solution du problème monétaire anglo-indien, communiquée à la section économique de l'Association britannique pour l'avancement des sciences, réunie à Manchester. (*Revue d'Economie Politique,* novembre–décembre) (Se trouve en anglais dans le compte rendu pour 1887 de la British Association [1888]) [X]

1889

96   Théorème de l'utilité maxima des capitaux neufs. (*Revue d'Economie Politique* [mai–juin] [XI]
97   *Eléments d'économie politique pure ou Théorie de la richesse sociale,* 2ème édition, revue, corrigée et augmentée. Avec une préface et une introduction: Des fonctions et de leur représentation géométrique. Théorie mathématique de la chute des corps. 8°, XXIV, 524 pp. Lausanne, Paris et Leipzig [VIII]
–   Opinions émises à la commission d'experts touchant la révision de la loi fédérale sur l'émission et le remboursement des billets de banque. (Inédit) [VII]

1890

98   Observation sur le principe de la théorie du prix de M. M. Auspitz et Lieben. (*Revue d'Economie Politique,* mai–juin) [VII^9]

1891

99   De l'échange de plusieurs marchandises entre elles. Mémoire lu à la Société des Ingénieurs Civils à Paris dans la séance du 17 octobre 1890. (*Mémoires et Compte-rendu des travaux de la Société,* janvier) [VIII^{10}]

1892

100   Théorie géométrique de la détermination des prix: De l'échange de produits et services entre eux. – De l'échange d'épargne contre capitaux neufs. (*Recueil inaugural de l'Université de Lausanne*) (Ce travail et le précédent ont paru en anglais sous le titre de *Geomet-*

rical Theory of the Determination of Prices dans les *Annals of the American Academy of Political and Social Science,* July 1892) [VIII[11]]

1893

101 Le problème monétaire anglo-indien. (*Gazette de Lausanne,* 24 juillet) [X]

1894

102 Le problème monétaire. (*Gazette de Lausanne,* 27 février) [X[12]]
103 La monnaie de papier. (*Gazette de Lausanne,* 3 décembre) [XIII]

1895

104 Le péril bimétalliste. (*Revue Socialiste,* 15 juillet) [X]
–   Biographie de mon père. (Inédit) [IV]

1896

105 *Eléments d'économie politique pure ou Théorie de la richesse sociale,* 3ème Edition. 8°, XXIV, 496 pp. Lausanne, Paris et Leipzig [VIII]
106 Prospectus [VII]
107 Note sur la réfutation de la théorie anglaise du fermage de M. Wicksteed. (Recueil publié par la faculté de Droit de l'Université de Lausanne) [VIII], [XI]
108 Méthode de conciliation ou de synthèse. (*Revue Socialiste,* 15 avril) [IX]
109 Théorie de la propriété. (*Revue Socialiste,* 15 juin et 15 juillet) [IX]
110 Le problème fiscal. (*Revue Socialiste,* 15 octobre et 15 novembre) [IX]
111 *Etudes d'économie sociale ou Théorie de la répartition de la richesse sociale.* 8°, VIII, 464 pp. Lausanne et Paris [IX]

1897

112 L'Etat et les chemins de fer. (*Revue du Droit Publique et de la Science Politique,* mai–juin et juillet–août) [X]
113 Théorie du libre échange. (*Revue d'Economie Politique,* juillet) [X]
114 L'économique appliquée et la défense des salaires. (*Revue d'Economie Politique,* décembre) [X]
–   Note sur la théorie de la quantité. (Inédit) [X]

1898

115   Théorie du crédit. (*Revue d'Economie Politique*, février) [X]
116   La caisse d'épargne postale de Vienne et le comptabilisme social. (*Revue d'Economie Politique*, mars) [X]
117   Politique française. – La prière du libre-penseur. (*Gazette de Lausanne*, 14 et 18 juillet) [X]
118   *Etudes d'économie politique appliquée* (*Théorie de la production de la richesse sociale*). 8°, 500 pp. Lausanne et Paris [X]

1899

119   Equations de la circulation. Mémoire lu à la Société Vaudoise des Sciences Naturelles à Lausanne (mai). [Lu dans la séance du 3 mai 1899 (*Bulletin de la Société Vaudoise des Sciences Naturelles*, vol. XXXV)] [XI]
120   Sur les équations de la circulation. (*Giornale degli Economisti* [traduction italienne de V. Pareto]) [XI]

1900

121   *Eléments d'économie politique pure ou Théorie de la richesse sociale*, 4ème édition. 8°, XX, 491 pp. Lausanne et Paris [VIII]
122   Equation du taux du revenu net. (*Bulletin de l'Institut des Actuaires français*, décembre) [XI]

1902

123   Lettre à M. P. Pic. (*Questions pratiques de législation ouvrière et d'économie sociale*, avril) [VII]
–   Autobiographie. (Inédit) [V]

1905

124   Cournot et l'économique mathématique. (*Gazette de Lausanne*, 13 juillet) [VII]

1907[13]

125   La paix par la justice sociale et le libre échange. (*Questions pratiques de législation ouvrière et d'économie sociale*, septembre) [VII]

1908

126   A.-A. Walras. (*Revue du Mois*, août) [IV]

1909

127   Economique et mécanique. [Mémoire lu à la Société Vaudoise des Sciences Naturelles à Lausanne dans la séance du 7 avril 1909.] (*Bulletin de la Société Vaudoise des Sciences Naturelles* [vol. XXXXV]) [VII]

128   Ruchonnet et le socialisme scientifique. (Jubilé. [*Gazette de Lausanne*, 13 avril]) [VII]

III

LETTER FROM LÉON WALRAS TO HERBERT SOMERTON FOXWELL

In this appendix we present an English translation of a letter from Walras to Foxwell.[1] The translation has been done from the copy in Walras's own handwriting in the Fonds Walras of Lausanne, where it is kept.

Lausanne, 13 March 1889

Dear Sir,

I had hoped to obtain some advice or indications from you and from your friends[2] with respect to my Theorem; but I see that the moment of having it printed will arrive without receiving a letter from you, and I decide the more so to it [i.e. to having it printed] now that the issue is completely clear to me.

As I wrote to you in my last letter, the key to the demonstration is that the *quantities produced of new capital goods* δ_k, $\delta_{k'}$, $\delta_{k''}$, ... are at the same time the *quantities consumed of the services* of these capital goods and that the differentials of these quantities of services consumed $\partial\delta_k$, $\partial\delta_{k'}$, $\partial\delta_{k''}$, ... are inversely proportional to the prices of their services, according to the equations

$$p_k\partial\delta_k = p_{k'}\cdot\partial\delta_{k'} = p_{k''}\cdot\partial\delta_{k''} = \ldots$$

where the differentials of the quantities produced of new capital goods $d\delta_k$, $d\delta_{k'}$, $d\delta_{k''}$, ... are inversely proportional to the prices of capital according to the equations

$$P_k d\delta_k = P_{k'}\cdot d\delta_{k'} = P_{k''}\cdot d\delta_{k''} = \ldots$$

These two systems of equations, when combined with the two [other] systems, the one of the maximum satisfaction of wants[3]

$$r_k\partial\delta_k = r_{k'}\cdot\partial\delta_{k'} = r_{k''}\cdot\partial\delta_{k''} = \ldots \tag{1}$$

[and] the other of maximum utility of new capital

148

$$r_k d\delta_k = r_{k'} d\delta_{k'} = r_{k''} d\delta_{k''} = \ldots \qquad (2)$$

yield the condition[4]

$$\frac{p_k}{P_k} = \frac{p_{k'}}{P_{k'}} = \frac{p_{k''}}{P_{k''}}.$$

This demonstration may be represented geometrically as follows.

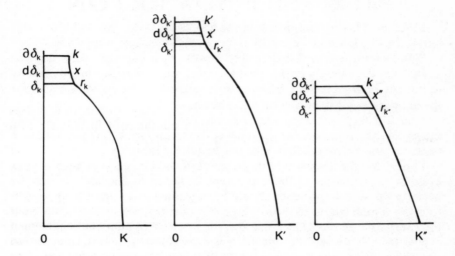

Kr_k, $K'r_{k'}$, $K''r_{k''}$	are the [marginal] utility curves or want curves
$0\delta_k$, $0\delta_{k'}$, $0\delta_{k''}$	are at the same time the *quantities produced of new capital goods* and the *quantities of services consumed*
$\delta_k r_k$, $\delta_{k'} r_{k'}$, $\delta_{k''} r_{k''}$	are the *intensities of the last wants satisfied* or the *raretés of the services*
$\delta_k \partial\delta_k[,\ldots]$	are the differentials of the *quantities of services consumed*
$\delta_k d\delta_k[,\ldots]$	are the differentials of the *quantities of new capital produced*[5]

The condition of maximum satisfaction of wants is the equality of the increments of effective [= total] utility represented by the areas $\delta_k \partial\delta_k kr_k$, ... [hedged by Walras].

The condition of maximum satisfaction of the new capital goods is the equality of the increments of effective utility represented by the areas $\delta_k d\delta_k xr_k$, ...

Since these areas have pairwise the same bases, the ratios of their heights are equal.

149

Consequently, we have

$$\frac{d\delta_k}{\partial\delta_k} = \frac{d\delta_{k'}}{\partial\delta_{k'}} = \frac{d\delta_{k''}}{\partial\delta_{k''}} = \ldots = \frac{p_k}{P_k}.$$

Hence

$$\frac{p_k}{P_k} = \frac{p_{k'}}{P_{k'}} = \frac{p_{k''}}{P_{k''}}.$$

I thought I had to distinguish in the text of my book, just as I did in this letter, the two kinds of differentials by two different symbols [d and ∂].

Simultaneously I included [galley proofs of] a passage which demonstrates that the equality of the rate of *net* income, substituted in the equality of the rate of *gross* income, charges the consumer of the capital services for the allowances for depreciation and insurance.

You will find the two corrections marked in red, just as two or three others on the galley proofs I am sending to you and which are the definitive ones, on which I am going to give the *Ready for Printing*.

I hope that the Theorem in its present form will be good enough in your eyes for presentation to the competent audience in England. It may be necessary that its importance should be explained and I am relying on you to make it understood to those who could possibly miss it. It is not a great discovery to have recognized that there is a benefit of utility in withdrawing capital from use where its revenue is less considerable and to bring it into use where its revenue is more considerable. But it is a great achievement to have furnished a mathematical demonstration of such a plausible and, one could say, evident fact, because this proves that satisfactory definitions and methods of analysis are at one's disposal. Consequently, here we have a result that helps in judging favourably the methods used in obtaining it; and my theorem, not only crowns but confirms my complete system of political economy. If this would be admitted by some of your compatriots, I shall not regret the time and the effort spent in arriving at it.

Believe me, always sincerely

Yours

LÉON WALRAS

IV

THE EQUATIONS OF WALRAS'S COMPLETE MODELS

THE MODEL WITH FIAT-MONEY

The following unknown variables are defined (all quantities are aggregates over all individuals).

Group 1

n quantities $O_t, \ldots, O_p, \ldots, O_k, \ldots$
(quantities of services of 'fixed' capital (T), ..., (P), ..., (K), ...)
n prices $p_t, \ldots, p_p, \ldots, p_k, \ldots$
m quantities $D_a, D_b, D_c, D_d, \ldots$
(quantities of (A), (B), (C), ... produced for consumption)
$m - 1$ prices $p_b, p_c, p_d, \ldots$
($p_a = 1$, (A) being the *numéraire*)

Group 2

1 quantity E
(gross savings)
1 price p_e
1 rate of net income i
l quantities $D_k, D_{k'}, D_{k''}, \ldots$
(quantities of newly produced capital goods proper)
l prices $P_k, P_{k'}, P_{k''}, \ldots$

Group 3

m quantities $O_{a'}, O_{b'}, O_{c'}, O_{d'}, \ldots$
(quantities supplied of circulating capital (A'), (B'), (C'), ...)
m prices $p_{a'}, p_{b'}, p_{c'}, p_{d'}, \ldots$
s prices $p_m, \ldots$
s prices $p_{m'}, \ldots$

151

(prices of the services of raw materials as circulating capital)

$m + s$ quantities $D_{a'}, D_{b'}, D_{c'}, D_{d'}, \ldots, D_{m'}, \ldots$

(quantities of products and raw materials produced, destined as circulating capital)

Group 4

1 quantity O_u

(quantity of money services offered)

1 price $p_{u'}$

(price of the service of money)

In total there are $5m + 2n + 2l + 3s + 4$ variables.

The equations of the system are the following.

n equations describing the total supply of the fixed-capital services, forming subsystem Ia:

$$O_t = F_t(p_t, \ldots, p_p, \ldots, p_k, p_{k'}, p_{k'}, \ldots, p_b, p_c, p_d, \ldots, p_e, p_{u'}),$$

$$\vdots$$

$$O_p = F_p(p_t, \ldots, p_p, \ldots, p_k, p_{k'}, p_{k'}, \ldots, p_b, p_c, p_d, \ldots, p_e, p_{u'}),$$

$$\vdots$$

$$O_k = F_k(p_t, \ldots, p_p, \ldots, p_k, p_{k'}, p_{k'}, \ldots, p_b, p_c, p_d, \ldots, p_e, p_{u'}),$$

$$\vdots$$

m equations describing the total supply of the services of circulating capital, forming subsystem Ib:

$$O_{a'} = F_{a'}(p_t, \ldots, p_p, \ldots, p_k, p_{k'}, p_{k'}, \ldots, p_b, p_c, p_d, \ldots, p_m, \ldots, p_e, p_{u'}),$$

$$O_{b'} = F_{b'}(p_t, \ldots, p_p, \ldots, p_k, p_{k'}, p_{k'}, \ldots, p_b, p_c, p_d, \ldots, p_m, \ldots, p_e, p_{u'}),$$

$$\vdots$$

1 equation describing the supply of money services, forming subsystem Ic:

$$O_u = Q_u - \frac{d_\alpha p_{a'} + d_\beta p_{b'} + d_\gamma p_{c'} + d_\delta p_{d'} + \ldots + d_\varepsilon}{p_{u'}}$$

or, alternatively,

$$O_u = F_u(p_t, \ldots, p_p, \ldots, p_k, p_{k'}, p_{k'}, \ldots, p_b, p_c, p_d, \ldots, p_{m'}, \ldots, p_e, p_{u'}).$$

m demand equations describing total consumption of the products (A), (B), (C), (D), ..., forming subsystem II:

$$D_b = F_b(p_t, \ldots, p_p, \ldots, p_k, p_{k'}, p_{k'}, \ldots, p_b, p_c, p_d, \ldots, p_e, p_{u'}),$$

$$D_c = F_c(p_t, \ldots, p_p, \ldots, p_k, p_{k'}, p_{k''}, \ldots, p_b, p_c, p_d, \ldots, p_e, p_{u'}),$$

$$D_d = F_d(p_t, \ldots, p_p, \ldots, p_k, p_{k'}, p_{k''}, \ldots, p_b, p_c, p_d, \ldots, p_e, p_{u'}),$$

$$\vdots$$

$$D_a = O_t p_t + \ldots + O_p p_p + \ldots + O_k p_k + O_{k'} p_{k'} + O_{k''} p_{k''} + \ldots$$
$$+ O_{a'} p_{a'} + O_{b'} p_{b'} + \ldots + Q_{m'} p_{m'} + \ldots + O_u p_{u'}$$
$$- (D_b p_b + D_c p_c + D_d p_d + \ldots + E),$$

E is defined by $E = D_e p_e + \Sigma_e$ and is explained in subsystem III:

$$E = F_e(p_t, \ldots, p_p, \ldots, p_k, p_{k'}, p_{k''}, \ldots, p_b, p_c, p_d, \ldots, p_e).$$

n equations expressing equality between the demand and supply of the services of fixed capital, forming subsystem IVa:

$$a_t(D_a + D_{a'}) + b_t(D_b + D_{b'}) + c_t(D_c + D_{c'}) + \ldots + m_t D_{m'} + \ldots$$
$$+ k_t D_k + \ldots = O_t,$$

$$\vdots$$

$$a_p(D_a + D_{a'}) + b_p(D_b + D_{b'}) + c_p(D_c + D_{c'}) + \ldots + m_p D_{m'} + \ldots$$
$$+ k_p D_k + \ldots = O_p,$$

$$\vdots$$

$$a_k(D_a + D_{a'}) + b_k(D_b + D_{b'}) + c_k(D_c + D_{c'}) + \ldots + m_k D_{m'} + \ldots$$
$$+ k_k D_k + \ldots = O_k,$$

$$\vdots$$

$m + s$ equations expressing equality between the demand and supply of the services of circulating capital, forming subsystem IVb:

$$a_{a'}(D_a + D_{a'}) + b_{a'}(D_b + D_{b'}) + \ldots + m_{a'} D_{m'} + \ldots + k_{a'} D_k + \ldots$$
$$= O_{a'},$$

$$a_{b'}(D_a + D_{a'}) + b_{b'}(D_b + D_{b'}) + \ldots + m_{b'} D_{m'} + \ldots + k_{b'} D_k + \ldots$$
$$= O_{b'},$$

$$\vdots$$

$$a_{m'}(D_a + D_{a'}) + b_{m'}(D_b + D_{b'}) + \ldots + m_{m'} D_{m'} + \ldots + k_{m'} D_k + \ldots$$
$$= Q_{m'}.$$

$$\vdots$$

1 equation expressing equality between the demand and supply of money services, forming subsystem IVc:

$$\frac{\delta_a p_{a'} + \delta_\beta p_{b'} + \ldots + \delta_\mu p_{m'} + \ldots + \delta_\kappa p_k + \ldots}{p_{u'}} = O_u.$$

$m + s + l$ equations expressing equality between prices and cost per unit of products (A), (B), ..., (M), ..., (K), ..., forming subsystem V:

$$a_t p_t + a_p p_p + a_k p_k + \ldots + a_{a'} p_{a'} + a_{b'} p_{b'} + \ldots + a_{m'} p_{m'} + \ldots + a_u$$
$$= 1,$$

$$b_t p_t + b_p p_p + b_k p_k + \ldots + b_{a'} p_{a'} + b_{b'} p_{b'} + \ldots + b_{m'} p_{m'} + \ldots + b_u$$
$$= p_b,$$

$$\vdots$$

$$m_t p_t + m_p p_p + m_k p_k + \ldots + m_{a'} p_{a'} + m_{b'} p_{b'} + \ldots + m_{m'} p_{m'}$$
$$+ \ldots + m_u = p_m,$$

$$\vdots$$

$$k_t p_t + k_p p_p + k_k p_k + \ldots + k_{a'} p_{a'} + k_{b'} p_{b'} + \ldots + k_{m'} p_{m'} + \ldots + k_u$$
$$= P_k,$$

$m + s$ equations which determine the prices of the services of circulating capital, forming subsystem VI:

$$p_{a'} = i, \qquad p_{b'} = p_b i, \qquad p_{c'} = p_c i, \qquad p_{d'} = p_d i, \qquad \ldots,$$
$$p_{m'} = p_m i, \qquad \ldots$$

1 equation stating the equilibrium between gross savings and investment, forming subsystem VII:

$$D_k P_k + D_{k'} P_{k'} + D_{k''} P_{k''} + \ldots + D_{a'} + D_{b'} p_b + \ldots + D_{m'} p_m + \ldots$$
$$= E.$$

l equations determining the prices of capital proper, forming subsystem VIII:

$$P_k = \frac{p_k}{i + \mu_k + \nu_k},$$

$$P_{k'} = \frac{p_{k'}}{i + \mu_{k'} + \nu_{k'}},$$

$$P_{k''} = \frac{p_{k''}}{i + \mu_{k''} + \nu_{k''}},$$

$$\vdots$$

1 equation establishing the relationship between p_e and i, forming subsystem IX:

$$p_e = \frac{1}{i}.$$

In total there are $5m + 2n + 2l + 3s + 5$ equations, of which one is dependent on other equations of the model.

THE MODEL WITH COMMODITY-BASED MONEY

The following unknown variables are defined (the quantities are aggregates over all individuals).

Groups 1 and 2 are the same as in the previous section.

Group 3

$m - 1$ quantities $O_{b'}, O_{c'}, O_{d'}, \ldots$
(quantities supplied of circulating capital (B'), (C'), …)
$m - 1$ prices $p_{b'}, p_{c'}, p_{d'}, \ldots$
s prices $p_m, \ldots$
s prices $p_{m'}, \ldots$
(prices of the *services* of raw materials as circulating capital)
$m + s - 1$ quantities $D_{b'}, D_{c'}, D_{d'}, \ldots, D_{m'}, \ldots$
(quantities of products and raw materials produced, destined as circulating capital)

Group 4

1 quantity O_u
(quantity of money services offered)
1 price p_u.
(price of the service of money)
1 quantity D_u
(total quantity of new money to be added to stocks)

The equations of the system are the following:

n equations describing total supply of the fixed-capital services, forming subsystem Ia, the same as in the previous section.

$m - 1$ equations describing the total supply of the services of circulating capital, forming subsystem Ib:

$$O_{b'} = F_{a'}(p_t, \ldots, p_p, \ldots, p_k, p_{k'}, p_{k\cdot}, \ldots, p_b, p_c, p_d, \ldots, p_m, \ldots, p_e, p_u),$$

$$O_{c'} = F_{b'}(p_t, \ldots, p_p, \ldots, p_k, p_{k'}, p_{k''}, \ldots, p_b, p_c, p_d, \ldots, p_m, \ldots, p_e, p_{u'}),$$

$$\vdots$$

1 equation describing the supply of money services, forming subsystem Ic:

$$O_u = Q_u - \frac{d_\beta p_{b'} + d_\gamma p_{c'} + d_\delta p_{d'} + \ldots + d_\varepsilon}{p_{u'}}$$

or, alternatively,

$$O_u = F_u(p_t, \ldots, p_p, \ldots, p_k, p_{k'}, p_{k''}, \ldots, p_b, p_c, p_d, \ldots, p_{m'}, \ldots, p_e, p_{u'}).$$

m demand equations describing total consumption of the products (A), (B), (C), (D), ..., forming subsystem II:

$$D_b = F_b(p_t, \ldots, p_p, \ldots, p_k, p_{k'}, p_{k''}, \ldots, p_b, p_c, p_d, \ldots, p_e, p_{u'})$$

$$D_c = F_c(p_t, \ldots, p_p, \ldots, p_k, p_{k'}, p_{k''}, \ldots, p_b, p_c, p_d, \ldots, p_e, p_{u'})$$

$$D_d = F_d(p_t, \ldots, p_p, \ldots, p_k, p_{k'}, p_{k''}, \ldots, p_b, p_c, p_d, \ldots, p_e, p_{u'})$$

$$\vdots$$

$$D_a = O_t p_t + \ldots + O_p p_p + \ldots + O_k p_k + O_{k'} p_{k'} + O_{k''} p_{k''} + \ldots$$

$$+ O_{b'} p_{b'} + O_{c'} p_{c'} + \ldots + Q_m p_{m'} + \ldots + O_u p_{u'}$$

$$- (D_b p_b + D_c p_c + D_d p_d + \ldots + E).$$

E is defined by $E = D_e p_e + \Sigma_e$ and is explained in subsystem III, the same as in the previous section.

n equations expressing equality between the demand and supply of the services of fixed capital, forming subsystem IVa:

$$a_t(D_a + D_u) + b_t(D_b + D_{b'}) + c_t(D_c + D_{c'}) + \ldots + m_t D_{m'} + \ldots$$

$$+ k_t D_k + \ldots$$

$$= O_t,$$

$$\vdots$$

$$a_p(D_a + D_u) + b_p(D_b + D_{b'}) + c_p(D_c + D_{c'}) + \ldots + m_p D_{m'} + \ldots$$

$$+ k_p D_k + \ldots$$

$$= O_p,$$

$$\vdots$$

$$a_k(D_a + D_u) + b_k(D_b + D_{b'}) + c_k(D_c + D_{c'}) + \ldots + m_k D_{m'} + \ldots$$

$$+ k_k D_k + \ldots$$

$$= O_k,$$

$$\vdots$$

$m + s - 1$ equations expressing equality between the demand and supply of the services of circulating capital, forming subsystem IVb:

$$a_{b'}(D_a + D_u) + b_{b'}(D_b + D_{b'}) + \ldots + m_{b'}D_{m'} + \ldots + k_{b'}D_k + \ldots$$
$$= O_{b'},$$

$$a_{c'}(D_a + D_u) + b_{c'}(D_b + D_{b'}) + \ldots + m_{c'}D_{m'} + \ldots + k_{c'}D_k + \ldots$$
$$= O_{c'},$$

$$\vdots$$

$$a_{m'}(D_a + D_u) + b_{m'}(D_b + D_{b'}) + \ldots + m_{m'}D_{m'} + \ldots + k_{m'}D_k + \ldots$$
$$= Q_{m'}.$$

$$\vdots$$

1 equation expressing equality between the demand and supply of money services, forming subsystem IVc:

$$\frac{\delta_\beta p_{b'} + \delta_\gamma p_{c'} + \ldots + \delta_\mu p_{m'} + \ldots + \delta_\kappa p_k + \ldots}{p_{u'}} = O_u.$$

$m + s + l$ equations expressing equality between prices and cost per unit of products (A), (B), ..., (M), ..., (K), ..., forming subsystem V:

$$a_t p_t + a_p p_p + a_k p_k + \ldots + a_{b'} p_{b'} + a_{c'} p_{c'} + \ldots + a_{m'} p_{m'} + \ldots + a_u$$
$$= 1,$$

$$b_t p_t + b_p p_p + b_k p_k + \ldots + b_{b'} p_{b'} + b_{c'} p_{c'} + \ldots + b_{m'} p_{m'} + \ldots + b_u$$
$$= p_b,$$

$$\vdots$$

$$m_t p_t + m_p p_p + m_k p_k + \ldots + m_{b'} p_{b'} + m_{c'} p_{c'} + \ldots + m_{m'} p_{m'} + \ldots$$
$$+ m_u = p_m,$$

$$\vdots$$

$$k_t p_t + k_p p_p + k_k p_k + \ldots + k_{b'} p_{b'} + k_{c'} p_{c'} + \ldots + k_{m'} p_{m'} + \ldots + k_u$$
$$= P_k,$$

$$\vdots$$

$m + s - 1$ equations which determine the prices of the services of circulating capital, forming subsystem VI:

$$p_{b'} = p_b i, \qquad p_{c'} = p_c i, \qquad p_{d'} = p_d i, \qquad \ldots, \qquad p_{m'} = p_m i, \qquad \ldots$$

1 equation stating the equilibrium between gross savings and investment, forming subsystem VII:

$$D_k P_k + D_{k'} P_{k'} + D_{k''} P_{k''} + \ldots + D_u + D_{b'} p_b + \ldots + D_{m'} p_m + \ldots$$
$$= E.$$

l equations determining the prices of capital proper, forming subsystem VIII, the same as in the previous section.

1 equation establishing the relationship between p_e and i, forming subsystem IX, the same as in the previous section.

V

ON THE EXISTENCE
OF EQUILIBRIUM AND ON
TÂTONNEMENT

In this book the models are mainly considered from the point of view that their solutions describe states of general economic equilibrium. In these states there are prices on which the individuals and the entrepreneurs base their optimal demand and supply. Because the state is an equilibrium state the total quantities supplied and demanded are such that for each good or service the market clears. We think that it makes sense to ask oneself whether such states exist and *a fortiori* we consider that this question has to be asked, and answered, before one discusses how the economy is moving to whatever state. Even when one is merely interested in movements, in dynamics, rather than in statics, or when one is interested in disequilibrium economics, it is important to know whether there is an equilibrium anyway. In our opinion, this might also have been the underlying idea of Walras. Consequently, it is most likely that for him, too, the 'question préalable' was the existence of a (mathematical) solution of his systems of general economic equilibrium. This appendix is devoted to this question.

Subsequently we shall discuss the method of counting variables and equations, the advanced mathematical proofs based on fixed-point theorems and *tâtonnement* as attempts at proving equilibrium.

COUNTING VARIABLES AND EQUATIONS

In accordance with the mathematical standards of his time, the existence of equilibrium was for Walras[1] ascertained when the system of equations contained just as many variables as there are independent equations. This method was considered satisfactory until far into the twentieth century[2] and model builders still consider it valuable as a first check.

However useful counting equations and variables may be for model building, it does not provide us with an unambiguous argument for the existence of a solution of a system of equations. Equality of equations and variables is neither necessary nor sufficient. It is not necessary because, for instance, the equation

$$(4 - x)^{1/2} + (9 - y)^{1/2} = 5 \tag{1}$$

can be solved $(x = y = 0)$ and it is not sufficient because systems with as many equations as variables may be inconsistent. Hence more subtle methods are required.

MODERN PROOFS

The present rigorous proofs of the existence of equilibrium are all based on so-called fixed-point methods. We shall illustrate the rationale of using fixed-point theorems by means of a simple example of a market in which a certain good is exchanged against money, with a demand function D and a supply function S both expressed in terms of the price p of the good. Let the problem be such that p can vary between zero and an upper bound $\bar{p}$. Take a value p_0 from the closed interval $[0, \bar{p}]$ and determine the quantity $D(p_0)$ demanded of the good in question. Now let p_1 in $[0, \bar{p}]$ be such that $S(p_1) = D(p_0)$. There may be more than one such price p_1; collect all these in a set called $f(p_0)$. So we have a procedure that connects every p from $[0, \bar{p}]$ to a set $f(p)$ also in $[0, \bar{p}]$. It is clear that an equilibrium price p^* in this market is such that p^* is in $f(p^*)$; hence p^* is a so-called fixed point of the 'mapping' f. This method can easily be extended to the case of exchange of two or more goods, as discussed in Chapter 5 above. In most intermediate textbooks on microeconomics one can find existence proofs for equilibrium in exchange economies.[3]

The history of general economic equilibrium theory has witnessed several attempts to prove the existence of equilibrium.[4] von Neumann's paper and those of Wald, dating from the 1930s,[5] are seminal in this respect. von Neumann's model has little to do with Walras's models of general economic equilibrium. Wald's model looks like Walras's model of production but, strictly speaking, it is quite different; Wald's model is the so-called Cassel–Schlesinger model with constant quantities of factors offered and prices of the goods as functions of the quantities demanded instead of the other way round. Proofs of existence of a solution of Walras's model of production[6] are incomplete or only valid under very restrictive conditions. The assertion that Walras's model is a special case of the model of Arrow and Debreu (1954) is not correct because Walras's cost minimization is not exactly the same as their profit maximization; nevertheless, the mathematics of Arrow and Debreu's model are such that for the case of constant returns to the scale of production Walras's production model can appear.[7]

In Van Daal *et al.* (1985) an attempt has been made to fill this surprising lack by providing a comprehensive rigorous proof of the existence of a solution of Walras's model of production with fixed coefficients of production, discussed in Chapter 9 above. The model was rearranged a little and generalized somewhat in order to include the possibility of zero prices and non-scarce goods.[8] Furthermore, a vector notation was adopted:

s is the vector $(O_t \ O_p \ O_k \ldots)'$,
d is the vector $(D_a \ D_b \ D_c \ldots)'$,
p is the vector $(p_a \ p_b \ p_c \ p_d \cdots p_t \ p_p \ p_q \ldots)'$ with subvectors $q = (p_a \ p_b \ p_c \ldots)'$ and $w = (p_t \ p_p \ p_k \ldots)'$,

Π is the matrix $\begin{bmatrix} a_t & b_t & c_t & \cdots \\ a_p & b_p & c_p & \cdots \\ a_k & b_k & c_k & \cdots \\ \vdots & & & \end{bmatrix}$.

Good (A) is no longer the *numéraire*, but now we take the vector p such that

$$p_a + p_b + p_c + \ldots + p_t + p_p + p_k + \ldots = 1 \tag{2}$$

and no prices are negative. P is the collection of vectors in the $(n + m)$-dimensional vector space satisfying the conditions mentioned in the preceding sentence. Mathematically, it makes no difference whether we normalize prices by taking them only from P or by taking (A) as the *numéraire*. Economically, taking p from P means that we consider as the *numéraire* a composite of all goods and factors, one unit of each.

The relations of the model together with some assumptions that will be discussed after the presentation of these relations are

$$s = G(p), \tag{3}$$

$$d = H(p), \tag{4}$$

$$q'd = w's, \tag{5}$$

$$\Pi d \leq s, \tag{6}$$

$$w'\Pi \geq q'; \tag{7}$$

if there is inequality in (6) for some $i \in \{1, \ldots, n\}$, then

$$w_i = 0; \tag{8}$$

if there is inequality in (7) for some $j \in \{1, \ldots, m\}$, then

$$d_j = 0. \tag{9}$$

In (3) one may recognize equation (6) of Chapter 9. G is a continuous n-dimensional vector-valued function that is positively zero-homogeneous, i.e. $\lambda > 0$ implies $G(\lambda p) = G(p)$. We assume $G_i(p) > 0$ for all i and all p. Equations (4) and (5) reflect subsystem (7) of Chapter 9. H is a continuous, positively zero-homogeneous m-dimensional vector-valued function that is defined for all p from P with subvectors q having no zeros and $w \neq 0$; it is assumed that then $H_i(p) \geq 0$ always, with $H_j(p) > 0$ for at least one j. Note that d (and therefore H) is m-dimensional and therefore contains a quantity of good (A) as a first component; this results in a dependence between equations (3), (4) and the budget restriction (5). This dependence is harmless, however, because we are not going to count equations. Furthermore, H has to fulfil some conditions in the cases where one or more prices of goods or the prices of all production factors are zero. The possibility of zero prices is necessary because we allow for goods or factors that eventually will turn out to be non-scarce, as follows from (6) and (7) together with (8) and (9). These conditions are only for mathematical convenience and read as follows.

1 If $\bar{p}$ in P is such that it has $\bar{q}_j = 0$ for some good j and $\bar{w} \neq 0$, then $H_j(p)$ tends to infinity if p (having no zeros in its subvector q) tends in P to $\bar{p}$.

2 If $\bar{p}$ in P is such that $\bar{q}_j > 0$ for some good j and $\bar{w} \neq 0$ then $\bar{p}$ has a neighbourhood N in P such that $H_j(\bar{p})$ is bounded for all p in N that have qs that contain no zeros.

3 If $\bar{p}$ in P is such that its subvector $\bar{w}$ is a vector of only zeros then $q_j H_j(p)$ tends to zero for all $j = 1, \ldots, m$ if p in P tends to $\bar{p}$.

Relations (6)–(9) are generalizations of subsystems (8) and (9) of Walras's original model as depicted in Chapter 9. In (6) and (8) we state that there must be enough factor supply for the production of goods, but that the existence of an excess supply of a factor will make that factor non-scarce and therefore without value in exchange (*Eléments*, Section 40). Relations (7) and (9) express that profits are never positive and that no good will be produced for negative profit (Section 188).

The proof of the existence of a solution of system (3)–(9) is based on Kakutani's fixed-point theorem[9] and in addition relies on arguments from linear-programming theory; we are not going to present the details of the proof in this appendix but confine ourselves to some remarks. In this much less simple case than the situation with which we opened this section, we constructed a complicated kind of mapping F from the set P into itself and proved that this mapping has some fixed point p^*. That the system (3)–(9) indeed has a solution, provided that the above conditions hold good, follows from the fact that the vectors s^* and d^*, which can be computed with (3) and (4) by substituting p^* for p, are such that they, together with p^*, fulfil all the relations of the system.

The mathematical problem here is mainly in the requirement that, in order to have a fixed point, our mapping has to be defined for all points of P, inclusive of border points, and that the sets $F(p)$ have to be convex. Furthermore, the mapping F has to be 'closed', which means that the $2(m + n)$-dimensional set consisting of *all* points (p, z) with p from P and z

from $F(p)$ contains its own border points. For the interior points of P we constructed, in line with Dorfman *et al.* (1958), economically meaningful convex sets $F(p)$ being complicated analogies of the $f(p)$ of the one-market model above. We did the same for the border points of P where the extension of the mapping F to the border points mentioned in 1, 2 or 3 above raised serious difficulties. The problem that we had to solve was finding meaningful sets $F(p)$ for the latter border points that do not contain their original point p, because otherwise such a point would be a fixed point which would preclude the investigation into the existence of other fixed points. An exact proof of the closedness of F and of its convexity has been presented in Van Daal *et al.* (1985), where it can also be seen how fastidiously one has to proceed in devising existence proofs.[10]

It can easily be proved that the above arguments can be extended to the case of flexible production coefficients under the provision that the form of the production equations has to be as Walras devised it initially.[11] This means that the optimal production coefficients do not change if the quantities produced change, given the prices of the production factors; in other words, constant returns to scale must prevail.

An existence proof for the model of capital formation is presented in Morishima (1960). We do not go into the details, but the reader may guess that the mathematical problems were similar. It can be argued that the model of circulating capital of Chapter 13 fits into the structure of Morishima's reasoning. Consequently, the existence of a solution of this model is also ascertained in a mathematically rigorous way. On the basis of the latter proof proofs can be devised for the existence of solutions of the two models with money. We shall not discuss these proofs here because the matter is purely technical and rather complicated, but uninteresting from an economics point of view.

TÂTONNEMENT

The notion of *tâtonnement* has become very famous. It has become so well known that one could easily overestimate its importance for the work of Walras itself. In devising it he aimed at demonstrating that the 'scientific solution' of the problem of equilibrium, i.e. the solution of the equations of the system concerned, is the same as that which will be reached in reality in the markets. For him the most important characteristic of the working of the markets was the phenomenon of underbidding of each other by the sellers if there was excess supply, and of outbidding of each other by the buyers if there was excess demand.

In the case of simple exchange (Chapter 5) Walras's reasoning was as follows (*Eléments*, Sections 126–30). Let p'_b, p'_c, p'_d, ... be 'prices cried at random'. Substituting these in equations (29) of Chapter 2 will yield in general

$$F_b(p_b', p_c', p_d', \ldots) \gtreqless 0,$$
$$F_c(p_b', p_c', p_d', \ldots) \gtreqless 0,$$
$$F_d(p_b', p_c', p_d', \ldots) \gtreqless 0, \tag{10}$$
$$\vdots$$

If, indeed, (10) displays inequalities, the prices p_b', p_c', p_d', ... are not equilibrium prices and there will be no trade, as Walras presupposed.

As we know, the Fs denote quantities of excess demand as functions of the prices. Hence F_b decreases if p_b increases, F_c decreases as p_c increases and so on. Now let p_b'' be such that

$$F_b(p_b'', p_c', p_d', \ldots) = 0. \tag{11}$$

It is always possible to find such a p_b'' because if p_b is low there is excess demand and if p_b is high there will be excess supply, given the other prices. Further let p_c'' be such that

$$F_c(p_b'', p_c'', p_d', \ldots) = 0, \tag{12}$$

let p_d'' be such that

$$F_d(p_b'', p_c'', p_d'', \ldots) = 0, \tag{13}$$

and so forth.

In general we shall again have

$$F_b(p_b'', p_c'', p_d'', \ldots) \gtreqless 0,$$
$$F_c(p_b'', p_c'', p_d'', \ldots) \gtreqless 0,$$
$$F_d(p_b'', p_c'', p_d'', \ldots) \gtreqless 0, \tag{14}$$
$$\vdots$$

where all prices now have double primes. But there is a difference between (10) and (14) in the sense that the latter inequalities are nearer to equality, as Walras argues. The equality in (11) will be offset by replacing p_c', p_d', ... by p_c'', p_d'', ... Similarly the equalities of (12), (13) and so on will be disturbed, but these secondary disturbances may be expected to be of smaller degree than the effects of the changes from p_b' to p_b'', p_c' to p_c'', p_d' to p_d'', and so on, which resulted in (11), (12), (13) and so on; moreover, the secondary effects may have different signs and therefore may cancel each other more or less.

Likewise there can be found prices p_b''', p_c''', p_d''', ... that will bring the inequalities still nearer to equality. This brought Walras to the conclusion that eventually there are prices that will bring exact equality. These prices are the equilibrium prices and transactions can start.

The process of prices 'groping' ('par *tâtonnement*', as Walras said) from

p'_b, p'_c, p'_d, ... to p''_b, p''_c, p''_d, ... and from this to p'''_b, p'''_c, p'''_d, ... and further to equilibrium prices may remind some people remotely of what happens in markets: if there is excess demand for some good, the price of it will be increased, and if there is excess supply, the price will be decreased. In the Bourse of Paris in Walras's time, for instance, transactions were only allowed if demand equalled supply and the process for coming to such a situation was for Walras, as he said, the inspiration to the reasoning above.

In fact, Walras did not prove exactly the existence of equilibrium prices in this way. It was Allais who was the first[12] to provide a (sufficient) condition under which existence of equilibrium (i.e. convergence of the prices to equilibrium) may be demonstrated rigorously. The condition is that of so-called gross substitutability: the derivatives of excess demand functions for each good with respect to the prices of the other goods have to be negative, a very restrictive condition.

For the model of production Walras developed a *tâtonnement* process that is much more complicated than the one above, as one may expect. An interesting point is that in the first three editions of the *Eléments* he admitted disequilibrium *production*. The process starts with arbitrary prices p'_t, p'_p, p'_k, ... of the production factors (T), (P), (K), ... and arbitrary quantities Ω_a, Ω_b, Ω_c, ... of products (A), (B), (C), ... In the first edition Walras supposed that during the process, i.e. before equilibrium is reached, the entrepreneurs in the first instance buy quantities of services of production factors in a foreign market. The idea in the first edition is the following. The prices p'_t, p'_p, p'_k, ... together with the production coefficients yield unit costs p'_a, p'_b, p'_c, ... of the products. The quantities of the services of (T), (P), (K), ... needed for the production of the quantities Ω_a, Ω_b, Ω_c, ... of (A), (B), (C), ... may be computed from the latter quantities together with the production coefficients. The quantities of services of production factors thus obtained are bought in a foreign market, and the quantities Ω_a, Ω_b, Ω_c, ... are produced and afterwards sold against prices that follow from the demand equations for products. Now it appears that the latter prices are in general not equal to p'_a, p'_b, p'_c, ..., respectively. Hence there are entrepreneurs who suffer losses and there are also entrepreneurs who make profits. This causes shifts in the quantities to be produced and, in a complicated way, new prices arise for (T), (P), (K), ...; these new prices and quantities, Walras argued, are closer to their equilibrium values. Taking them as a starting point for a new step in the *tâtonnement* process, we eventually obtain prices for the consumption goods and quantities of goods and services that are also nearer to equilibrium. This has to be continued until equilibrium is reached.

Allowing disequilibrium production may lead to inconsistencies in the sense that the eventual equilibrium is not the one described by a solution of the equations of the system; for that same reason Walras had excluded the possibility of disequilibrium transactions in the case of exchange only. He therefore amended the expositions from the fourth edition onwards in the sense that now disequilibrium production will no longer occur, but instead the consumers and the entrepreneurs produce *pledges*,[13] indicating the action they would undertake in answer to the crying of prices and quantities. This play of crying and producing pledges stops when equilibrium is reached after which production and the ensuing transactions may take place. It is clear that in this way *tâtonnement* was reduced to a mathematical device for proving the existence of equilibrium – no more, no less. The same applies to the *tâtonnement* processes for the other models of Walras's chain.

For further expositions on *tâtonnement* in Walras's work we refer to the many authoritative papers by Walker, mentioned in the list of references.

NOTES

PREFACE

1 These books are republished in *Auguste et Léon Walras: Oeuvres économiques complètes*, edited under the auspices of the Centre Walras in the University of Lyon 2; see Appendix II. The excellent editorial work makes them much more accessible, but an English translation is still badly lacking.

1 ON THE USE OF MATHEMATICS IN ECONOMIC *ANALYSIS*

1 This chapter is based on our article 'Léon Walras's mathematical economics and the mechanical analogies', *History of Economics Society Bulletin*, 11 (1) (Spring 1989): 25–32.
2 This has been explained excellently in the article 'Une branche nouvelle de la mathématique' (A new branch of mathematics). In our opinion this is one of the most interesting articles by Walras; it remained unpublished in French until recently, however (*Mélanges*, pp. 291–329). An Italian translation appeared in 1876 (Walras 1876). The article contains Walras's explanation how one should interpret different uses of mathematics. The mathematical method, he argued further, would supply a more rigorous analysis than 'ordinary logic' would make possible.
3 Descartes, *Regulae ad directionem ingenii*, quoted from Gaukroger (1980: 43).
4 ibid.
5 The citations in this quotation are from Part II of Descartes's *Discours de la méthode*.
6 This is one of the earliest texts of Walras's pure economics. This section can be found in his second 'Tentative', dating from 1870; see Chapter 3 later.
7 These objections are reviewed by Jaffé in note 2 to Letter 1509 of the *Correspondence* (Jaffé 1965).
8 See, for instance, Mirowski (1984) and Mirowski and Cook (1989).

2 FREE COMPETITION AND GENERAL EQUILIBRIUM

1 See *Mélanges*, pp. 270, 316.
2 See also Walker (1990a, b, c, d, 1991).
3 See, for example, Ingrao and Israel (1990: chs 2, 3).
4 See Walras (1860c, 1870, 1871); see also Chapter 3 later. See in particular Walras (1993).

5 In its eighth edition (Paris, 1842).

6 Jaffé (1965: Letter 1483, note 7).

7 It is interesting to note that Jaffé refers to Haton's book as Walras's mathematical *vade mecum.*

3 ON THE NOTION OF UTILITY AS DEVELOPED BY WALRAS

1 'Il y a des valeurs antérieures à la production. Et ici les faits sont pour moi; ... Les fruits spontanés de la terre, tels que les arbres, les plantes, les animaux sauvages, la terre ou le sol cultivable consideré comme un agent de la production agricole, le travail lui-même, ou l'ensemble des facultés industrielles de l'homme considérées dans ce qu'elles ont de primitif et de *naturel*, sont autant de choses qui ont certainement de la valeur, et qui ne sont cependant pas des produits du travail' (A. Walras, 'Mémoire sur l'origine de la valeur d'échange', 1849).

2 The notation in the following formulae is that of Walras, found in the 'Tentatives'. Little of this notation eventually found a place in the notational system of the *Eléments*, as can be inferred from other chapters of this book.

3 'Le rapport v_b/v_a est celui de la valeur absolue de l'espèce B à la valeur absolue de l'espèce A, ou la valeur relative de l'espèce B à l'espèce A, ou le *prix* de l'unité de B en unités d'A' ('Applications', 1ère tentative).

4 '*Théorème: Personne n'est demandeur d'une certaine quantité de richesse qu'à la condition d'être offreur d'une certain autre quantité de richesse équivalente*' ('Applications', 1ère tentative; italics in original).

5 It may be observed that this definition of value corresponds exactly to the definition of value given by Auguste Walras in a letter of May 18, 1861, to his son: 'la rareté [absolute value] est un rapport entre la somme des besoins et la somme des provisions ou, comme on le dit quelquefois, entre la quantité offerte et la quantité demandée' (*rareté* [absolute value] is the ratio between the sum of the wants and the sum of the provisions, or, as it is said sometimes, between the quantity offered and the quantity demanded).

6 'Il n'y a pas d'unité de demand et de besoin. Il suit de là qu'on ne peut pas dire absolument d'une espèce de la richesse qu'elle a une valeur résultant de telle demande comparée à telle offre. En d'autres termes, il n'y a pas de valeur absolue, il n'y a que des valeurs relatives' ('Applications', 1ère tentative).

7 As indicated on the cover of the manuscript, this 'tentative' was meant to supplement Walras's *Recherche de l'idéal social* with three more lessons. There is even a third 'tentative', dating from the end of 1871, as has been detected by the second author of this book. We shall not go into the details here; see, however, Jolink (1991: 92ff.).

8 'L'utilité d'une marchandise est supposée être en raison de la somme des besoins qu'elle satisfait – ou la somme des besoins est en raison de l'utilité' ('Applications', 2e tentative).

9 'Appelons en effet rareté d'une marchandise le rapport de l'*utilité* que possède cette marchandise à la *quantité* qui en existe, autrement dit le rapport de la *somme des besoins* auxquelles elle répond à la *somme de provisions* qui s'en produisent sur le marché, ou le rapport de la *demande* à l'*offre*' (Namely, let us call the rareté of a commodity the ratio of the *utility* that it possesses to the *quantity* existing of it, in other words, the ratio of the *sum of the wants* which the commodity satisfies to the *sum of the provisions* that come to the market, or the ratio of the *demand* to the *supply*) ('Applications', 2e tentative; Walras's italics).

10 'La valeur d'échange se mesure avec un mètre qui varie de grandeur entre nos

mains' ('Applications', 2e tentative).

11 'La difficulté véritable pour apprécier la rareté c'est le manque d'une unité d'utilité. L'utilité ne se pèse pas. Le besoin ne se mesure pas. L'utilité est parmi les choses, comme le besoin, qui sont en nous.... Et voilà pourquoi la rareté peut non plus être directement mesurée. On ne mesure que la rareté relative' ('Applications', 2e tentative).

12 These germs of his later theory can be found in the third 'tentative'.

13 The extensive utility is depicted in Figure 3.1 as the length of the ordinate of $\alpha_{q,1}$, illustrating the consumption of good (A) if it is a free good.

14 This note can be found in the Fonds Walras of Lausanne, FW Vb, Carton 22. The original text is: 'Observation à M. Gide (juin 98). 1° Distinction de l'*utilité finale* (incrément d'utilité effective) et du *degré final d'utilité* (rareté). L'*utilité finale* est le produit de l'incrément [dq] de quantité supposée infiniment petite (positif ou negatif, demande ou offre) par le *degré final* [r] *d'utilité* (rareté): utilité finale = d$q \times r$. 2° Le maximum d'utilité effective de (A) et (B) pour un échangeur a lieu par l'égalité des utilités finales aux *prix criés*: d$q_a \times r_a$ = d$q_b \times r_b$ [ou] r_a/r_b = dq_b/dq_a = $p_{a,b}$. Cette condition ne détermine pas l'échange, mais seulement la *demande* et l'*offre*' (Walras's emphasis).

4 WALRAS'S GRAPHIC ANALYSIS OF THE EXCHANGE OF TWO GOODS

1 See also Van Daal and Walker (1990).
2 Cournot (1838: Section 22).
3 Walras did not speak in terms of elasticities; this stems from Marshall.
4 Here Walras made an exception to his assumption that the demand curves cut both axes.

5 WALRAS'S EXCHANGE MODEL

1 See Chapters 1 and 3; see also Jolink and Van Daal (1989a, b) and Van Daal and Jolink (1990).

2 It was L. von Bortkiewicz who suggested (7) to Walras, in a letter dated 9 May 1888 (Jaffé 1965: Letter 831). For whatever reason it has not been inserted in the second edition (1889) nor in the third one (1896a).

3 Because of an incorrect translation of the first sentence this has been more or less lost in the English version of the *Eléments*. Walras speaks of 'demande partielle' and has in mind the total demand for a certain good in exchange for a specific other good (D_{ab} for example); Jaffé translated this term as 'individual demand', which is obviously incorrect.

4 In the two-goods case p_b is unambiguously determined as the quantity of good (A) that has to be given in exchange for one unit of (B). This determinateness disappears when more than two goods are considered. Hence Walras chose $p_a = 1$ and measured all prices in *numéraire* (A).

5 As we already indicated above, this result can also be obtained by simply remarking that, if (25) does not hold for one or more goods, it is advantageous for individual (1) to buy or sell some of these goods. For instance, if the left-hand side of one of equations (25) is less than its right-hand side, then (1) adds to his utility by selling some of the good on the left-hand side for (A), and if the left-hand side is greater, it is advantageous to buy that good in exchange for (A). Of course, this has repercussions for the other equations, entailing further exchanges until (25) is completely satisfied. This, Walras's, argumentation is a further illustration that he always had something like a monetary economy in the

back of his mind, because in this reasoning the good (A) is always an intermediary in the exchange between any two other goods.

6 This does not mean that such an allegation is completely incomprehensible. See Part III. In fact, evidence shows that Walras was of the opinion that the process of haggling in competitive markets leads to a 'conditional maximum'. This was in contradiction, for instance, with Gossen's ideas (Gossen 1854: 85), according to which the individual endowments are first collected, as it were, and then redistributed such that total social utility is maximized. Gossen's device, according to Walras, is a violation of the individual's right of property; 'the economy is no picnic', he said on page 211 of the *EES*.

7 Exchange out of equilibrium is assumed never to take place in Walras's system. This is a reflection of how business was done at the Bourse of Paris in Walras's time, the best example of free competition in his eyes, where disequilibrium transactions were not allowed.

6 THE NOTION OF CAPITAL

1 A. A. Walras, *Théorie de la richesse sociale, ou résumé des principes fondamentaux de l'économie politique*, Paris, 1849, Chapter IV, pp. 53–70.

2 This will be dealt with in Chapters 13 onwards. When we speak of capital without adjective we will always mean 'fixed-capital goods'. In neglecting circulating capital Walras had to make the assumption that the element of time in production may be ignored.

3 Strictly speaking, we should say 'capitalists proper', because every individual has human capital at his disposal and may, in addition, own some land and/or capital proper, which makes him a capitalist by definition. In the latter context, however, we shall use the term 'capital-owner'.

4 In Walras's own French:

1	(i) capital foncier	(ii) rente	(iii) fermage
2	(i) capital personnel	(ii) travail	(iii) salaire
3	(i) capital proprement dit	(ii) profit	(iii) intérêt

7 THE ENTREPRENEUR

1 See Chapter 9.

2 The possibility of abstracting from the entrepreneur in Walras's theory only applies to the state of equilibrium in a system of free competition. Clearly in a state of disequilibrium or in the case of monopoly entrepreneurs play an essential role. In a state of disequilibrium, however, Walras believed a tendency existed to reduce profits to zero, which serves for an efficient allocation of production factors. In the case of monopoly this profit-reducing tendency, by necessity, does not exist since the condition that the selling price equal the cost of inputs is impaired. The latter case, however, is not included in Walras's models.

8 PRODUCTION

1 According to Jaffé, A. N. Isnard was possibly the very first, in 1781; see Jaffé (1969).

2 Strictly speaking one should write (T), ..., (P), ..., (K), ..., expressing that all three categories (land, human capital and capital proper) may consist of more than one specific type.

3 In Walras's model with circulating capital (see Chapter 13) it is supposed that also some quantities of raw materials will be produced to be set apart in the form of circulating capital. This means that we shall then also explicitly deal with raw materials. (See Chapter 13.)
4 This section is largely based upon Van Daal (1989).
5 Albeit as an afterthought.
6 Our italics; the italicized part of this quotation can only be found in the first edition of Walras's *Eléments*. See also Walras (1988: 305).
7 In the first instance Walras simply used the word 'equation' but later (Walras 1926) this was changed to 'production equation'. Note that Jaffé did not always translate this consistently; in Walras (1954: 385) the translation 'production function' is used, which might be a slip.
8 Jaffé (1965: Letter 364).
9 A first version of the appendix was published in the 1896 volume of the *Recueil publié par le Faculté de Droit de l'Université de Lausanne*. Translated by Jaffé, it has been added to the English translation of the *Eléments* (Walras 1954: 489–95).
10 See also Barone's letter to L. Walras dated 20 September 1894 (Jaffé 1965: Letter 1191).
11 They did not mention the exact place. It is likely, however, that they became acquainted with Pareto's formula (5) by oral communication. The idea was published in print for the first time, as far as we know, in Pareto (1895: 489).
12 For a given quantity Q of good (B) to be produced the cost minimization problem can be formalized as follows:

minimize $\qquad p_t T + p_p P + p_k K + \ldots$

subject to $\qquad Q = \phi(T, P, K, \ldots).$ $\qquad\qquad$ (A1)

The variables to be calculated in this problem are the quantities $T, P, K, \ldots$ of the factors (T), (P), (K), $\ldots$; the prices $p_t, p_p, p_k, \ldots$ are given. Furthermore, the following relation must hold:

$$p_b Q = p_t T + p_p P + p_k K + \ldots, \qquad\qquad (A2)$$

where p_b, likewise given, is the price of good (B). Relation (A2) expresses the zero-profit condition.

The first-order conditions for (A1) are

$$p_t = \lambda \frac{\partial \phi}{\partial T}, \qquad p_p = \lambda \frac{\partial \phi}{\partial P}, \qquad p_k = \lambda \frac{\partial \phi}{\partial K}, \qquad \ldots \qquad (A3)$$

$$Q = \phi(T, P, K, \ldots)$$

Differentiating the last relation with respect to Q gives

$$1 = \frac{\partial \phi}{\partial T}\frac{\partial T}{\partial Q} + \frac{\partial \phi}{\partial P}\frac{\partial P}{\partial Q} + \frac{\partial \phi}{\partial K}\frac{\partial K}{\partial Q} + \ldots, \qquad\qquad (A4)$$

or, multiplying both sides of (A4) by λ and using the first of equations (A3),

$$\lambda = p_t \frac{\partial T}{\partial Q} + p_p \frac{\partial P}{\partial Q} + p_k \frac{\partial K}{\partial Q} + \ldots, \qquad\qquad (A5)$$

which is a well-known result of mathematical programming theory which states that the Lagrange multiplier expresses the rate of change of the objective function (here the costs of producing Q units of (B) with respect to an expansion or contraction of the restriction (here the second of equations (A3)). Differentiation of (A2) with respect to Q yields

$$p_b = p_t \frac{\partial T}{\partial Q} + p_p \frac{\partial P}{\partial Q} + p_k \frac{\partial K}{\partial Q} + \dots \qquad (A6)$$

Combining this with (A5) leads us to the conclusion that

$$p_b = \lambda. \qquad (A7)$$

This means that producing one unit more of (B) results in an additional cost p_b, i.e. there is marginal as well as average product exhaustion. Inserting (A7) into the first of equations (A3) and putting the result into (A2) yields, after dividing both sides by p_b,

$$Q = T \frac{\partial \phi}{\partial T} + P \frac{\partial \phi}{\partial P} + K \frac{\partial \phi}{\partial K} + \dots \qquad (A8)$$

which must hold for the solution of (A1) irrespective of constancy of returns.

13 It is well known from modern literature on general equilibrium theory that ever-increasing returns to scale (here $\partial b_t / \partial Q < 0$, $\partial b_p / \partial Q < 0$ etc.) are not consistent with free competition, an essential feature of Walrasian equilibrium theory (see, for example, Arrow and Hahn 1971). When the cost functions are U-shaped with a minimum that is (infinitesimally) low compared with the market demand, an equilibrium may exist under certain circumstances (see Novshek and Sonnenschein 1980). In the latter case, however, Walras's original aggregative setting has to be abandoned.

14 In a letter to Wicksell, dated 2 November 1900, he wrote with respect to marginal productivity: 'I prefer to restrict myself to only pointing to it, leaving it outside of my theory. With respect to the latter, I answer you that it deals with *Grenznutzen* [marginal utility], investigated to its last details in economic equilibrium' (Jaffé 1965: Letter 1465).

9 WALRAS'S PRODUCTION MODEL

1 See Chapter 7. It cannot be stressed enough that this idea has made it possible to link production and consumption in a simple mathematical model in which the interdependence can be clearly seen and discussed. As we see it at present, direct modelling of the maximizing behaviour of all agents would have raised mathematical problems that could not be solved adequately before the work of Arrow and Debreu and their immediate predecessors. See also Weintraub (1985: ch. 6).

2 We omit the index 1 when no confusion can arise.

3 A quantity offered of a service may be negative. This then means that the individual wishes to consume more than he has at his disposal at the outset of the period in question.

4 Irving Fisher (1892) already used such general utility functions, where the marginal utility of each good depends on all quantities consumed; Pareto, at the time, also used this kind of utility function in his articles in the *Giornale degli Economisti*.

5 See, for instance, Figure 5, plate II, in Walras (1926) (Walras 1954: Figure 17).

6 Walras is likewise silent about the issue in his other publications and in his correspondence. To Walras and those with whom he corresponded, aggregation

either did not appear to be problematic and therefore did not arise as a subject for discussion, or was considered to be subordinate to difficult issues such as utility maximization, general economic equilibrium, capital, money, and marginal productivity. See Van Daal and Walker (1990); see also Van Daal and Merkies (1984).

7 The terms 'individual' and 'household' are used interchangeably.

8 Multiply both sides of equations (8) by p_t, p_p, p_k, ..., respectively, add the results and compare this with the sum of equations (9) multiplied consecutively by D_a, D_b, D_c, D_d, ...

10 THE RATE OF NET INCOME AND THE FUTURE

1 We shall see later (Chapter 12) that it is highly questionable whether Walras himself was fully aware of this important consequence of his set-up.

2 In the first edition these amounts were assumed to be fixed, independent of the price of the capital good.

3 Here Walras apparently departed from his normal custom of denoting by the term income revenue in kind only.

4 See Chapter 5, equations (25), and Chapter 9, equations (2) and (3).

5 'Le théorème (de l'utilité maxima des capitaux neufs) est le couronnement de toute l'économie politique pure. Ne serait-il pas possible d'en donner une démonstration élémentaire par le moyen d'une représentation géométrique des incréments totaux d'utilité des produits et des incréments partiels d'utilité des services producteurs qui entrent dans la confection des produits?

OUI

à condition de généraliser la formule de satisfaction maximum.'

This is one of Walras's many 'personal carnets', pieces of paper with all kinds of remarks that can be found throughout his books, papers and manuscripts in the Walras Archives at Lausanne. The present one can be found in Section V, Carton 22. See also Appendix III, where a similar statement can be found.

6 This model will be further discussed in Chapter 12.

7 Note that one unit of capital provides one unit of services.

8 In the mathematical model we have to strip (E) from all the varieties it has in Walras's verbal expositions. See, for instance, the *Eléments*, Section 270; see also pages 74–6.

9 Walras calls good (E) 'revenu net perpétuel' and states that this good as well as its price p_e are simply measured in units of *numéraire* (*Eléments*, Section 242). This is erroneous, however, because then the value $d_e p_e$ of a quantity d_e demanded of (E) would be of the dimension $[N]^2$ (*numéraire* squared). In our opinion (E) has to be measured as money (*numéraire*) per period and must therefore have the dimension $[N][T]^{-1}$ (money divided by time). According to (5) p_e, being the inverse of i, must have the dimension $[T]$. Then $d_e p_e$ has the correct dimension, i.e. $[N][T]^{-1}[T] = [N]$.

The germ of this concept can already be found in the nineteenth-century model as we saw above in equation (2): a unit of *numéraire* spent on buying some capital good always results in the expectation of a stream of i francs of net income in all the periods in which the capital good will bear fruit. In the preface to the second edition Walras even alluded to what was going to come in the fourth edition. Comparing his system with Böhm-Bawerk's he remarked that the choice between consumption and saving is the same as the choice between consuming a value of one unit of *numéraire* during the period in question and consuming a value (in *numéraire*) of i year in year out from the subsequent period onwards.

10 For d_e to be positive the individual's savings must exceed the provisions necessary for keeping intact his initial quantity q_e of (E); in other words, depreciation and destruction have to be completely neutralized first. For the time being we shall make the bold assumption that during each period the fraction $\mu_k + \nu_k$ precisely of each capital good (K) is lost by wear and tear or accidental destruction. Hence the amounts set aside for replacement of capital proper are immediately used up. In this way no funds are needed for replacement nor do possible future price changes of the capital goods play a role.

11 As far as we are aware, this mistake was pointed out for the first time by Floss (1957); it is further discussed by Montgomery (1971), who considered it unimportant. Suggestions for eliminating it were never given as far as we know.

The mistake has repercussions on the resulting variables of the macro model, in particular total savings. In Walras's macro model of capital formation of the last two editions of the *Eléments* the same symbol E was used for denoting total *net* savings (4th and 5th editions, Section 242) and total *gross* savings (last equation of [2] (Walras's numbering) in Section 245). Walras apparently did not notice the inconsistency and continued considering E further as total gross savings. This did not make the macro model *as such* inconsistent, yet it was not based anymore on the foregoing microeconomic premises, strictly speaking. Certainly this could not have been Walras's intention.

12 Jaffé (1942); italics added.

13 We omitted the word 'and', which might be a slip in the original text.

11 WALRAS'S MODEL OF CAPITAL FORMATION

1 Just as in the preceding chapters, the italicized capitals in all the subsystems denote the aggregates of the micro variables indicated by the corresponding lower case letter. The functions F in subsystems I and II likewise correspond to the functions f in (4), (5) and (6). Some subsystems consist of only one equation.

2 This notation is somewhat confusing; E is an amount of *numéraire*, while (E) denotes a type of commodity. $F_e(.)$ is the sum of the amounts $p_e f_e(.)$ to which has been added Σ_e, the total amount needed to cover wear and tear. Note that the last argument in F_e is not p_e as in I and II but i ($= 1/p_e$); this has no mathematical significance. In fact, the equation $E = D_e p_e + \Sigma_e$ and the definition of Σ_e as the aggregate of the σ_es also belong to the model.

3 Later, in subsystem VII, these quantities will also appear as quantities demanded.

4 The rigid way in which uncertainty is treated in the last chapter of Debreu (1959) does not change this.

5 This becomes even more apparent from his models of money circulation, which also have been revised considerably from the fourth edition onwards; see the next chapters.

6 One must not forget, however, that Walras suggested as an element of his whole theory a monetary system with gold as the principal money-commodity and with silver money for regulation of the value of money to be brought in or withdrawn by the state in adequate quantities (*EPA*, pp. 107ff.). This kind of open-market policy *avant la lettre* should keep the price level more or less constant.

7 Where Walras kept the quantity of land as given, it is questionable whether his sequence of temporary equilibria might eventually become a steady-state growth. It seemed that Walras was already charmed by that type of growth, or at

least by the idea that the development of the economy in question may be characterized by some simple features. In Part VII of the *Eléments* he discussed verbally what will happen in the model when population rises while natural resources are limited and technology improves in the sense that the technical coefficients for land diminish and the quantities of capital goods proper increase proportionally more than population. In such an economy, Walras argued, the price of labour will remain constant, the price of land services will rise considerably and the price of the services of capital goods proper will fall. This means that in general the prices of the products will not change but the rate of net income will fall. Consequently people may spend the same amount on consumption goods (whose prices did not change) as before. Their amount of savings will then be higher because there are more capital goods than before; this will enable them to continue the expansion of the set of capital goods proper. It must be said, however, that Walras was committing here the same sin as he reproached the 'économiste' with, namely treating science as literature.

8 The *O*s in subsystem I are (aggregate) quantities offered by the capital owners, whereas in subsystem IV these same *O*s denote quantities demanded by the entrepreneurs. The *D*s in subsystem II are quantities demanded by the consumers and in subsystem IV they denote quantities offered by the entrepreneurs.

9 It is interesting to note that Walker (1987a: 857) uses the same citations to come to a conclusion differing from ours.

10 That is, this period's revenues minus this period's costs.

11 See also on this point Hicks (1965: 32ff.).

12 See also on this point Kuenne (1961).

13 This is sometimes the case even in his more verbal analysis. For instance, in his 'Théorie du crédit' (*EPA*, Part IV) he states that in many cases the entrepreneurs are also capitalists and that it is just the combination of these two qualities that turns out to be fruitful in acquiring funds for investment.

12 ON THE FUTILITY OF LESSONS 26 AND 27 OF THE *ÉLÉMENTS*

1 'I promised to show that, subject to a certain constraint, the condition of equality of ratios between the net incomes and the prices of new capital goods was the condition of the maximum effective utility obtainable from the services of these capital goods on which the social excess of income over consumption was spent, just as the condition of equality of the ratios between the *raretés* and the prices of [consumers'] goods and services was the condition of the maximum effective utility obtainable from these goods and services, on which the individual incomes were spent' (opening sentence of Lesson 26 of the *Eléments* from the second edition onwards). This was the subject of Lesson 26 of the second and third editions, split into Lessons 26 and 27 of the fourth and fifth editions.

2 Relation (4) is the same as (13) of Chapter 11.

3 See also Walras (1988: 412–13).

4 There is yet another specific case, which was dealt with by Walras in Lesson 27 of the fourth and fifth editions of the *Eléments*. This second specific case is that in which the quantities of newly produced capital goods are exactly equal to those quantities of capital goods already existing that are used for the production of consumption goods; we shall not deal with this case here.

It is a moot question why Walras only studied these two cases. Possibly he was of the opinion that every situation of equilibrium is a mixture of the two specific cases. Alternatively, one might guess that he had the idea that the general truth of his assertion would already have been ascertained if it is true for at least one case. At least the two cases gave him concrete instances about which something could be said.

5 Walras's printers must have been admirably patient persons. In the Walras archives of Lausanne (Carton 22) we found seven substantially different versions of these galley proofs and there might have been more because the last one still differs from the definitive text of the second edition.

6 In order to give a full example of Walras's argumentation, we present a translation into English of this letter in Appendix III.

7 The macro budget restriction does hold in the specific situation, but Walras disaggregated it incorrectly.

8 That is, the amount reserved for depreciation and insurance during the period in question divided by the rate of net income, where it is assumed that prices are invariable. It was assumed by Walras that an item of capital will exist in perpetuity with maintenance and insurance. Note that the technology is assumed to be invariable. See Jaffé (1980; in Walker 1983: 357, n. 29). See also Letter 918 in Jaffé (1965), from Bortkiewicz to Walras, 12 September 1889.

9 It was Claude Mouchot who directed our attention to this point.

10 The same applies to the second specific case.

11 Jaffé (1942; 1953) and Walker (1984a) paid attention to Lessons 26 and 27 of the *Eléments*. In his first article Jaffé considered Walras's theory of capital formation as incomplete and unsatisfactory. In his second article he was less negative and tried to explain Walras's reasoning; the latter article is partly reproduced as a note to the translation of the *Eléments* (Walras 1954: 536–41). In his discussion of Walras's theorem, however, Jaffé completely lost his way in the labyrinth of formulae. He vainly attempted to clarify Walras's exposition in Lesson 27 by supposing that in Walras's second case the economy is in a stationary state in the sense that there are just as many capital goods produced as are needed to balance wear and tear, which is virtually impossible.

Walker (1984a) deals with the correspondence between Walras and the latter's colleagues to whom galley proofs of Lesson 26 of the second edition of the *Eléments* had been sent (Böhm-Bawerk, Bortkiewicz, Edgeworth, Foxwell and others). He relates this critically to the assertions by Jaffé (1953). He does not give a global negative judgement on Walras's proof of the theorem as we do in the present chapter because he considers the two specific cases as less stringent than we do. He interprets them in the sense that Walras subsequently would have considered new capital produced for consumptive use by their owners and new capital destined for productive use, a pedagogical split of two simultaneous processes, which is at least questionable.

13 CIRCULATING CAPITAL

1 Money will be treated separately in the three subsequent chapters. Therefore, we shall denote by the term circulating capital only non-monetary stocks.

2 *Eléments*, 4th and 5th editions, Section 207.

3 Walras (1954: 315–24).

4 Even Jaffé was put on the wrong track. He missed some technical errors made by Walras. Moreover, note 16 of Lesson 29 in Walras (1954) is completely beside the point. In this note, dealing with counting variables and equations, Jaffé confuses quantities of produced goods destined to be held as circulating capital with quantities of services of circulating capital offered. It is remarkable,

however, how few of such slips can be found in Jaffé's translation and in the annotations.

5 Introduced for the first time in the fourth edition of the *Eléments*; see the preface to the fourth edition (Walras 1988: 5, 7). See also Appendix V.

6 Raw materials should now be taken explicitly into consideration in the sense that their production for use as circulating capital becomes 'visible'. The production of raw materials for production purposes may remain 'hidden', as set out on page 50.

7 Alternatively, one could suppose that the units of circulating capital in stock as such do not remain the same throughout the period. For instance, an individual wishing to keep his stock intact could consume the stock during the period and replace it at the end of the period by fresh, newly produced units.

8 The services of circulating capital are measured such that one unit of capital delivers one unit of services, just as for fixed capital.

9 If one of these amounts is negative then the individual is demanding services of availability in addition to the services that he has already at his disposal. We shall disregard this.

10 Denoting the supply of newly produced circulating capital by $D_{a'}$, $D_{b'}$, $D_{c'}$, ... is at first sight confusing. But as always this is a consequence of Walras's way of expressing market demand mathematically: the same symbols $D_{a'}$, $D_{b'}$, $D_{c'}$, ... will also be used to denote the quantities of circulating capital demanded by individuals. As we already remarked, Walras's Ds (Os) always denote in the first instance quantities demanded (offered) by individual consumer-capitalists; at the same time, in the second instance they denote, because of market clearing, quantities offered (demanded) by the entrepreneurs. The extra confusion here is caused by the circumstance that there are both $D_{a'}$, $D_{b'}$, $D_{c'}$, ... and $O_{a'}$, $O_{b'}$, $O_{c'}$, ..., that denote, respectively, quantities of circulating capital and quantities of services of circulating capital. The mistake made by Jaffé in note 16 to Lesson 29 is that he considered these Ds and Os as demand and supply in the same markets, which is not the case.

11 For instance, the first equation of subsystem IV of Chapter 11 now becomes

$$a_t(D_a + D_{a'}) + b_t(D_b + D_{b'}) + \ldots + m_t D_{m'} + \ldots + k_t D_k + k'_t D_{k'} + \ldots$$
$$= O_t.$$

It seems that Walras was not aware of the need to add the terms $m_t D_{m'}$, ..., which is a consequence of including raw materials in the stocks of circulating capital.

12 Walras overlooked these prices and their equations in counting.

14 A PRELUDE TO THE MONEY MODELS

1 *The Purchasing Power of Money* (1911).

2 The latter booklet has been republished with minor changes in the *EES*.

3 Walras retained the cash balance approach which he had developed from the second edition onwards. On the other hand, he also maintained elements of the quantity theory approach. This hybrid combination of monetary thoughts led to a confusing way of modelling in the final editions of the *Eléments*. In fact, one may distinguish several models rather than one single model, as we shall set out below.

4 This will only be done in this chapter.

5 See page 78.

6 *H* was derived in the first instance in a way similar to (2) above:

$$Q_a'' P_a = aP_a + b + cp_c + dp_d + \ldots + TP_t + \ldots + PP_p + \ldots + KP_k$$
$$+ K'P_{k'} + K''P_{k''} + \ldots + tp_t + \ldots + pp_p + \ldots + kp_k + k'p_{k'} +$$
$$k'p_{k''} + \ldots + mp_m + \ldots$$
$$= H + a(P_a - p_a).$$

The amount *a* was assumed to be small in comparison with *H*, which allowed Walras to neglect it and to consider *H* as 'predetermined'.

In the fourth edition of the *Eléments* this argumentation was deleted, but it was not replaced by an alternative derivation. Relation (3) was maintained by Walras without any argumentation about the predetermined nature of *H*.

7 See Lesson 26 of the first edition and Lesson 15 of the second to fifth editions.

8 In the next two chapters we shall see that the macro money model becomes even more untenable in the light of Walras's twentieth-century models of general economic equilibrium money models.

9 'Théorie mathématique du billet de banque', *EPA*, pp. 339–75.

10 *Eléments*, Lesson 32.

11 The state regulates the total quantity of money by issuing or withdrawing silver money in order to stabilize the price level; *EPA*, Part I. This a kind of open-market policy *avant la lettre*.

15 WALRAS'S EQUILIBRIUM MODEL WITH FIAT-MONEY

1 See the quotation on page 90.

2 This resembles his assumptions in the production model, in which the individuals are assumed to have fixed initial endowments q_t, q_p, q_k, ... of capital (T), (P), (K), ... that do not change from period to period.

The unrealistic invariability of the individuals' holdings of money illustrates the plausibility of our assertion that Walras's models with fiat-money have been devised for pedagogical purposes only.

3 The prices in *numéraire* of the availability in money of products are $p_{a'}$, $p_{b'}$, $p_{c'}$, ...; they are already known from Chapter 13. The price $p_{e'}$ of the availability in money of a perpetual net income of one unit of *numéraire* per period is, in our opinion, equal to unity, because $p_{c'} = ip_c = i(1/i) = 1$. Walras erroneously took $p_{c'} = p_{a'}$. We changed his formulae accordingly.

4 Just as in the case of circulating capital of Chapter 13, Walras preferred a set-up in which the optimal money stock kept for own use by an individual may differ from that strictly needed and foreseeable; see page 84.

5 Again, the utility functions have been supposed to be additively separable.

6 See note 3 above.

7 Walras did not use this form because he needed (7) in his further analysis, as we shall set out below.

8 Walras did not indicate the entrepreneurs' demand for money services explicitly by means of a separate symbol. The symbol D_u would have been inconsistent with Walras's system of notation as we already set out in Chapter 13, note 10.

9 Walras supposed that the entrepreneurs need capital goods proper as circulating capital in the form of money but, of course, not in kind; see Chapter 13, relations (7) and (8). Note that δ_x is a quantity of (K) in the form of money. Because (K) is already capital, it is meaningless to speak of (K') in this respect; moreover, this would be inconsistent with earlier notation: (K') is another type

of capital proper. Since the opportunity cost of holding one unit of (K) available during the period is equal to p_k, the price of one unit of (K) available in the form of money is also equal to that amount.

10 Preliminary results, which eventually led to Lesson 29 of the fourth edition of the *Eléments*, were published in Walras (1899).

11 This slip has been pointed out in T. Yasui, *Kinko bunseki no kihon mondai (Basic Problems in Equilibrium Analysis)*, Tokyo: Iwanami, 1955; see Morishima (1977: 125).

12 He is silent about the fact that he wrote $p_{u'}$ also as an argument of the equations for α, β, γ, δ, ..., ε; see (4) above. Furthermore, one should not forget that $p_{u'}$ is an argument of all the other demand functions and of all the supply functions.

13 Alternatively, we could have derived the Cambridge formula $M = kY$ by defining Y as $(O_t p_t + \ldots + O_p p_p + \ldots + O_k p_k + O_{k'} p_{k'} + O_{k'} p_{k'} + \ldots + O_a p_a + O_{b'} p_{b'} + \ldots + Q_m p_{m'} + \ldots + O_u p_{u'})P$ and k as the quotient of $H_a i$ and the expression within parentheses in the definition of Y.

16 WALRAS'S EQUILIBRIUM MODEL WITH COMMODITY-MONEY

1 Note that O_u and D_u are not supply and demand of some good in the same market but magnitudes that relate to different markets. O_u is a quantity of money services, whereas D_u is an amount of money. We already pointed to this consequence of Walras's notation in earlier chapters.

2 A. W. Marget (1931, 1935) was the first to point in a positive way to Walras's monetary achievements.

3 It might be, however, that Walras would not have been happy with a conclusion that prevented him from making such instructive pictures as Figure 14.1. This figure is not only present in the *Eléments* from the first edition onwards, it can also be found in his applied work (e.g. in his 'Théorie mathématique du billet de banque' (1880)) and as the basis of his considerations on bimetallism in the *Eléments* from the second edition onwards.

This story might perhaps be 'saved' by amending it twofold. First, equation (5) in Chapter 14 should be replaced by a general formula $q = H(p)$, expressing the demand for (A) as money as a function of its price in (B). Second, instead of introducing the total fixed amount Q_a of (A), a total supply curve for (A) should be introduced, replacing the horizontal line through A by some increasing graph. The picture would then make clear how the price of (A) in (B) is affected by making (A) the money-commodity.

4 Money is not the only store of value; it is only one of the types of capital and all types of capital may serve as a store of value.

5 See the *Eléments*, fourth and fifth editions, Section 274.

6 In this respect we disagree with Rijnvos (1988: 10–11) and Negishi (1987: 591).

17 REALITY AND REALISTIC UTOPIAS

1 See Jaffé (1977) and Walker (1984b).

2 Jaffé characterizes Walras's model as a 'realistic utopia'.

3 Chapter 2.

4 See page 5.

5 'L'ensemble des rapports nécessaires qui dérivent de la nature des choses' (*Mélanges*, pp. 248–9). Walras derives this notion of 'law' from Montesquieu's *L'esprit des lois* (1748).

6 Notably Chapters 5, 9, 11, 15 and 16.

7 In discussing dynamic properties of the market, Walras observed that there is a tendency towards equilibrium although equilibrium itself is hardly ever attained.

8 See Jolink (1991).

9 Jaffé (1977).

10 In this respect, it seems more appropriate to speak of a utopian reality than of a realistic utopia.

18 FREE COMPETITION REVISITED

1 See Chapters 2 and 17.

2 These subjects are grouped in Walras's *EPA*.

3 These subjects are grouped in Walras's *EES*.

4 Letter 548 in Jaffé (1965), from L. Walras to W. Lexis.

5 Letter 836 in Jaffé (1965), from L. Walras to Ch. Gide.

6 A continuation of this process, however, may be explained, for instance, by assuming that entrepreneurs will try to maximize their revenues rather than their profits.

7 The reason why some entrepreneurs do sell their products and why some do not cannot be explained by the model and, in fact, remains enigmatic in Walras's text also.

8 Walras referred to this type of monopoly as a 'natural monopoly'. In addition, he distinguished 'necessary monopolies', relating to situations in which, by necessity, only one enterprise could or was allowed to exist.

9 *Eléments*, Lesson 41. Note that the maximization of net receipts is equivalent to the maximization of profits per unit of product in the case of a single supplier:

$$\text{net receipts} = O_b p_b - O_b(b_t p_t + b_p p_p + b_k p_k + \dots)$$
$$= O_b[p_b - (b_t p_t + b_p p_p + b_k p_k + \dots)].$$

Since a high O_b corresponds to a low p_b and vice versa, a monopolist is able to fix a level of production so as to maximize total profits.

10 That is, natural and necessary monopolies.

11 See also Jaffé (1977), who distinguishes commutative justice and distributive justice.

12 This also implied that inequality of effort necessarily implied an inequality of reward.

13 In particular in A. Walras (1835); see also Jolink (1991: ch. 6). See also Clark (1993) for a survey of natural law concepts in economics.

19 WALRAS'S 'GENERAL GENERAL EQUILIBRIUM MODEL'

1 This chapter is largely based on our article 'On Walras's "general general equilibrium model"', originally published as Chapter 9 in *Perspectives on the History of Economic Thought*, vol. IX, Aldershot: Edward Elgar, 1993.

2 Chapter 16.

3 See, for example, Jaffé (1977).

4 In fact, Walras used additively separable utility functions. This made his reasoning considerably simpler.

I A LIFE SKETCH OF LÉON WALRAS

1 Léon Walras wrote, in a letter to L. von Bortkiewicz, the following P.S.: 'Mon nom se prononce Walrasse' (Letter 999 of Jaffé 1965).
2 This and other biographical details we borrow from Jaffé (1965, 1984).
3 Walras (1908: 170).
4 Léon Walras's maternal grandmother's maiden name was Peluche.
5 Jaffé (1965: vol. I, p. 2).
6 Walras (1859, 1860a).
7 Walras (1860b).
8 This common friend was director of the *Bibliothèque de l'Arsenal.*
9 In 1863 their child Marie Aline was born. In September 1869 they decided to marry. On the occasion of their marriage, Léon Walras legitimized his wife's son Georges as his own. Both children remained unmarried.
10 At a much later stage these lectures were reprinted in the *EES.*
11 The Academy of Lausanne became the University of Lausanne in 1890.
12 'To Léon Walras, born in Evreux, professor at the Academy and at the University of Lausanne, who was the first to establish the general conditions of the economic equilibrium, thus founding the School of Lausanne. To honour 50 years of unselfish work.'

II ON WALRAS'S WORKS

1 See, for instance, the general introduction to A. Walras (1990). That the indifference with respect to the work and the person of Léon Walras from his own university belongs to the past is illustrated by the recent foundation (and the first activities) of the 'Centre Walras–Pareto' in the University of Lausanne in 1991.
2 This book was ready for publication at the time of Walras's death, but it had never been published. The Walras Centre therefore decided to bring out the *Mélanges* first. See Hébert and Potier (1987).
3 Although most of his publications are on the list, it is not totally accurate. The best and most complete bibliography of Walras's writings is Walker (1987d). It corrects some errors made by Walras. The latter bibliography also contains the (re)publications and translations dating from after Walras's death; moreover, it also contains Walras's non-economic writings, some dozens of titles.
4 We thank Jean-Pierre Potier for checking these indications.
5 The *Complete Economic Works*, incidentally, contain more than is reported in the autobibliography. The *Abrégé* is included in Part VIII, for instance, whereas the 'Tentatives' (see Chapter 4) have found a place in Volume XI.
6 In abridged form, pp. 483–4, n. 27.
7 Pages 457–8. (See also Letter 645 in Jaffé (1965).)
8 Annexe I.
9 Appendice II.
10 Appendice I, I.
11 Appendice I.
12 Under the title 'Le problème monétaire en Europe et aux Etats-Unis'.
13 The entries 1907, 1908 and 1909 were later added in Walras's own hand.

III LETTER FROM LÉON WALRAS TO HERBERT SOMERTON FOXWELL

1 Letter 869 in Jaffé (1965). The italics are Walras's.

2 In a former letter Walras had asked Foxwell to transmit the galley proofs for comments to his colleagues, among which was Edgeworth.
3 The *rs* denote *raretés*. The numbering has been added.
4 Walras made here the error of considering the corresponding *rs* in (1) and (2) as equal or proportional. The *rs* in (1) and (2), however, relate to different objects.
5 Jaffé transcribed Walras's shorthand at this place as 'quantities of capital consumed', which is in our opinion an error.

V ON THE EXISTENCE OF EQUILIBRIUM AND ON
TÂTONNEMENT

1 As Jaffé has pointed out, Walras's first inspiration (at the age of 19 years) to try to put the economic system in a mathematical system of just as many equations as there are variables was provoked by his reading of Poinsot's *Eléments de Statique* in its eighth edition (1842). The chapter that must have inspired Walras most is certainly Chapter II, entitled 'Des conditions de l'équilibre, exprimées par des equations' (Of the conditions of equilibrium as expressed by equations, pages 93–174). See Jaffé (1968; Walker 1983: 132). See also Letters 1483 and 1495 in Jaffé (1965).
2 See, for example, Bowley (1924).
3 See, for example, Varian (1984: 193–7).
4 See, for example, Ingrao and Israel (1990).
5 See von Neumann (1945) and, for example, Wald (1936); see also Weintraub (1983).
6 Dorfman, Samuelson and Solow (1958: 366ff.) and Lancaster (1968: 145–9) for instance.
7 Arrow and Debreu's model is in many aspects much more general than Walras's. In particular, the former can be such that an equilibrium state arises in which there are positive profits. This can occur when the production possibility sets show strict convexities; see, for instance, the simple but illustrative examples in Cornwall (1984: 20–4, 83–5).
8 This does not harm Walras's underlying idea that it is just scarce goods that are worthwhile considering. The only difference with the original Walrasian model is that in the model below scarcity becomes endogenous.
9 See, for example, Debreu (1982: Theorem 1).
10 The proof inspired Bidard and Franke (1987) to devise an elegant alternative existence proof based on the so-called Gale–Nikaido–Debreu lemma. Bidard and Franke's proof, however, is of the same mathematical depth, because it can be proved that the lemma is equivalent to Kakutani's fixed-point theorem (Uzawa 1962). Further, it can be proved that the lemma is equivalent to the existence of equilibrium; see also Debreu (1982: 719–20). This, in fact, means that it is impossible to prove the existence of general economic equilibrium in a mathematically more elementary way. In other words, it is not mathematical pedantry that leads economists to the use of fixed-point theorems.
11 That is, based on equations of the type of equations (1) in Chapter 8.
12 Allais (1943: vol. 2, pp. 489ff.).
13 The French word is *bon*; Jaffé's translation is 'ticket'. The more exact translation 'pledge' for *bon* has been proposed by Walker (1987a: 859).

REFERENCES

Allais, M. (1943) *Traité d'économie politique pure*, 2 vols, Paris: Imprimerie Nationale.

Arrow, K. J. and Debreu, G. (1954) 'Existence of equilibrium for a competitive economy', *Econometrica* 22: 265–90.

Arrow, K. J. and Hahn, F. (1971) *General Competitive Analysis*, San Francisco, CA: Holden-Day.

Barone, E. (1895) 'Sur une livre de récent de Wicksteed', translated from Italian by L. Walras (October 1895); published as note 4 to Letter 1215 (from Walras to Barone) in Jaffé, W. (ed.) (1965) *Correspondence of Léon Walras and Related Papers*, vol. II, Amsterdam: North-Holland.

Bidard, C. and Franke, R. (1987) 'On Walras' model of general equilibrium: a simpler way to demonstrate existence', *Zeitschrift für Nationalökonomie* 47: 315–19.

Bowley, A. L. (1924) *The Mathematical Groundwork of Economics*, Oxford: Clarendon.

Clark, C. M. A. (1993) *Economic Theory and Natural Philosophy*, Aldershot: Edward Elgar.

Cornwall, R. R. (1984) *Introduction to the Use of General Equilibrium Anaysis*, Amsterdam: North-Holland.

Cournot, A. (1838) *Recherches sur les principes mathématiques de la théorie des richesses*, Paris: Hachette.

Debreu, G. (1959) *Theory of Value*, New York: Wiley.

—— (1982) 'Existence of competitive equilibrium', in K. J. Arrow and M. D. Intriligator (eds) *Handbook of Mathematical Economics*, vol. II, Amsterdam: North-Holland, pp. 697–743.

Dorfman, R., Samuelson, P. and Solow, R. (1958) *Linear Programming and Economic Analysis*, New York: McGraw-Hill.

Fisher, I. (1892) *Mathematical Investigation in the Theory of Value and Prices*, New Haven, CT: Connecticut Academy of Arts and Science; *Transactions*, 9.

—— (1911) *The Purchasing Power of Money*, New York: Macmillan.

Floss, L. (1957) 'Some notes on Léon Walras' theory of capital and credit', *Metroeconomica* 9: 52–69.

Gaukroger, S. (1980) *Descartes. Philosophy, Mathematics and Physics*, Brighton: Harvester Press.

Gossen, H. H. (1854) *Entwickelung der Gesetze des menschlichen Verkehrs und der daraus fliessenden Regeln für menschliches Handeln*, Braunschweig: Vieweg. (Reprinted Liberac, Amsterdam, 1967; English translation by R. C. Blitz, *The Laws of Human Relations*, Cambridge, MA: MIT Press, 1983.)

Hébert, C. and Potier, J.-P. (1987) 'The surprising history of the *Mélanges d'économie politique et sociale*', *History of Economics Society Bulletin* 9: 67–79.

Hicks, J. R. (1965) *Capital and Growth*, Oxford: Clarendon.

Ingrao, B. and Israel, G. (1990) *The Invisible Hand. Economic Equilibrium in the History of Science*, translated from Italian by I. McGilvray, Cambridge, MA: MIT Press.

Jaffé, W. (1942) 'Léon Walras' theory of capital accumulation', in O. Lange, F. McIntyre and Th. O. Yntema (eds) *Studies in Mathematical Economics and Econometrics*, Chicago, IL: University of Chicago Press, pp. 37–48. (Reprinted in Walker, D. A. (ed.) (1983) *William Jaffé's Essays on Walras*, Cambridge: Cambridge University Press, ch. 9.)

—— (1953) 'La théorie de la capitalisation chez Walras dans le cadre de sa théorie de l'équilibre général', *Economie Appliquée* 6: 289–317. (Reprinted in English, translated by D. A. Walker, in Walker, D. A. (ed.) (1983) *William Jaffé's Essays on Walras*, Cambridge: Cambridge University Press, ch. 10.)

—— (ed.) (1965) *Correspondence of Léon Walras and Related Papers*, 3 vols, Amsterdam: North-Holland.

—— (1968) 'Léon Walras', in D. L. Sills (ed.) *International Encyclopedia of the Social Sciences*, New York: Macmillan, pp. 447–53. (An abridged version of this paper appears in Walker, D. A. (ed.) (1983) *William Jaffé's Essays on Walras*, Cambridge: Cambridge University Press, ch. 7.)

—— (1969) 'A. N. Isnard, Progenitor of the Walrasian general equilibrium model', *History of Political Economy* 1: 19–43. (Reprinted in Walker, D. A. (ed.) (1983) *William Jaffé's Essays on Walras*, Cambridge: Cambridge University Press, ch. 3.)

—— (1977) 'The normative bias of the Walrassian model: Walras versus Gossen', *Quarterly Journal of Economics* 91: 371–87. (Reprinted in Walker, D. A. (ed.) (1983) *William Jaffé's Essays on Walras*, Cambridge: Cambridge University Press, ch. 18.)

—— (1980) 'Walras's economics as others see it', *Journal of Economic Literature* 18: 528–49. (Reprinted in Walker, D. A. (ed.) (1983) *William Jaffé's Essays on Walras*, Cambridge: Cambridge University Press, ch. 19.)

—— (1984) 'The antecedents and early life of Léon Walras', edited by D. A. Walker, *History of Political Economy* 16: 1–43.

Jolink, A. (1991) 'Liberté, égalité, rareté; the evolutionary economics of Léon Walras: an analytical reconstruction', Ph. D. Thesis, Erasmus University Rotterdam.

Jolink, A. and van Daal, J. (1989a) 'Léon Walras' latest book: mélanges d'économie politique et sociale', *De Economist* 137: 351–9.

—— and —— (1989b) 'Léon Walras's mathematical economics and the mechanical analogies', *History of Economics Society Bulletin* 11: 25–32.

Kuenne, R. E. (1961) 'The Walrasian theory of money: an interpretation and reconstruction', *Metroeconomica* 13: 94–105.

Lancaster, K. (1968) *Mathematical Economics*, New York: Macmillan.

Lipsey, R. G. and Lancaster, K. (1956) 'The general theory of second best', *Review of Economic Studies* 24: 11–32.

Marget, A. W. (1931) 'Léon Walras and the "cash-balance approach" to the problem of the value of money', *Journal of Political Economy* 39: 569–600.

—— (1935) 'The monetary aspects of the Walrasian system', *Journal of Political Economy* 43: 145–86.

Mirowski, P. (1984) 'Physics and the "marginal revolution"', *Cambridge Journal of Economics* 8: 361–79.

Mirowski, P. and Cook, P. (1989) 'Walras's "Economics and mechanics": translation, commentary, context', in W. Samuels (ed.) *Economics as Rhetorics*, The Hague: Kluwer.

Montgomery, W. D. (1971) 'An interpretation of Walras' theory of capital as a model of economic growth', *History of Political Economy* 3: 278–97.

Morishima, M. (1960) 'Existence of solution to the Walrasian system of capital formation and credit', *Zeitschrift für Nationalökonomie* 20: 238–43. (Reprinted in Morishima, M. (1964) *Equilibrium, Stability and Growth. A Multisectoral Analysis*, Oxford: Clarendon, Note to chapter III.)

—— (1964) *Equilibrium, Stability and Growth. A Multisectoral Analysis*, Oxford: Clarendon Press.

—— (1977) *Walras' Economics: a Pure Theory of Capital and Money*, Cambridge: Cambridge University Press.

Negishi, T. (1987) 'Tâtonnement and recontracting', in J. Eatwell, M. Milgate and P. Newman (eds) *The New Palgrave Dictionary of Economics*, Basingstoke: Macmillan, Part 4, pp. 589–95.

von Neumann, J. (1945) 'A model of general economic equilibrium', *Review of Economic Studies* 13: 1–9. (Translated from the German paper of 1937.)

Novshek, W. and Sonnenschein, H. (1980) 'Small efficient scale as a foundation for Walrasian equilibrium', *Journal of Economic Theory* 22: 243–55.

Pareto, V. (1895) 'Teoria matematica del commercio internationale', *Giornale degli Economisti* 10: 476–98.

Poinsot, L. (1842) *Eléments de statique*, 8th edn, Paris: Bachelier. (The first edition appeared in 1803.)

Rijnvos, C. J. (1988) *Monetaire filosofie*, Leiden/Antwerpen: Stenfert Kroeze.

Uzawa, H. (1962) 'Walras's existence theorem and Brouwer's fixed point theorem', *Economic Studies Quarterly* 8: 59–62.

Van Daal, J. (1989) 'Walras' model of general economic equilibrium with flexible coefficients of production', in F. Muller and W. J. Zwezerijnen (eds) *The Role of Economic Policy in Society*, The Hague: Rotterdam University Press, ch. 13.

Van Daal, J. and Jolink, A. (1990) 'Une note sur l'article "Economique et Mécanique" de Léon Walras', *Economie Appliquée* 43 (2): 83–94.

—— and —— (1992) 'On Walras's "general general equilibrium model"', in R. F. Hebert (ed.) *Perspectives on the History of Economic Thought*, vol. IX, Aldershot: Edward Elgar, ch. 9.

Van Daal, J. and Merkies, A. H. Q. M. (1984) *Aggregation in Economic Research*, Dordrecht: Reidel.

Van Daal, J. and Walker, D. A. (1990) 'The problem of aggregation in Walrasian general equilibrium theory', *History of Political Economy* 22: 489–505.

Van Daal, J., Henderiks, R. E. D. and Vorst, A. C. F. (1985) 'On Walras' model of general economic equilibrium', *Zeitschrift für Nationalökonomie* 45: 219–44.

Varian, H. (1984) *Microeconomic Analysis*, 2nd edn, New York: Norton.

Wald, A. (1936) 'Uber einige Gleichungssysteme der mathematischen Okonomie', *Zeitschrift für Nationalökonomie* 7: 637–70.

Walker, D. A. (ed.) (1983) *William Jaffé's Essays on Walras*, Cambridge: Cambridge University Press.

—— (1984a) 'Walras and his critics on the maximum utility of capital goods', *History of Political Economy* 16: 529–54.

—— (1984b) 'Is Walras's theory of general equilibrium a normative scheme?', *History of Political Economy* 16: 445–69.

—— (1986) 'Walras's theory of the entrepreneur', *De Economist* 134: 1–24.

—— (1987a) 'Walras, Léon (1834–1910)', in J. Eatwell, M. Milgate and P.

Newman (eds) *The New Palgrave Dictionary of Economics*, Basingstoke: Macmillan, Part 4, pp. 852–63.

—— (1987b) 'Walras's theories of tâtonnement', *Journal of Political Economy* 95: 758–74.

—— (1987c) 'Edgeworth versus Walras on the theory of tâtonnement', *Eastern Economic Journal* 13: 155–65.

—— (1987d) 'Bibliography of the writings of Léon Walras', *History of Political Economy* 19: 667–702.

—— (1988) 'Iteration in Walras's theory of tâtonnement', *De Economist* 136: 299–316.

—— (1990a) 'Institutions and participants in Walras's model of oral pledges markets', *Revue Economique* 41: 651–67.

—— (1990b) 'Disequilibrium and equilibrium in Walras's model of oral pledges markets', *Revue Economique* 41: 961–78.

—— (1990c) 'The structure of Walras's barter model of written pledges markets', *Revue d'Economie Politique* 100: 618–41.

—— (1990d) 'The equilibrating process in Walras's barter model of written pledges', *Revue d'Economie Politique* 100: 786–807.

—— (1991) 'The structure and the behavior of Walras's last monetary model of markets', *Economie Appliquée* 44 (2): 87–107.

Walras, A. (1831) *De la nature de la richesse sociale*, Evreux: Ancelle fils; Paris: Johanneau.

—— (1835) *Réfutation des doctrines de Hobbes*, Evreux: Ancelle fils.

—— (1849) *Théorie de la richesse sociale ou résumé des principes fondamentaux de l'économie politique*, Paris: Guillaumin.

—— (1990) *Richesse, liberté et société*, prepared by Pierre-Henri Goutte and Jean-Michel Servet under the auspices of the Centre Auguste et Léon Walras in the University of Lyon 2; *Auguste et Léon Walras, Oeuvres économiques complètes*, vol. I, Paris: Economica.

Walras, L. (1859) 'De la propriété intellectuelle. Position de la question économique', *Journal des Economistes, 2nd series* 24: 392–407.

—— (1860a) 'Philosophie des sciences économiques', *Journal des Economistes, 2nd series* 25: 196–206.

—— (1860b) *L'économie politique et la justice. Examen critique et réfutation des doctrines économiques de M. P.-J. Proudhon*, Paris: Guillaumin.

—— (1860c) 'Application des mathématiques à l'économie politique (1ère tentative)', Manuscript, preserved in the Fonds Walras of Lausanne (FW Vb) published in *Auguste et Léon Walras, Oeuvres économiques complètes*, Paris: Economica, 1993, pp. 329–39.

—— (1870) 'Application des mathématiques à l'économie politique (2ème tentative 1869–1870)', Manuscript, preserved in the Fonds Walras of Lausanne (FW Vb) published in *Auguste et Léon Walras, Oeuvres économiques complètes*, Paris: Economica, 1993, pp. 341–59.

—— (1871) 'Application des mathématiques à l'économie politique (1871), 3e tentative', Manuscript, preserved in the Fonds Walras of Lausanne (FW Vb) published in *Auguste et Léon Walras, Oeuvres économiques complètes*, Paris: Economica, 1993, pp. 385–409.

—— (1874) *Eléments d'économie politique pure, ou théorie de la richesse sociale*, first instalment, Lausanne: L. Corbaz; Paris: Guillaumin; Basel: H. Georg.

—— (1876) 'Un nuovo ramo della matematica. – Dell' applicazione delle matematiche all' economia politica', *Giornale degli Economisti* 3: 1–40.

—— (1877) *Eléments d'économie politique pure, ou théorie de la richesse sociale*,

second instalment, Lausanne: L. Corbaz; Paris: Guillaumin; Basel: H. Georg.
— (1880) 'Théorie mathématique du billet de banque', *Bulletin de la Société Vaudoise des Sciences Naturelles, 2nd series* 16: 553–92.
— (1886) *Théorie de la monnaie*, Lausanne: L. Corbaz; Paris: Larose et Forcel; Rome: Loescher; Leipzig: Von Duncker & Humblot.
— (1889) *Eléments d'économie politique pure, ou théorie de la richesse sociale*, 2nd edn, Lausanne: Rouge; Paris: Guillaumin; Leipzig: Von Duncker & Humblot.
— (1896a) *Eléments d'économie politique pure, ou théorie de la richesse sociale*, 3rd edn, Lausanne: Rouge; Paris: F. Pichon; Leipzig: Von Duncker & Humblot.
— (1896b) *Etudes d'économie sociale (théorie de la répartition de la richesse sociale)*, Lausanne: Rouge; Paris: F. Pichon.
— (1898) *Etudes d'économie politique appliquée (théorie de la production de la richesse sociale)*, Lausanne: Rouge; Paris: F. Pichon.
— (1899) 'Equations de circulation', *Bulletin de la Société Vaudoise des Sciences Naturelles* 35: 85–103.
— (1900) *Eléments d'économie politique pure, ou théorie de la richesse sociale*, 4th edn, Lausanne: Rouge; Paris: F. Pichon.
— (1908) 'Un initiateur en économie politique: A. A. Walras', *Revue du Mois* 32: 170–83.
— (1909) 'Economique et mécanique', *Bulletin de la Société Vaudoise des Sciences Naturelles* 45: 313–27. (Reprinted in *Metroeconomica* 12 (1960) and in Walras, L. (1987) *Mélanges d'économie politique et sociale*, prepared by Claude Hébert et Jean-Pierre Potier under the auspices of the Centre Auguste et Léon Walras in the University of Lyon 2; *Auguste et Léon Walras, Oeuvres économiques complètes*, vol. VII, Paris: Economica.)
— (1926) *Eléments d'économie politique pure, ou théorie de la richesse sociale*, édition définitive, revue par l'auteur, Paris: R. Pichon & R. Durand-Auzias; Lausanne: Rouge. (Reprinted in 1952.)
— (1954) *Elements of Pure Economics, or the Theory of Social Wealth*, translated and annotated by W. Jaffé, Homewood, IL: Irwin; London: Allen & Unwin.
— (1987) *Mélanges d'économie politique et sociale*, prepared by Claude Hébert et Jean-Pierre Potier under the auspices of the Centre Auguste et Léon Walras in the University of Lyon 2; *Auguste et Léon Walras, Oeuvres économiques complètes*, vol. VII, Paris: Economica.
— (1988) *Eléments d'économie politique pure, ou théorie de la richesse sociale*, variorum edition, prepared by Claude Mouchot under the auspices of the Centre Auguste et Léon Walras in the University of Lyon 2; *Auguste et Léon Walras, Oeuvres économiques complètes*, vol. VIII, Paris: Economica.
— (1993) *Théorie mathématique de la richesse sociale (et autres écrits mathématiques et d'économie pure)*, prepared by Claude Mouchot under the auspices of the Centre Auguste et Léon Walras in the University of Lyon 2; *Auguste et Léon Walras, Oeuvres économiques complètes*, vol. XI, Paris: Economica.
Weintraub, E. R. (1983) 'On the existence of a competitive equilibrium', *Journal of Economic Literature* 21: 1–39.
— (1985) *General Equilibrium Analysis*, Cambridge: Cambridge University Press.
Wicksteed, P. H. (1894) *An Essay on the Co-ordination of the Laws of Distribution*, London: Macmillan. (Reprinted by the London School of Economics and Political Science, 1932.)

INDEX OF NAMES

189

SUBJECT INDEX